Get the Results

Illustrated Science Dictionary

Years 5–8 | Ages 10–14

Elise Masters

PASCAL PRESS

© Elise Masters and Pascal Press 2006
Reprinted 2007, 2008, 2010

Updated in 2014 for the Australian Curriculum

ISBN 978 1 74125 222 4

Pascal Press
PO Box 250
Glebe NSW 2037
(02) 8585 4044
www.pascalpress.com.au

Publisher: Vivienne Joannou
Project editors: Ian Rohr and Leanne Poll
Edited by Christine Eslick and Karen Pearce
Reviewed by Geoffrey Thickett
Typeset by Grizzly Graphics (Leanne Richters)
Cover and page design by DiZign Pty Ltd
Photos by Dreamstime
Printed by Green Giant Press

Reproduction and communication for educational purposes
The Australian *Copyright Act 1968* (the Act) allows a maximum of one chapter or 10% of the pages of this work, whichever is the greater, to be reproduced and/or communicated by any educational institution for its educational purposes provided that the educational institution (or the body that administers it) has given a remuneration notice to Copyright Agency Limited (CAL) under the Act.

For details of the CAL licence for educational institutions contact:

Copyright Agency Limited
Level 15, 233 Castlereagh Street
Sydney NSW 2000
Telephone: (02) 9394 7600
Facsimile: (02) 9394 7601
E-mail: enquiry@copyright.com.au

Reproduction and communication for other purposes
Except as permitted under the Act (for example a fair dealing for the purposes of study, research, criticism or review) no part of this book may be reproduced, stored in a retrieval system, communicated or transmitted in any form or by any means without prior written permission. All inquiries should be made to the publisher at the address above.

All care has been taken in the preparation of this study guide, but please check with your teacher or the relevant Board of Studies about the exact requirements of the course you are studying as they can change from year to year.

Contents

A	1
B	8
C	14
D	32
E	37
F	51
G	59
H	64
I	68
J	71
K	72
L	74
M	80
N	92
O	94
P	98
R	111
S	122
T	141
U	146
V	148
W	152
X	158
Y	159

Excel Illustrated Science Dictionary Years 5–8

Introduction

This book has been written specifically for the Australian Curriculum and is suitable for primary school students in Years 5 and 6 and secondary school students in Years 7 and 8 studying Science. It contains an alphabetical list of common words and phrases applicable to the new Australian Curriculum Science course for Years 5–8. Coloured, labelled diagrams and illustrations, as well as numerous examples, have been included to aid understanding and learning.

Words in *italics* indicate where more information is included elsewhere in the book. Other related material is listed at the end of each entry in **bold** print.

absorption

absorption

See **heat absorption**.

acceleration

occurs when an object increases its *speed*. When the object slows down, it decelerates. Acceleration and deceleration are measured in metres per second per second (m/s²).

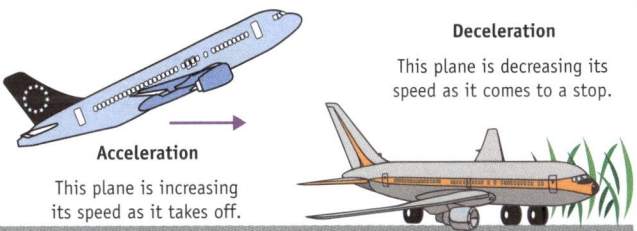

Acceleration
This plane is increasing its speed as it takes off.

Deceleration
This plane is decreasing its speed as it comes to a stop.

acids

form an important group of chemical *compounds*. They can be detected using indicators (e.g. litmus and universal indicator). Universal indicator changes colour in different levels of acidity.

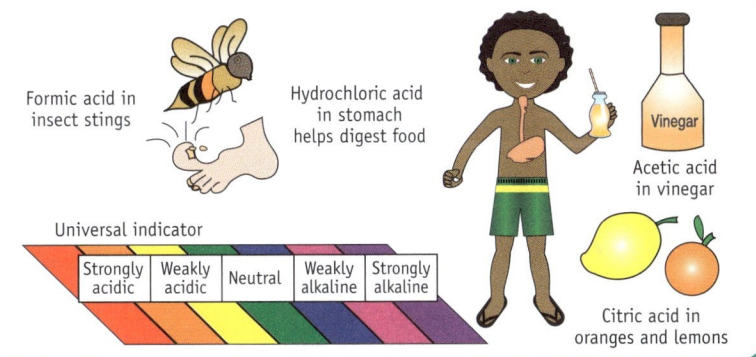

Formic acid in insect stings

Hydrochloric acid in stomach helps digest food

Acetic acid in vinegar

Citric acid in oranges and lemons

Universal indicator: Strongly acidic | Weakly acidic | Neutral | Weakly alkaline | Strongly alkaline

adaptation

is a behaviour or feature that helps *living things* to survive. A behavioural adaptation is an action such as burrowing to stay cool. A structural adaptation is a feature such as thick fur to stay warm. See **reproductive adaptations**; **survival features**; **adaptations in Australia**.

A adaptations in Australia

adaptations in Australia

help *plants* and animals survive harsh environmental conditions. The range of adaptations is vast. Some mammals are *nocturnal*. This helps them to survive high temperatures and avoid predators. Many plants have leaves covered with a thick cuticle layer which reduces water loss. Some plants on sand dunes have silvery leaves which reflect heat.

air

is a *mixture* of *gases* that extends about 50 km around the *Earth*. Important gases are nitrogen (78%), *oxygen* (21%) and *carbon dioxide* (0.04%).

Carbon dioxide and other gases such as argon, neon and helium 1%
Oxygen 21%
Nitrogen 78%

air currents

See **global air currents**.

air pressure

or atmospheric pressure is the *pressure* of the *air* on its surroundings. Air pressure is measured with a *barometer*. It is measured in kilopascals (kPa) and hectopascals (hPa), millibars (mB) and millimetres of mercury (mm of Hg). See **aneroid barometer; high pressure system; low pressure system**.

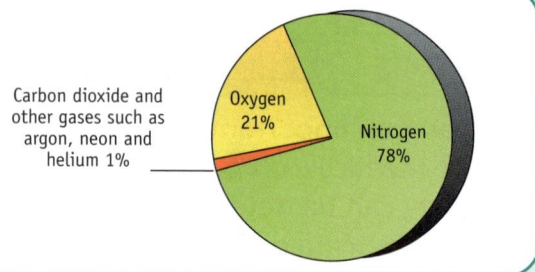

Examples
Air pressure holds a suction cap to the wall.
← Air pressure
← Air pressure

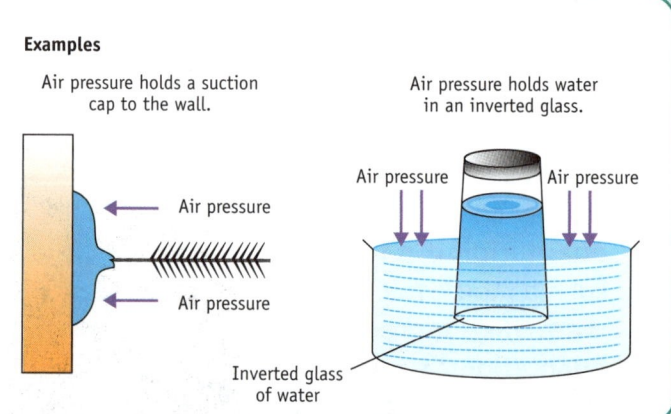

Air pressure holds water in an inverted glass.
Air pressure ↓ ↓ Air pressure
Inverted glass of water

air pressure and weather

See **high pressure system; low pressure system**.

air resistance

air resistance

occurs when *air* slows the movement of an object. Planes, racing cars and birds are streamlined to reduce air resistance. Parachutes use air resistance to slow movement. See **friction reduction**.

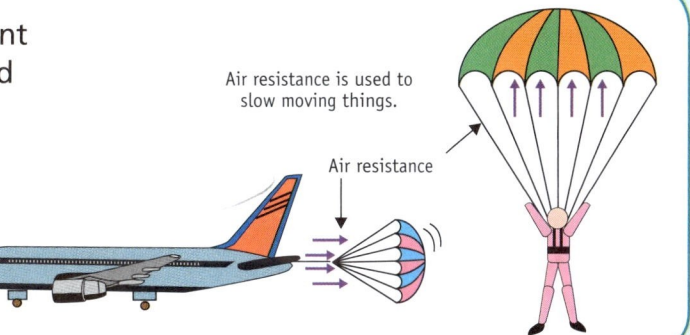

Air resistance is used to slow moving things.

alloys

are *mixtures* of different *metals*. Making metals into alloys gives them different *properties* and makes them useful for certain jobs (e.g. stainless steel made of iron, chromium and nickel is stronger than iron and does not *rust*).

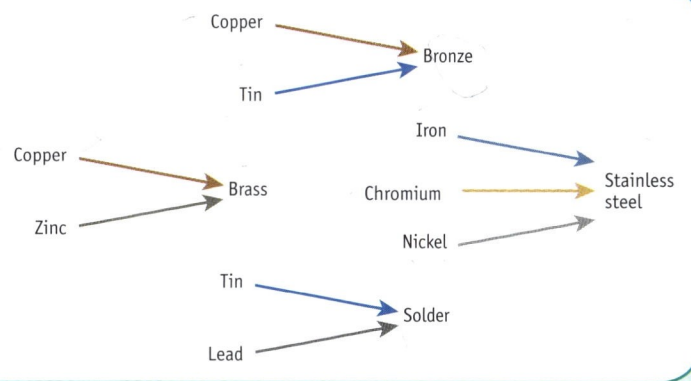

alternating current (AC)

is when the *current* or *charge* moves backwards and forwards. Many *generators* produce this type of current. Compare **direct current (DC)**.

anemometer

measures the *speed* of *wind*. Wind from any direction will make the cups on the anemometer spin. Anemometers may be connected to computers for accurate readings.

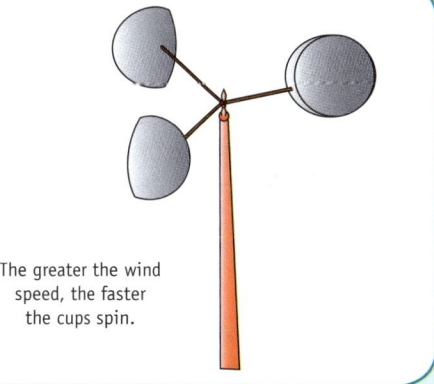

The greater the wind speed, the faster the cups spin.

Excel Illustrated Science Dictionary Years 5–8

A

aneroid barometer

aneroid barometer

measures *air pressure*. It contains a sealed box with most of its *air* removed. When the surrounding air pressure changes, the box becomes larger or smaller. These changes in the size of the box are recorded on a dial.

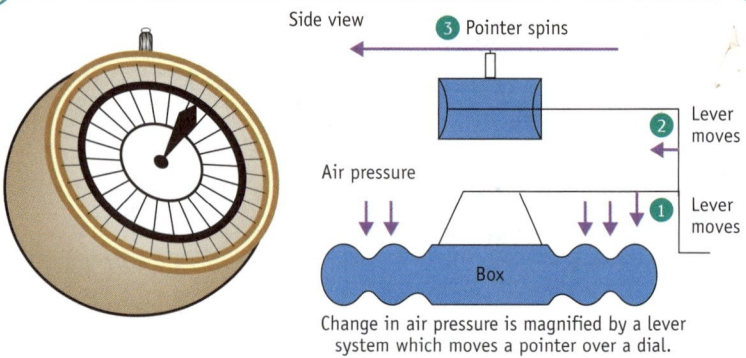

Change in air pressure is magnified by a lever system which moves a pointer over a dial.

animals

are *organisms* that obtain their *food* by eating *plants* or other animals. Generally they move about and react quickly to changes. Their *cells* have no wall. See **vertebrates; invertebrates**.

animals in Australia

See **biodiversity** in Australia.

Antarctica

is a large continent covered by ice, approximately 1.8 km thick. It is in the southern hemisphere and contains the south pole. It provides unique opportunities for *science* research by scientists from around the world. Research includes *climate*, astrophysics, marine biology, ecology, geology and meteorology. For instance, the cold, dry, stable air here allows astronomers to make clear observations.

aquatic

refers to anything living or growing in water (fresh or salt). Aquatic *environments* include seas, oceans, estuaries, rivers, lakes and rock pools.

Excel Illustrated Science Dictionary Years 5–8

asexual reproduction

asexual reproduction

is when new *organisms* are produced by the simple dividing of *cells*. They are copies of the parent. Compare **sexual reproduction**.

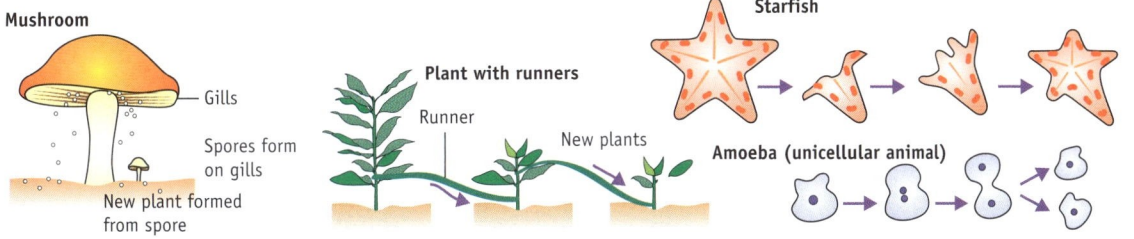

asteroids

are large rock fragments in a band *orbiting* the *Sun*. They are mainly between *Mars* and *Jupiter*. See **solar system**.

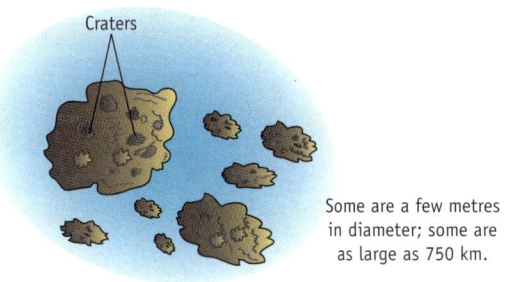

Some are a few metres in diameter; some are as large as 750 km.

asthenosphere

is an area in the upper *mantle* of the *Earth* that is less rigid than the *lithosphere* and slowly oozes. It allows the plates that make up the lithosphere to move.

astronomy

is the study of the *universe*. Early Greeks (350 BC) believed the Sun and planets moved around the *Earth*. In the 2nd century, Ptolemy proposed a model showing this. In the 10th century Al-Battani of Iraq determined the length of the *year* and seasons, and the possibility of solar *eclipses*. In the 11th century Khayyam of Persia very accurately calculated the length of a year. In the 16th century Polish astronomer Copernicus proposed that the planets moved around the Sun. Galileo supported his ideas in Italy in the 17th century. See **solar system**.

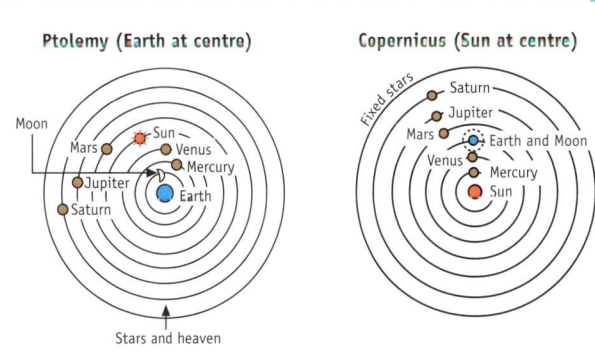

Excel Illustrated Science Dictionary Years 5–8

A astronomy and Aboriginal and Torres Strait Islander peoples

astronomy and Aboriginal and Torres Strait Islander peoples

are linked in Dreamtime stories. In these stories, the sky is believed to be the home of spirits who watch over the people. Generally the *Sun*, *Moon* and *stars* are people or animals that have fled from the Earth because of some event. For example, one story describes the Sun as a woman carrying a torch. She wanders around Earth looking for her child. This produces *day and night*. The objects in the sky were also used for navigation. The Australian Indigenous people used their positions and movements to help guide them through the bush at night.

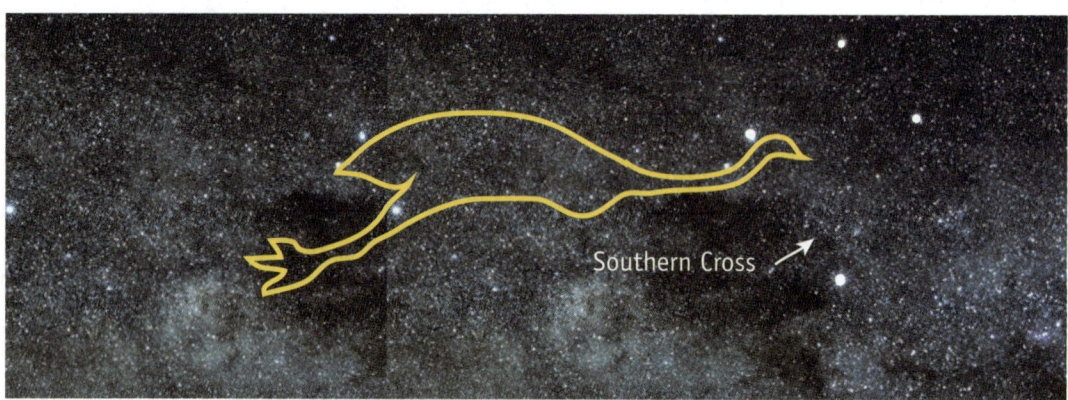

atmosphere

is a blanket of *gases* surrounding a *planet*. The *Earth's* atmosphere extends about 800 km. Most of the *air* is in the first 50 km. The atmosphere protects the Earth from *meteors* and harmful rays (e.g. *ultraviolet rays*). The atmosphere is made up of layers. See **atmosphere changes**.

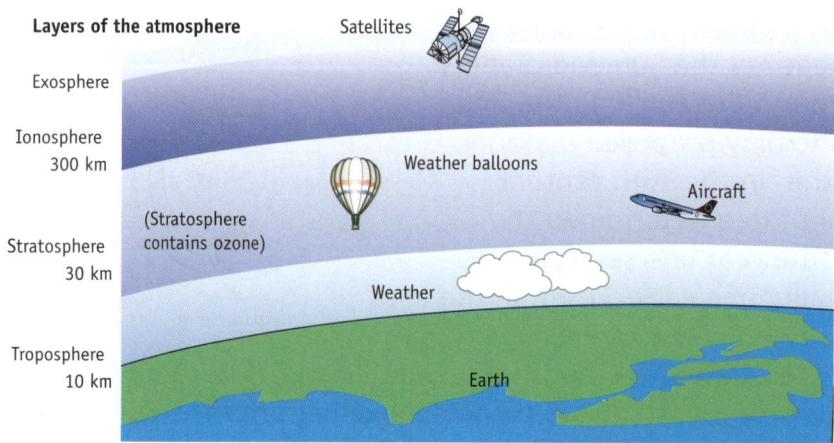

atmosphere changes

atmosphere changes

have occurred over time. When the *Earth* was formed the atmosphere was mainly made up of *carbon dioxide*. Today, the atmosphere is mainly nitrogen and *oxygen*. The present atmosphere is maintained by the activities of *plants* and *animals*.

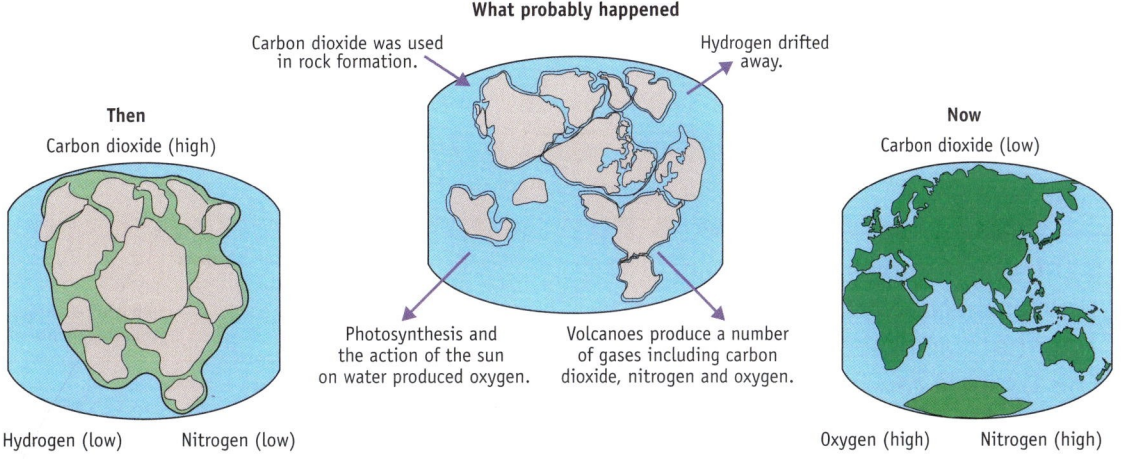

atoms

are extremely small particles that make up *matter*. An atom contains charged particles, positive protons and negative electrons. All the atoms in an *element* are the same. The atoms of one element are different from those of a different element (e.g. the atoms in iron are different from those in copper). Compare with **molecule**. See **charge**.

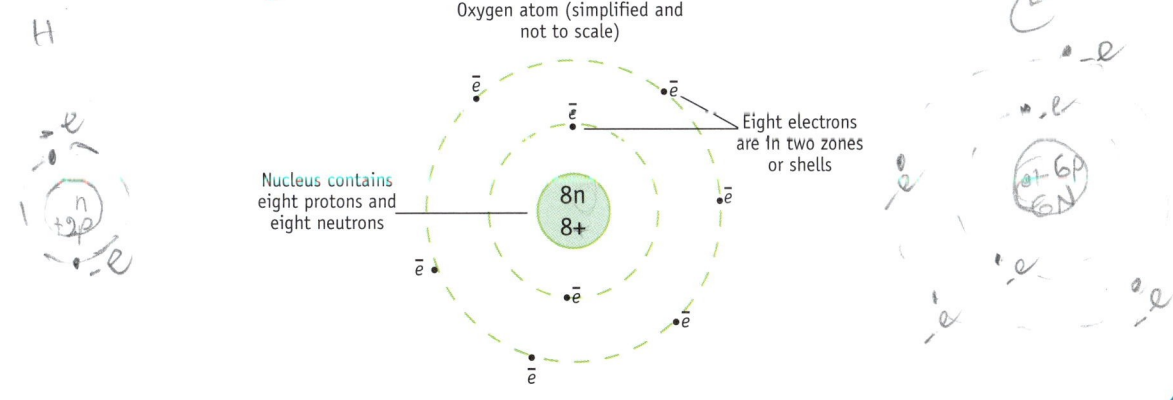

Excel Illustrated Science Dictionary Years 5–8

B bacteria

bacteria (singular: bacterium)

are microscopic, *unicellular organisms*. Some cause disease, but many are useful (e.g. they break down dead organisms and *recycle* nutrients). See **microorganisms**.

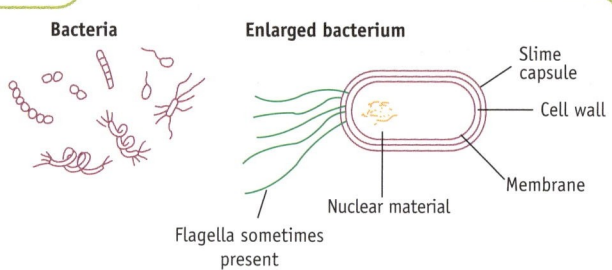

balance of nature

is the way *organisms* coexist in a natural *ecosystem* in such a way that each *species* survives. This balance can be upset and survival threatened by changing the *environment*.

Ways the balance can be upset

balanced and unbalanced forces

determine whether an object will move. When an object is not moving (is at rest), the *forces* acting on it are balanced. To make an object move or change its speed, one force must be greater than the others—the forces must be unbalanced.

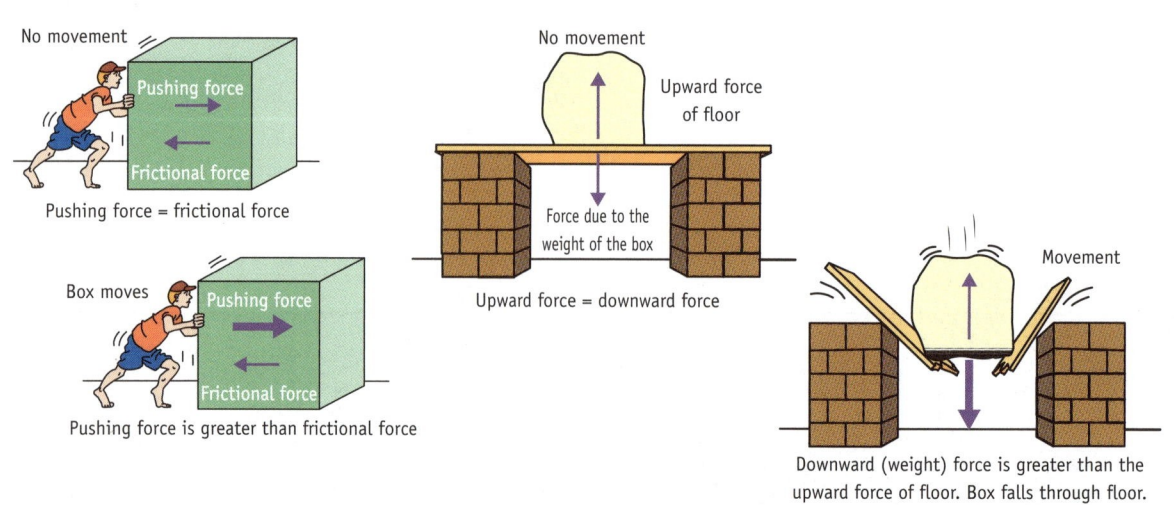

Excel Illustrated Science Dictionary Years 5–8

barometer

barometer

is an instrument for measuring *air* (atmospheric) pressure. A simple mercury barometer uses *air pressure* to hold up a column of mercury in a glass tube. If the air pressure is low, the column drops. See **aneroid barometer**.

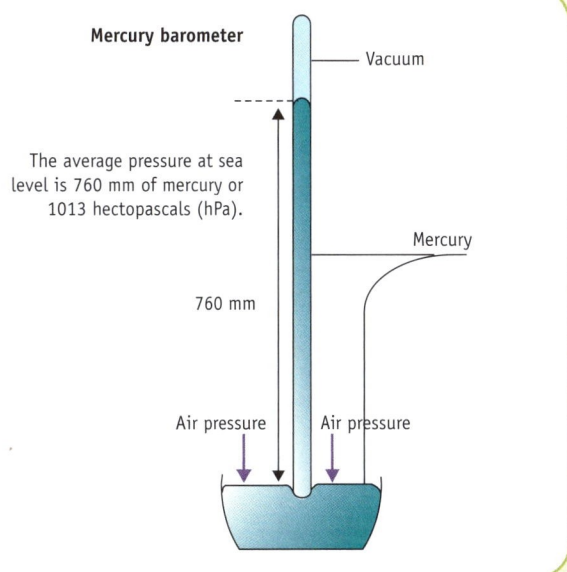

Mercury barometer

The average pressure at sea level is 760 mm of mercury or 1013 hectopascals (hPa).

basalt

See **igneous rocks**.

batteries

are made of two or more electric cells (or dry cells). Chemical reactions in the cells create electrical energy. See **voltage**.

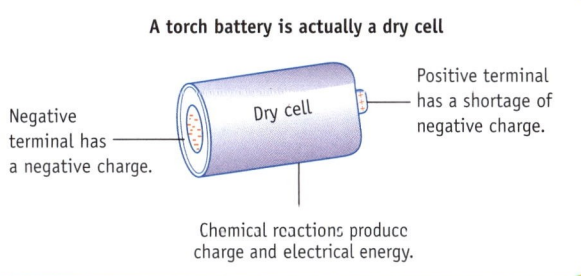

A torch battery is actually a dry cell

batteries in parallel

is when batteries are placed in parallel in a *circuit*. Their *voltage* or electrical push is not combined but the *current* is increased. Compare **batteries in series**.

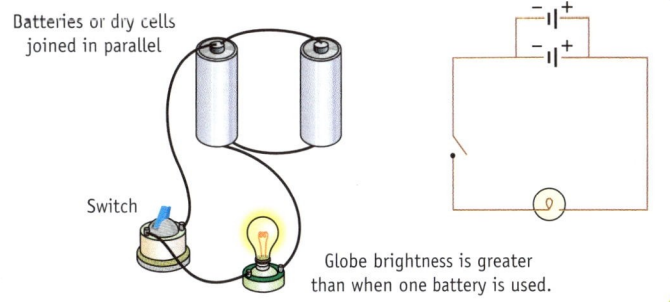

Globe brightness is greater than when one battery is used.

Excel Illustrated Science Dictionary Years 5–8

B batteries in series

batteries in series

is when batteries are placed in a row in a *circuit*. Their *voltage* or electrical push is combined and more *current* can flow. Compare **batteries in parallel**.

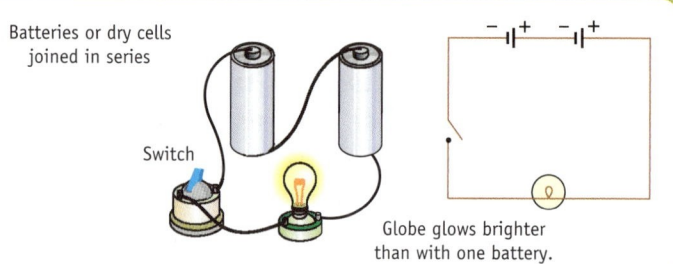

Batteries or dry cells joined in series

Switch

Globe glows brighter than with one battery.

biodegradable

refers to a material that can be broken down or decomposed by *living things* such as bacteria. Decomposing the material makes it harmless so that it will not pollute. Some *plastics* are now biodegradable. See **decomposers; soaps and detergents**.

biodiversity

is the variety of *living things* living on *Earth*. Variety is reduced by human activities that destroy *organisms*, their shelters and *food* (e.g. by hunting, removing forests and setting up farms and cities). See **biodiversity in Australia; extinction**.

biodiversity in Australia

is made up of an unusual variety of *organisms* that do not live naturally elsewhere. See **megafauna**.

Pouched mammals (marsupials)

Egg-laying mammals (monotremes)

Koala Wombat Tasmanian devil Echidna Platypus

biofuel

is an *energy source* obtained from living things (e.g. canola). Manure and waste plant products from the palm oil industry in Indonesia are used to produce methane gas. The gas is burned to heat water which produces steam used to drive a *generator*.

biosphere

is the region of the Earth's surface (including the sea and air) that is inhabited. The biosphere is affected by *natural disasters*.

black hole

is the remains of a *star*. It has very powerful *gravity* so that nearby objects are sucked into it. Nothing can escape from a black hole, including *light*, thus making it black and invisible. Astronomers detect black holes by the effect of their gravity on nearby bodies in space.

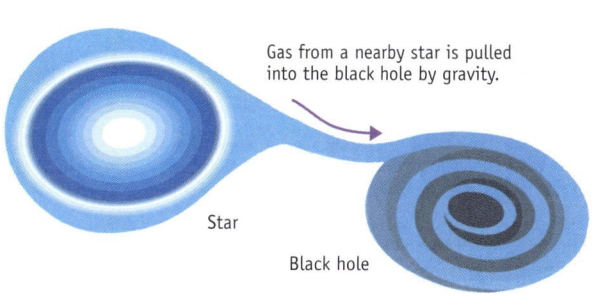

boiling

occurs when the particles in a *liquid* separate and form *gas* bubbles. The bubbles rise to the surface. A change of state occurs during boiling. Compare **melting**. See **boiling point; state of matter, change**.

boiling point

is the *temperature* at which a substance boils and turns to a *gas*. A *liquid* with strong *bonds* between its particles has a high boiling point (e.g. iron boils at 2750 °C). A liquid with weak bonds has a low boiling point (e.g. water boils at 100 °C). Compare **melting point; freezing point**.

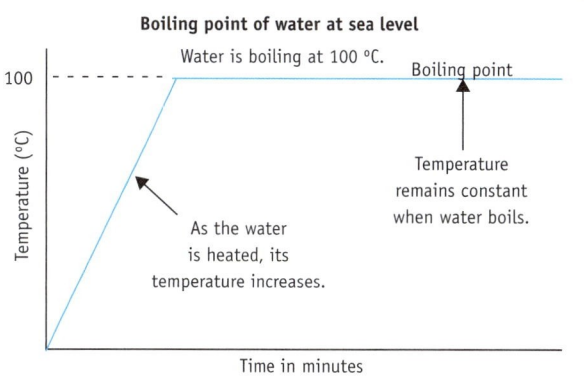

 bonds

bonds

are forces between particles in matter. They hold the particles together and give a substance its *properties* (e.g. *boiling point*, hardness and *melting point*).

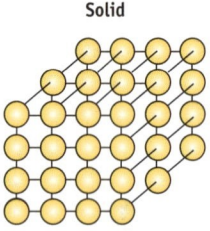
Solid
Bonds are strong and so the solid keeps its shape.

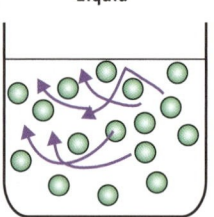
Liquid
Bonds are weak and so particles move about.

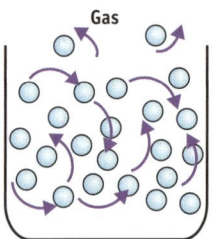
Gas
Bonds are very weak and particles move rapidly.

breathing

is the process of taking in *oxygen* and giving out *carbon dioxide*. Land *vertebrates* use lungs to breathe, fish use gills and insects have small pores down the sides of their bodies.

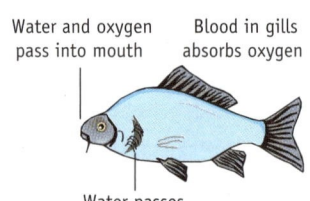
Water and oxygen pass into mouth
Blood in gills absorbs oxygen
Water passes out gill slit

Spiracles are small pores along the body for breathing

bridges

exert *forces* on the foundation and surrounding *rock*. See **tension and compression.**

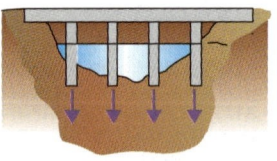
Pier bridges
Pier bridges exert downward forces that are spread over the base rock. They can be built on most rock types.

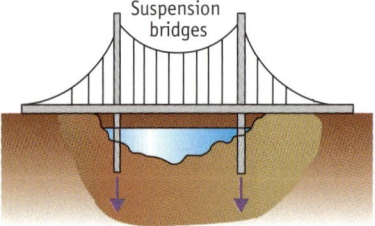
Suspension bridges
The pressure under the towers is great and the foundation rock needs to be strong.

Arch bridges
Arch bridges exert downward and sideways forces so the rock foundations need to be strong in all directions.

buoyancy

is a force that pushes an object in a liquid upwards, making it hard to *sink*. The object is said to be buoyant. An object is more buoyant in salt water than fresh water. See **float; sink.**

12

Excel Illustrated Science Dictionary Years 5–8

burning

burning (combustion)

is a *chemical reaction* that occurs when a substance is heated and combines with *oxygen* in the *air*. It produces *heat, light, sound* and new chemicals. The reaction cannot be reversed. Compare **state of matter, change**.

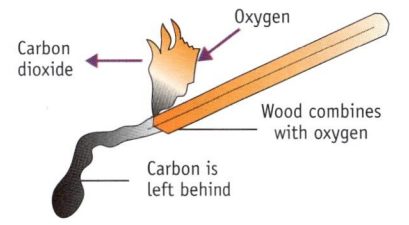

bushfires and floods

change *ecosystems*. They kill *plants* and *animals* and destroy *food* and places where animals can hide from *predators*. They damage the *soil* and cause *erosion* by killing and removing plants.

Excel Illustrated Science Dictionary Years 5–8

carbohydrates

are *organic compounds* such as sugar, starch and glucose. They are used in *respiration* to provide *energy* for activities and *cell* functioning. Glucose is made by *plants* during *photosynthesis* and it may change to starch for storage. See **nutrients**.

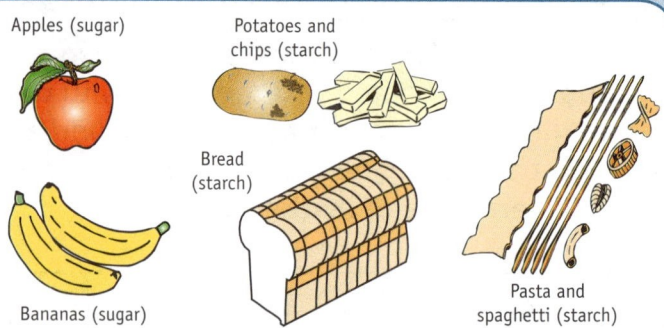

carbon dioxide (CO_2)

is a *gas* found in the *atmosphere*. *Plants* use it to make their *food* supply. Both plants and *animals* make carbon dioxide in *respiration*. Burning wood and *fossil fuels* releases carbon dioxide. See **greenhouse effect**.

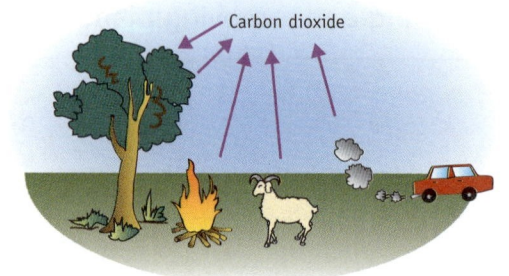

carnivore

is an *animal* that eats the flesh of other animals (e.g. cat, lizard).

catalyst

is a chemical that speeds up reactions but does not take part in them. Some *chemical reactions* would take years without a catalyst. *Enzymes* are catalysts.

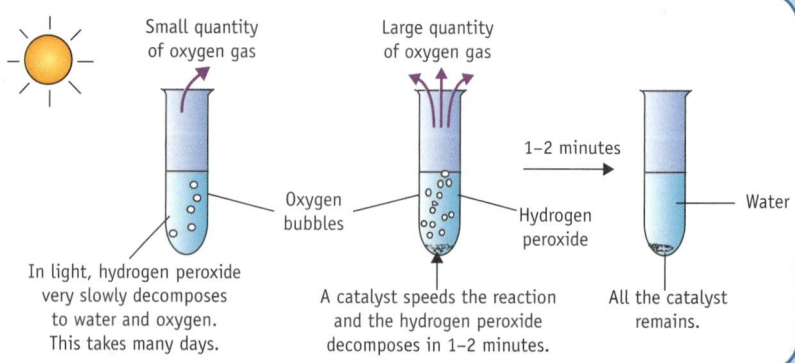

cell

See **cells in living things; electric cells**.

cell division

cell division

is the process by which *cells in living things* reproduce. This results in growth and repair of *tissues*. The division of body cells is called mitosis.

cell types in living things

are many and varied. Each type has its own particular job (function). For examples of cells in *plants* see **xylem**; **stomates**.

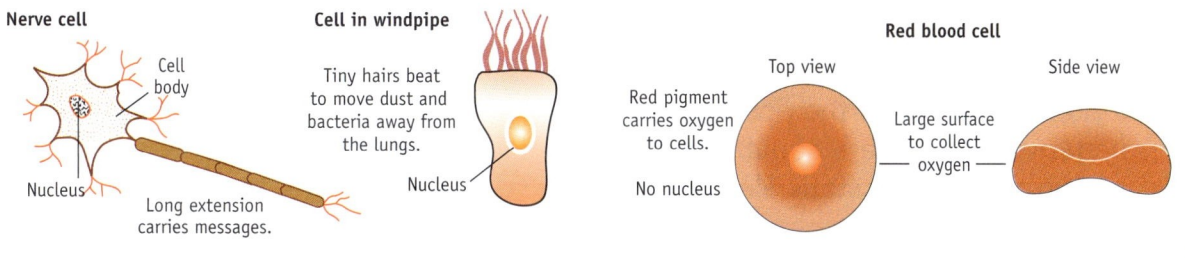

cells in living things

are small structures that make up the whole. Most are microscopic. The diagram shows details of cells seen with a *light* microscope. See **cell types in living things**; **fungus**; **unicellular organisms**.

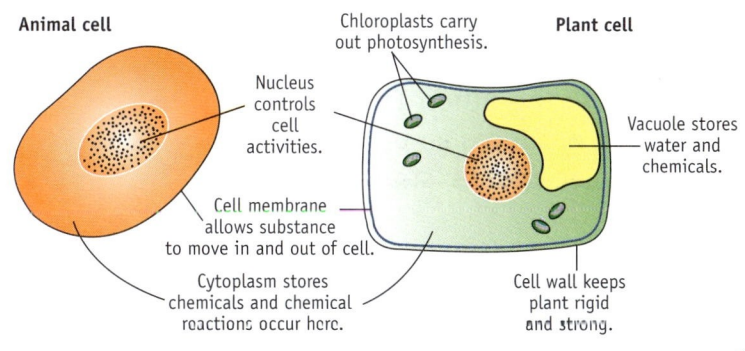

centrifuge

is a *machine* used to separate different *solids* or to separate *liquids* from solids by spinning. A washing machine spins to separate the water from the clothes; in laboratories centrifuges separate red blood *cells* from blood plasma.

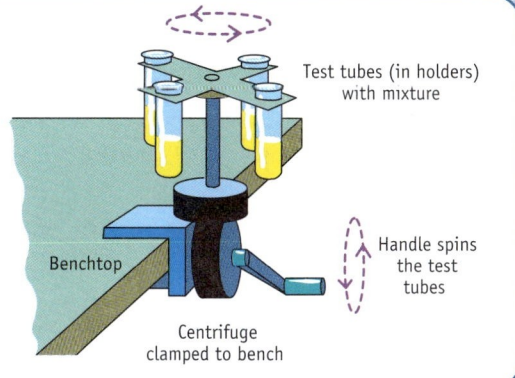

Excel Illustrated Science Dictionary Years 5–8

change of state

See **state of matter, change**.

charge

is positive or negative. *Matter* in an object contains positive and negative particles. If there are more negative than positive particles, the object has a negative charge. If there are more positive particles than negative, it has a positive charge. If the positive and negative particles are equal, the object has no charge. See **static electricity; electrostatic force**.

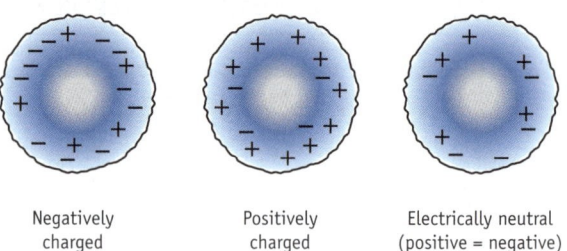

Negatively charged — Positively charged — Electrically neutral (positive = negative)

charging an object

may be done by rubbing it with another object. Rubbing causes the negative charge to move from one object to the other. The excess charge produces an *electrostatic force*. See **charge; static electricity**.

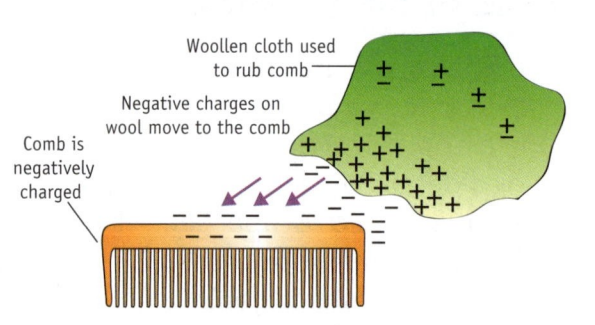

chemical element symbols

are used to represent *elements*. The first letter of the chemical's Latin name is used (e.g. potassium, *kalium* in Latin, has the symbol K). When there are two elements with the same letter, another letter is added (e.g. copper, *cuprum* in Latin, is Cu). See **periodic table**.

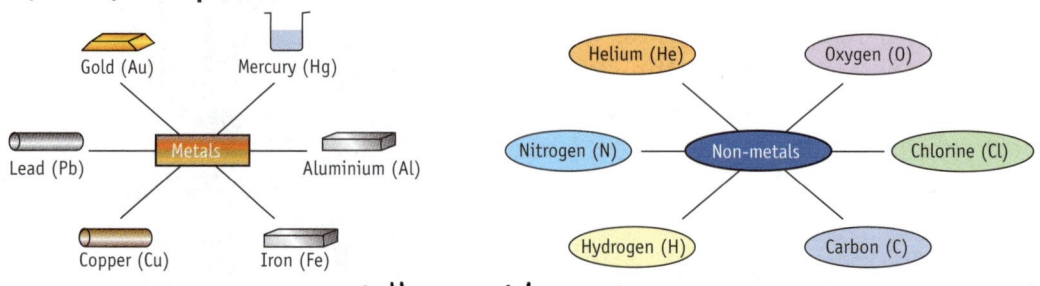

Salt → NaCl
Na → Sodium

chemical energy

chemical energy

is stored in substances such as *food* and fuels. *Chemical reactions* release the *energy*. See **energy transformation**.

chemical properties

See **properties**.

chemical reaction (change)

occurs when particles in substances are rearranged to form a new substance(s) with different *properties*. For example, when wood burns, it combines with *oxygen* to form *carbon dioxide*. The stored *energy* in the wood is changed to *heat* energy, *light energy* and *sound* energy. A chemical change is often difficult to reverse. Compare **physical change**. See **decomposition**; **word equations**.

chemical reaction speed

can be fast (e.g. a match *burning*) or slow (a nail *rusting*; milk going sour). It will go faster if the *temperature* is increased, the concentration of the chemicals is increased, the chemicals are ground into small pieces or a powder, or a *catalyst* is added.

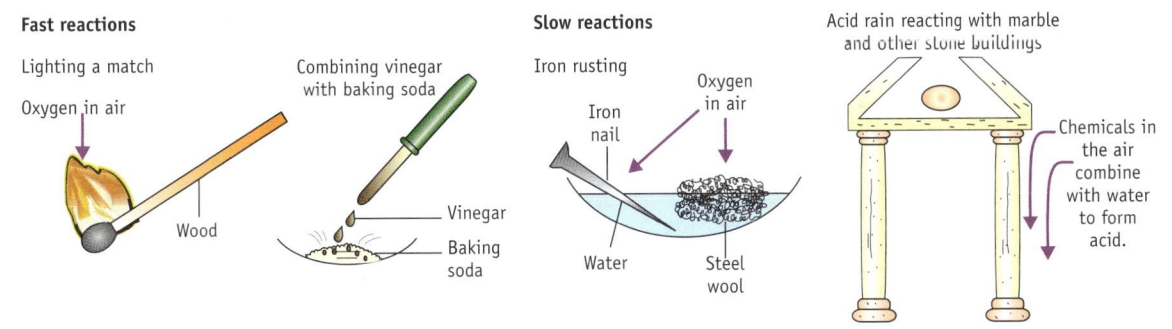

Excel Illustrated Science Dictionary Years 5–8

chemical weathering

occurs when chemicals in water or the *air* react with *minerals* in *rock*. The chemical change weakens the rock so that it crumbles. If the crumbled particles are blown or washed away the whole process is called *erosion*.

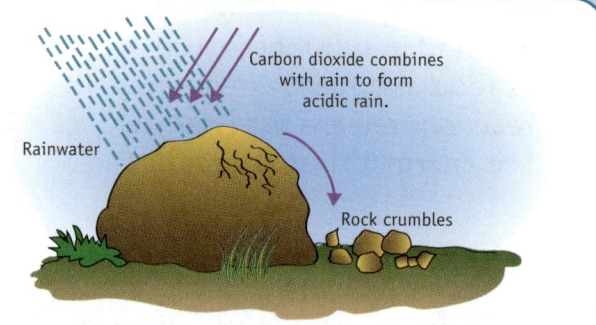

chloroplast

is a structure in plant *cells* where *photosynthesis* occurs. It contains green pigment that collects the *Sun*'s energy needed for this process. See **cells in living things**.

chromatography

is used to separate and detect small amounts of chemicals in *mixtures* (e.g. chemicals in urine samples). A drop of the mixture is placed on special absorbent paper, which is dipped into a *solvent*. The solvent then separates each chemical.

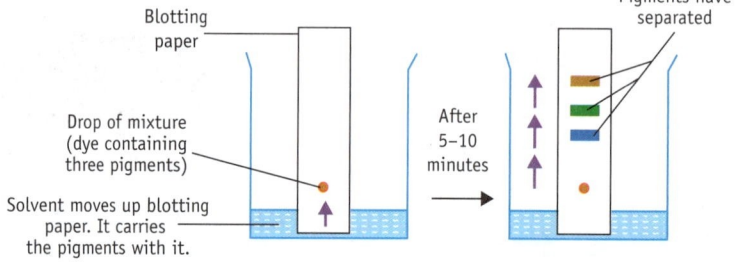

circuit

is the continuous pathway along which *electricity* flows. Electricity will not flow if there is a break or gap in the circuit. Circuits can be open or closed by a switch. See **circuit diagrams; circuit components in series; circuit components in parallel; switch**.

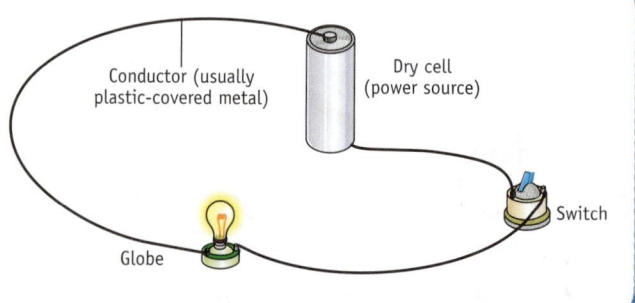

circuit components in parallel

circuit components in parallel

is when some of the components (or parts) in a *circuit* are parallel to each other. A meter to measure *voltage* is placed in parallel. Compare **circuit components in series**. See **batteries in parallel**.

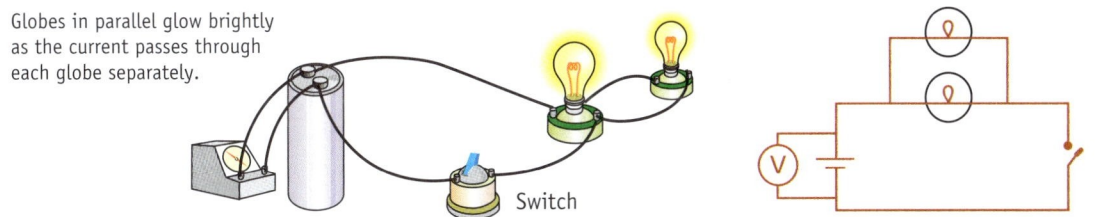

Globes in parallel glow brightly as the current passes through each globe separately.

Switch

circuit components in series

is when components (or parts) of the *circuit* are joined in line. Compare **circuit components in parallel**. See **batteries in series**.

 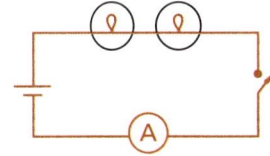

Meter to measure current is always joined in series.

Globes in series glow dimly as the current is pushed through two globes.

Dry cell   Switch

circuit diagrams

use symbols to show components (parts) of a *circuit*. See **electrical symbols**.

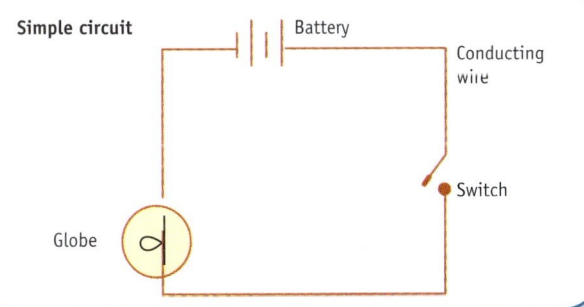

Simple circuit   Battery
Conducting wire
Switch
Globe

circulatory system

in humans consists of heart, blood and vessels (arteries, veins and capillaries). The heart pumps blood around the body in blood vessels. The blood carries *food* and *oxygen* to *cells* and collects wastes (e.g. *carbon dioxide*) and takes them to the *excretory system*.

(cont.)

Excel **Illustrated Science Dictionary Years 5–8**

circulatory system (cont.)

Circulatory system

- Blood is carried away from the heart in arteries and to the heart in veins.
- Blood passes through the heart twice during one circulation of the body.

— Blood with oxygen
— Blood lacking oxygen

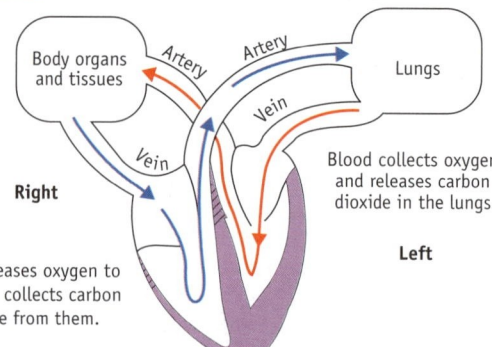

Body organs and tissues. Lungs. Blood collects oxygen and releases carbon dioxide in the lungs. Blood releases oxygen to cells and collects carbon dioxide from them. Right. Left.

classification groups (hierarchy)

help with identification and show relationships between *organisms*. Each organism is placed the following groups.
- Kingdom: *animals* and *plants* are in different kingdoms and are distantly related.
- Phylum: animals with backbones are in the same phylum; other animals are in different phyla.
- Class: all mammals are in the same class; reptiles and birds are in different classes.
- Order: carnivorous mammals are in the same order; herbivores are in different orders.
- Family: dogs and foxes are in the same family; cats are in a different family.
- Genus: dogs and dingos are in the genus *Canis*; foxes are in the genus *Vulpes*.
- Species: organisms in the same species are very similar and closely related; the dingo is in species *Canis dingo* while domestic dogs are in species *Canis familiaris*.

See **classification of living things; kingdoms; species; species name**.

classification of elements

See **periodic table**.

classification of living things

is the grouping of *living things* by their similarities in structure (e.g. body covering, *flowers* or cones produced, number of legs). *Organisms* in the same group are usually closely related. See **kingdoms; species; keys; classification groups (hierarchy)**.

Jointed invertebrates have different numbers of legs.

Insects have six legs.

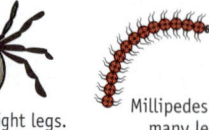
Spiders have eight legs.

Millipedes have many legs.

Vertebrates have different body coverings.

Fish have scales.

Birds have feathers.

Mammals have fur or hair.

Excel Illustrated Science Dictionary Years 5–8

climate

climate

is the average weather conditions in an area over many years. *Temperature* and rainfall are commonly used to define climate zones (e.g. tropical, dry or arid, temperate or mild, and snowy or polar). Climate influences the types of *plants* and *animals* that can live in an area.

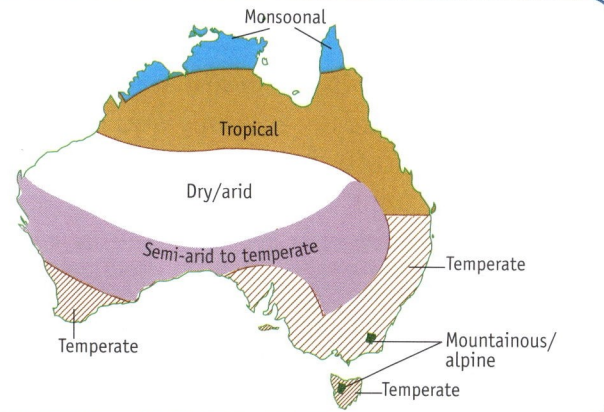

cloning

produces offspring that are identical to the parent. A breeder of *organisms* can select the features desired and then clone them (e.g. large, juicy corncobs).

cloud

is formed when moisture in the *air* cools and condenses on dust. Clouds are made of millions of very fine water droplets. See **cloud formation**; **cloud types**.

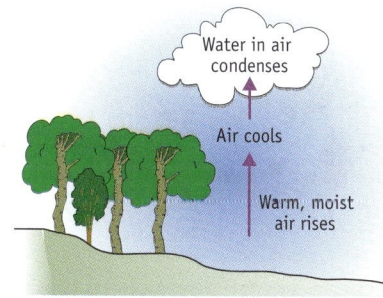

cloud formation

is the process of making *clouds*. When warm *air* rises, it cools and moisture condenses to form clouds. Warm air rises by:

See **cloud types**.

Excel Illustrated Science Dictionary Years 5–8   21

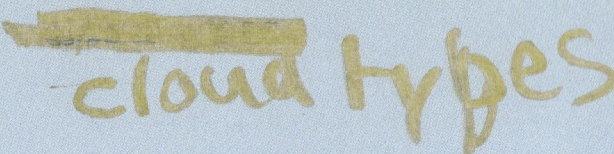

cloud types

are named by their height, shape and colour. Cirrus clouds are high, white, feathery strands. They are made up of ice. They usually indicate fine *weather*. Cumulus clouds are woolly and constantly change their shape. Small cumulus clouds indicate fine weather but if they grow large they may bring *rain* or thunderstorms. Stratus clouds are low, grey and uniform. They often produce drizzle.

Cirrus

Cumulus

Stratus

coal

is a *fossil fuel*. It is used for heating and to produce *electricity* and *gas*.

How coal is formed

Plants fall into swamps where they cannot decay.

Sediments are compressed by layers of soil and so form peat.

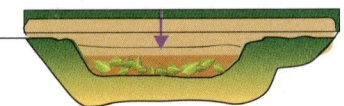
More compression changes the peat to coal.

collaboration in ecosystems

See **cooperation (collaboration) in ecosystems**.

colloid

is a *mixture* with the particles of a substance finely and evenly spread through another substance (e.g. fog, paint). The particles will not settle out and cannot be separated by filtering. See **emulsion**.

Paint is pigment spread through a solvent.

Fog is made of fine water particles in air.

Excel Illustrated Science Dictionary Years 5–8

colony

colony

is a group of *organisms* in the same *species* living closely together. Termites, ants and some bees and wasps have complex societies. In termite colonies, the reproductive male fertilises the queen (reproductive female). She produces *eggs* that hatch into workers; they build the nest, gather *food* and care for the young. Some become soldiers that protect the colony.

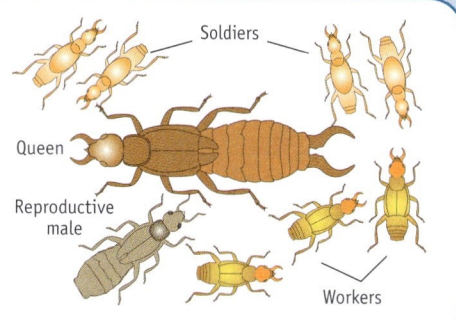

colours

come from white light, which is the name for *light* from the *Sun*, light bulbs and fluorescent tubes. All the colours (red, orange, yellow, green, blue, indigo and violet) combine to make white light. White light passing through a prism or raindrops is separated into these different colours to form a spectrum of light or a rainbow. This is known as dispersion of light.

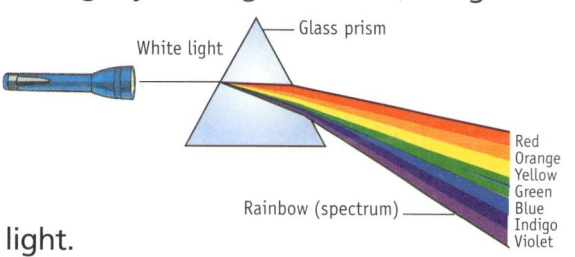

We see coloured objects because coloured light is reflected from them and enters our eyes (e.g. a red shoe reflects red light and absorbs the others). An object that reflects all light is white and one that absorbs all light is black. See **rainbow**.

 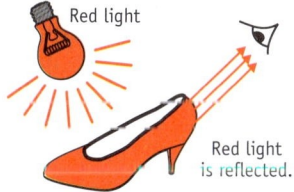  

comet

is a body of dust, rock and frozen *gas* that travels around the *Sun*. When a comet is close to the Sun, it warms up and glows, and forms a tail of dust and *gas*, which points away from the Sun.

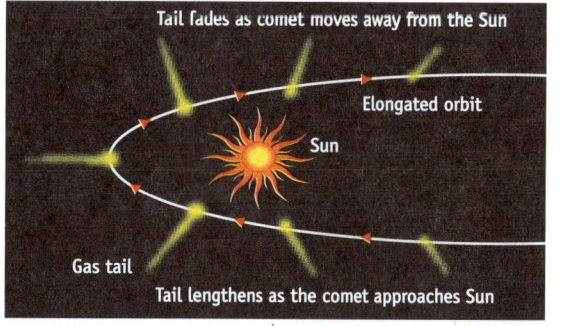

Excel **Illustrated Science Dictionary Years 5–8**

23

competition

occurs when *organisms* in an *ecosystem* fight each other for *food*, water, space and shelter, especially if they are in short supply or difficult to obtain.

compost

is a *mixture* of decaying *matter* such as leaves, grass and manure. It is useful for fertilising *soil*.

compound

is a pure substance made of elements joined by chemical bonds. The elements occur in fixed proportions.

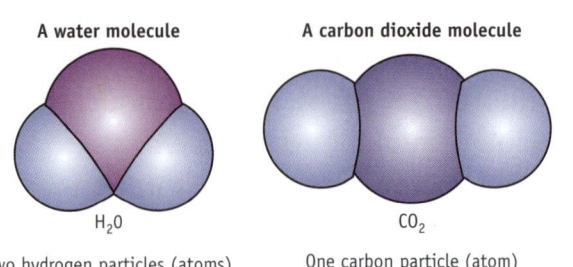

A water molecule — H$_2$O — Two hydrogen particles (atoms) and one oxygen particle

A carbon dioxide molecule — CO$_2$ — One carbon particle (atom) and two oxygen particles

compression of matter

is when particles are pressed into a smaller space. *Gases* can be compressed, but *liquids* and *solids* cannot be compressed because their particles are already packed closely together.
See **particle theory of matter; pressure and the particle theory**.

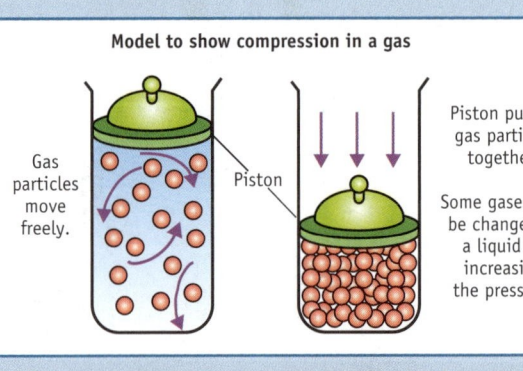

Model to show compression in a gas

Gas particles move freely.

Piston

Piston pushes gas particles together.

Some gases may be changed to a liquid by increasing the pressure.

concentrated solution

has a large amount of *solid* or *solute* (e.g. sugar) *dissolved* in a *liquid* or *solvent* (e.g. water). Compare **dilute solution; saturated solution**. See **solution**.

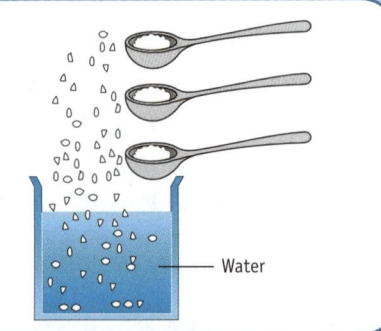

Concentrated sugar solution

A large quantity of sugar is stirred into the water.

Water

condensation

condensation

is a *change of state* from a *gas* to a *liquid* (e.g. water *vapour* on a cold surface will collect as water droplets). Condensation is used in *distillation*, for separating substances in *mixtures*.

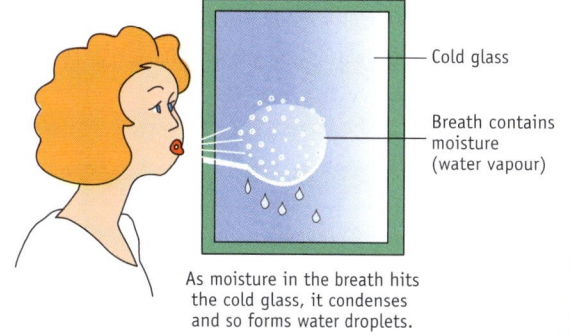

As moisture in the breath hits the cold glass, it condenses and so forms water droplets.

conduction of heat

is one way *heat* is moved (transferred) from one place to another. When a substance is heated, its particles vibrate more and pass on their *energy* by bumping the next particles. See **conductors of heat**.

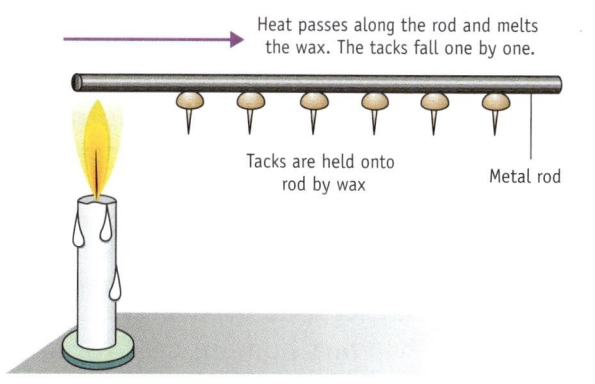

conductors of electricity

transfer *electricity* from one place to another. All *metals* conduct electricity. Copper is commonly used to carry *currents* in *circuits*. See **insulators of electricity**.

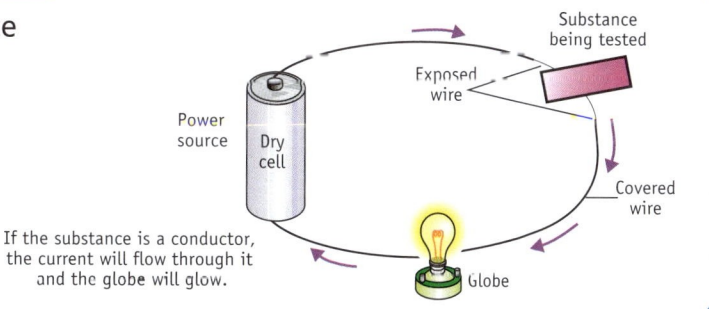

If the substance is a conductor, the current will flow through it and the globe will glow.

conductors of heat

transfer *heat* from one place to another. *Metals* are good conductors of heat, but most other *solids*, *liquids* and *gases* are generally poor conductors. See **conduction of heat**; **insulators of heat**.

Excel Illustrated Science Dictionary Years 5–8

25

conglomerate

conglomerate (puddingstone)

is a *sedimentary rock* containing pebbles, which have been deposited by fast flowing water.

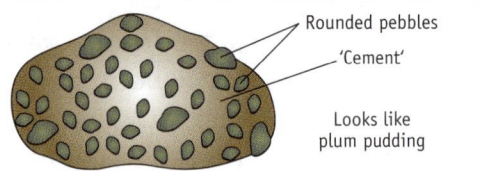

conservation

means preserving or protecting something (e.g. *energy* or the *environment*).

conservation of energy

means the total amount of *energy* in the *universe* remains the same. Energy is not created or destroyed. It may be moved to another place or changed into another form of energy. See **energy transfer**; **energy transformation**; **conservation of non-renewable resources**.

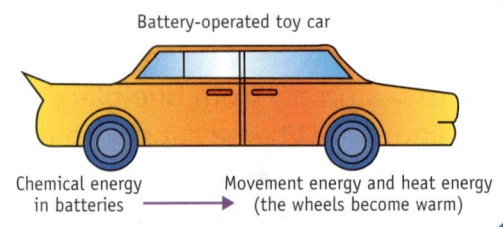

conservation of the environment

refers to the ways humans care for and protect the land, the *environment* and its *resources*. Many industries are now managed so that they help with conservation. For example, the timber industry regenerates forests and restricts wood harvesting. See **sustainable**.

conservation of fossil fuels

See **conservation of non-renewable resources**; **conservation of petrol**.

conservation of mass

During *physical* and *chemical changes*, no *matter* (*mass*) is created, lost or destroyed. The total mass remains unchanged.

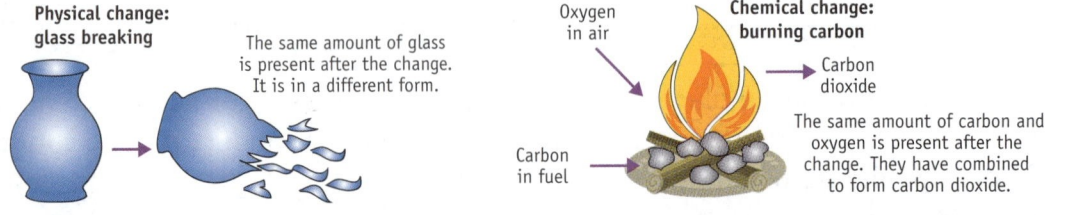

26

Excel Illustrated Science Dictionary Years 5–8

conservation of non-renewable resources

conservation of non-renewable resources

means conserving (protecting) *materials* by recycling and reusing them, or using materials that are renewable (e.g. using natural fibres like wool and cotton instead of *synthetics*, which are made from *fossil fuel*). See **sustainable**; **conservation of petrol**; **non-renewable resources**.

conservation of petrol

is when alternatives are used to replace petrol in cars. They include *electricity* from batteries, alcohol produced from crops, *gas* from *animal* manure or rotting garbage, and oils from *seeds* and *fruits* or oil *shale*. See **sustainable**.

Using muscles conserves petrol.

conservation of soil

See **soil conservation**.

constellation

is a cluster of *stars* forming a pattern or shape. Ancient people saw these patterns as pictures (e.g. scorpion, bear, Orion the hunter, the Southern Cross). Modern star charts show 88 constellations in the sky.

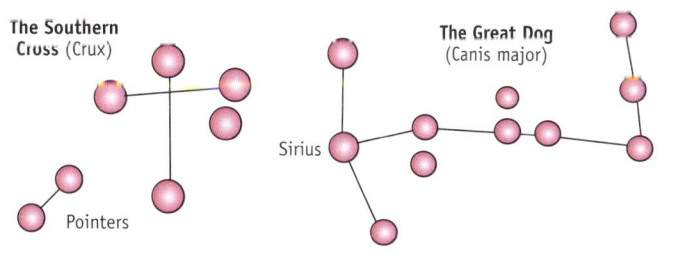

consumers

are *living things* that obtain their *energy* by feeding on other living things. *Animals* are consumers and they may be *herbivores*, *carnivores* or omnivores. Compare **producers**; **decomposers**. See **food chain**.

Excel Illustrated Science Dictionary Years 5–8

contraction of matter

occurs when *matter* is cooled. It takes up less space. Cooling slows down the movement of particles so that they do not bounce off each other as much and they spread out less. See **particle theory of matter**.

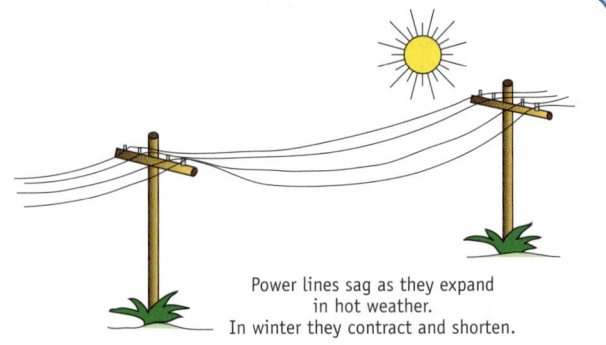

Power lines sag as they expand in hot weather.
In winter they contract and shorten.

control (in an experiment or fair test)

is used as a comparison. In an *experiment* to see if water evaporates faster in *wind*, a wet cloth is set up in wind and another (the control) is set up without wind. They are then compared. See **scientific method**.

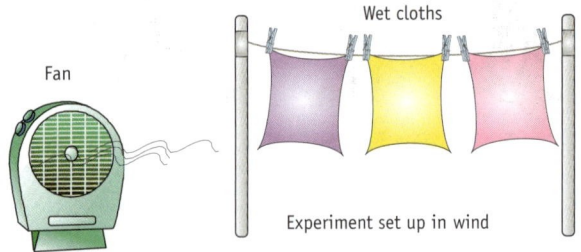

Experiment set up in wind

Control group set up without wind

convection

is one way *heat* travels in *liquids* and *gases*. When a gas or liquid is heated, the particles move faster and spread out. They become less dense and rise. Cooler, denser particles move in to take their place. Compare **conduction**; **radiation of heat**. See *convection in the atmosphere*.

Convection in air

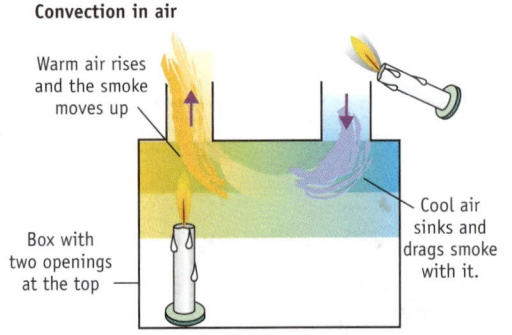

Convection in liquid

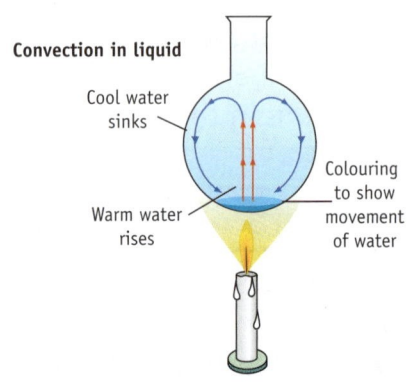

convection in the
atmosphere

convection in the atmosphere

occurs when the *Sun* heats the *air* near the ground. This makes the air expand and become less dense (lighter), so that it rises. The *temperature* of the atmosphere decreases with height from the *Earth*. As the air rises, it cools, becomes heavier and then falls. See **global air currents**; **cloud**.

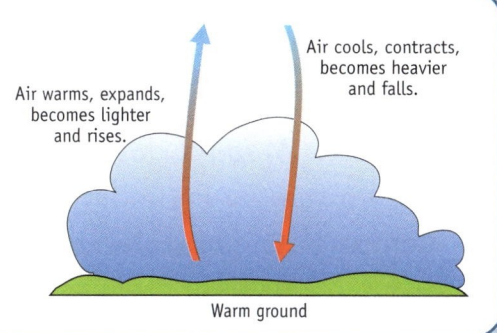

cooling substances

See **state of matter, change**.

cooperation (collaboration) in ecosystems

is when *organisms* work together to increase their survival rate (e.g. wolves hunt in packs; male yaks surround the females and young when *predators* threaten; dolphins surround schools of fish to catch them). See **colony**.

core

is at the central region of a *planet*. See **Earth**.

corrasion

occurs when *rock* fragments carried by *wind*, water or ice beat against the rocks or grind into them, causing them to crumble. See **erosion from wind**; **erosion from water**.

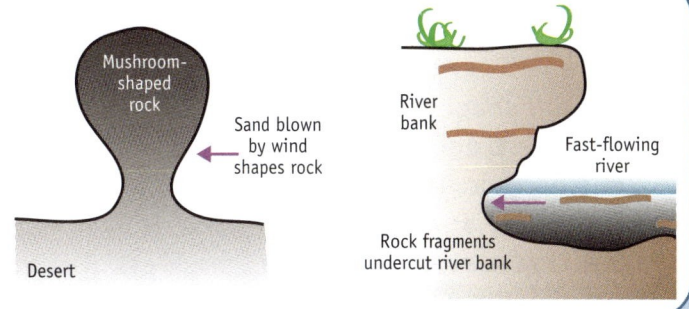

Excel Illustrated Science Dictionary Years 5–8

29

corrosion

occurs when a *metal* reacts with other chemicals. For example, iron slowly combines with *oxygen* and water to form *rust*. This reaction cannot be reversed. *Word equation*:

iron + oxygen + water → hydrated iron oxide (rust)

Compare **state of matter, change**. See **rust proofing**.

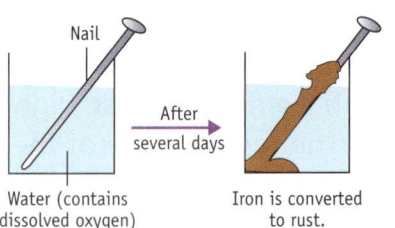

courtship

is behaviour that occurs before mating. It ensures *animals* mate with the same *species* and encourages the female to receive the male. In birds, courtship often includes elaborate song, display of feathers and dancing. For example, the male lyrebird mimics sounds and performs elaborate displays.

The male bower bird builds a bower for mating. He decorates it with coloured objects such as feathers, berries, leaves and shells.

crust

is the outermost solid layer of the *Earth* and is made up of the oceanic crust and continental crust. See **lithosphere**.

crustal plates

make up the *Earth's* surface. They are composed of the *crust* and upper layers of the *mantle* (the *lithosphere*). The plates move slowly on the soft *asthenosphere*, which is almost at *melting point*. The plates rub and cause *earthquakes* and *volcanoes* and collide to produce mountains and trenches.

crystal

is a *solid* substance that contains regular shapes with flat surfaces and sharp edges. Crystals may be microscopic. The particles in a crystal are arranged in a lattice. See **crystal formation**.

Crystal shapes

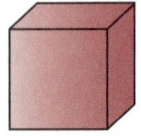 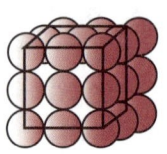 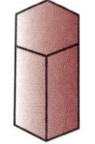 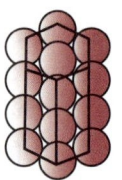

Cubic (e.g. salt) | Particles inside crystals | Hexagonal (e.g. quartz) | Particles inside crystals

The arrangement of particles inside the crystal gives it shape.

crystal formation (crystallisation)

occurs when a molten substance cools and solidifies, and when a *liquid* is evaporated from a *solution* (e.g. salt water). The slower the process, the larger the *crystals*. See **igneous rocks**; **crystal**.

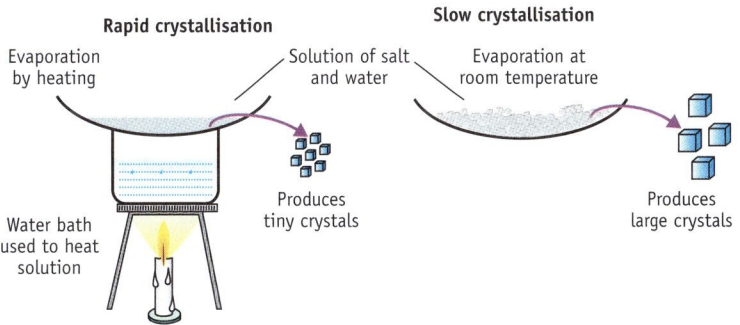

current

See **electric current**; **current electricity**; **global air currents**; **ocean currents**.

current electricity

is moving *charge*. Electricity is produced by batteries and *generator*s and is transferred from one place to another by a *current* in an electric *circuit*. Compare **static electricity**.

cyclone

is a very intense whirlpool of *wind* that forms over the ocean. It can travel at *speeds* greater than 200 km/hr and can also cause huge waves and massive damage.

day and night

day and night

is the length of time for a planet to spin or rotate on its axis. The side facing the *Sun* is in daytime. The side away from the Sun is in darkness or night. The Earth rotates once in about 24 hours.

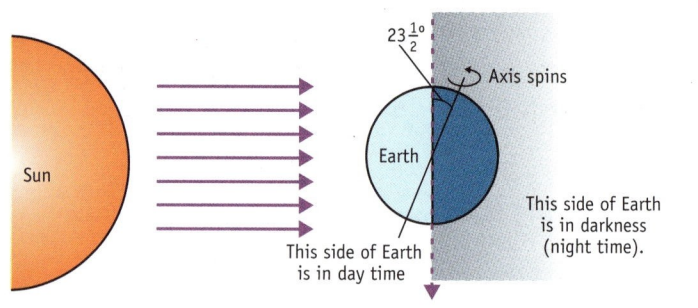

decanting

See **sedimentation and decanting**.

decomposers

break down dead *plants* or *animals* and their wastes and cause them to decay, releasing *nutrients* into the *soil*. *Bacteria* and *fungi* are decomposers. See **decomposition**.

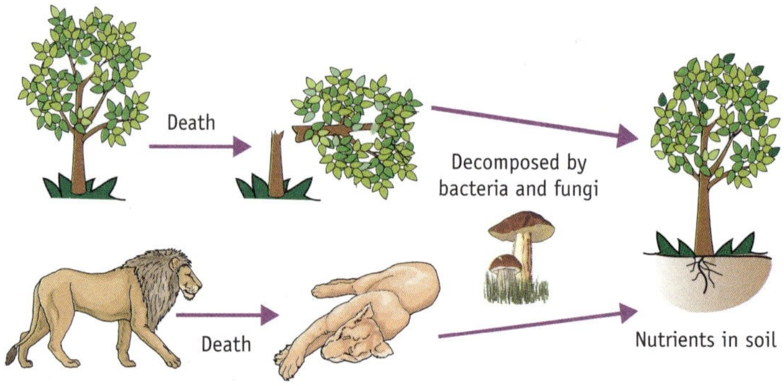

decomposition

is a *chemical reaction* where a substance is broken down into two or more new substances. For instance, heating sugar breaks it down to carbon and water. See **decomposers; food preservation**.

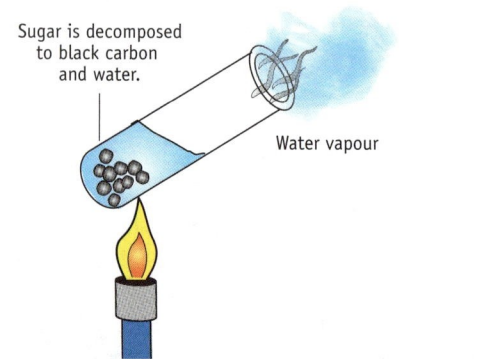

32

Excel Illustrated Science Dictionary Years 5–8

density

is the amount of *matter* or *mass* in a certain *volume* or space. A bag full of glass marbles feels heavier than the same bag when it is filled with corks. This is because glass is denser than cork (the glass particles are more closely packed than the cork particles). Density is measured in g/mL or g/cm^3.

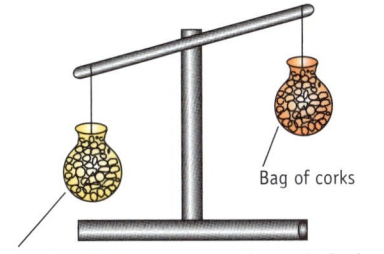

Bag of corks

Bag of marbles has more mass than a similar bag of corks because the marbles are more dense.

detergents

See **soaps and detergents**.

diffusion

is the spreading and mixing of one substance into another. Diffusion is caused by the natural movement of particles. Diffusion *speeds* up if the *temperature* increases.

Cooking smells spread by diffusion.

Smells of perfume spread by diffusion.

Undisturbed water

Dissolving tablet spreads slowly through the water by diffusion.

digestion

(in humans) occurs when *food* is broken down in the *digestive system* into small particles so that it can pass through the intestine walls into the blood. See **digestive system**; **digestion, mechanical**; **digestion, chemical**.

digestion, chemical

occurs in the mouth, stomach and small intestines. Chemicals called *enzymes* react with *food* and break it into small particles. In the stomach hydrochloric *acid* helps with this digestion. See **digestion, mechanical**; **digestive system**.

digestion, mechanical

is the breaking up of *food* into small pieces. The teeth grind food into small pieces. Bile breaks *fats* into small lumps. See **digestion, chemical**; **digestive system**.

Excel Illustrated Science Dictionary Years 5–8

digestive system

(in humans) breaks down *food* into small particles so that they can pass through the walls of the small intestines, into the blood. Compare **herbivore**. See **digestion**.

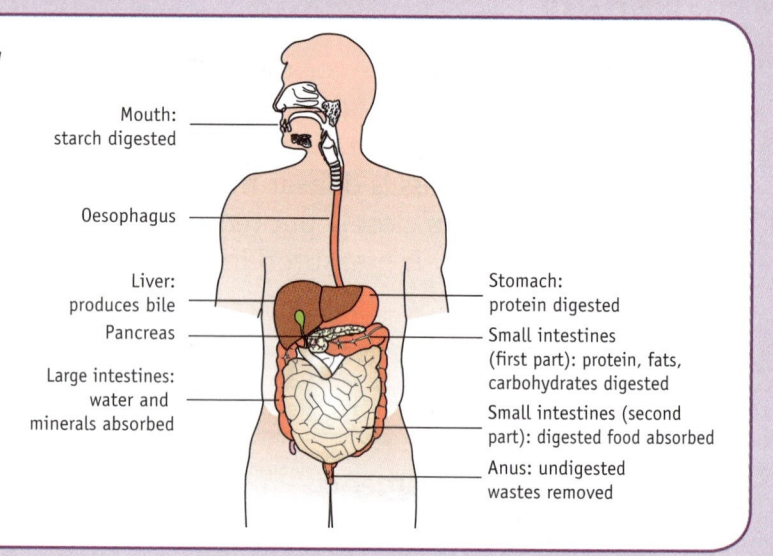

Mouth: starch digested
Oesophagus
Liver: produces bile
Pancreas
Large intestines: water and minerals absorbed
Stomach: protein digested
Small intestines (first part): protein, fats, carbohydrates digested
Small intestines (second part): digested food absorbed
Anus: undigested wastes removed

dilute solution

has a small amount of *solid dissolved* in the *liquid*. Compare **concentrated solution; saturated solution**. See **solution**.

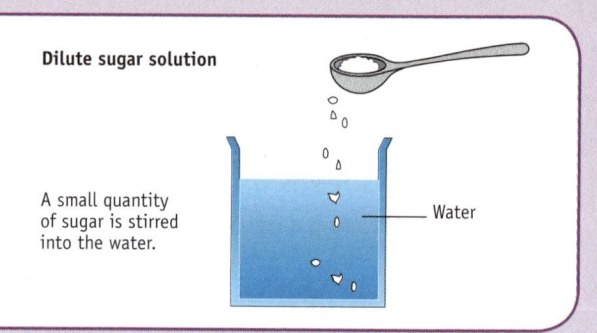

Dilute sugar solution

A small quantity of sugar is stirred into the water.
Water

dinosaurs

were prehistoric reptiles that lived about 150 million years ago. *Fossil* remains show that dinosaurs ranged from the size of a chicken to 30 m in length. See **rock age**.

Tyrannosaurus
Pterodactyl
Triceratops

direct current (DC)

is a steady *current* flowing in one direction. It is produced by batteries. Compare **alternating current (AC)**.

34

Excel Illustrated Science Dictionary Years 5–8

disposal of wastes

disposal of wastes

See **waste disposal**.

dissolve

is what happens when a solid breaks down in a liquid into tiny particles that are too small to see. A *solution* is formed. For example, sugar stirred in hot water dissolves. See **soluble**.

distance in space

See **light year**.

distillation

is a method of separating *liquids* from *mixtures*. The *solution* is heated and as each substance boils at a different temperature, the *vapours* formed can be condensed and collected separately. Distillation is used to obtain fresh water from sea water, to separate perfumes and oils from *plant* materials, to collect petrol, kerosene and diesel oil from *petroleum* and to purify and concentrate alcohols.

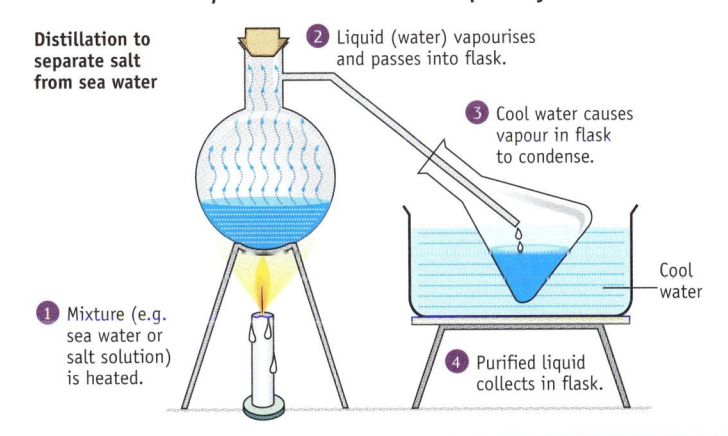

Distillation to separate salt from sea water

1. Mixture (e.g. sea water or salt solution) is heated.
2. Liquid (water) vapourises and passes into flask.
3. Cool water causes vapour in flask to condense.
4. Purified liquid collects in flask.

diurnal

means active during the *day*. Most animals are diurnal. Compare **nocturnal**.

diversity

See **biodiversity**.

Excel Illustrated Science Dictionary Years 5–8

drought

drought

occurs when there is a long period without *rain*. Droughts have a devastating effect on the natural *environment* and on farming and the production of *food*. They kill *plants* and *animals* and destroy places where animals can hide from *predators*. Droughts damage the soil and cause erosion by killing and removing plants.

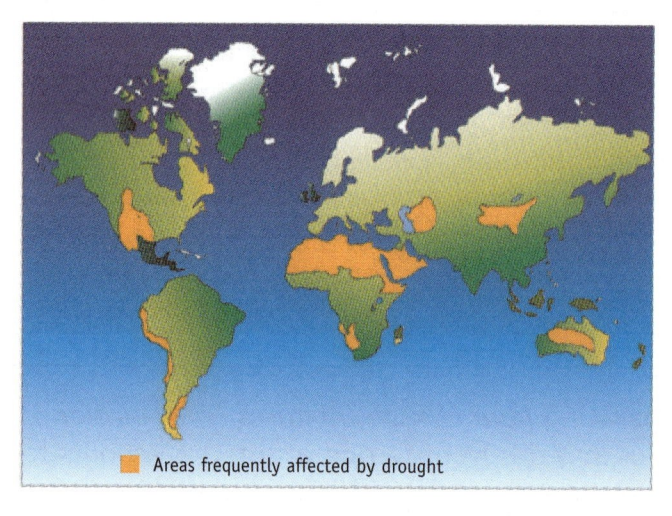

Areas frequently affected by drought

dry cell

See **electric cell**.

Earth

Earth

is the third *planet* from the *Sun*. It is a sphere slightly flattened at the poles and bulging at the equator. The outer zones of the Earth are the *atmosphere*, *lithosphere*, *hydrosphere* and *asthenosphere*. See **rotate**; **biosphere**; **crustal plates**.

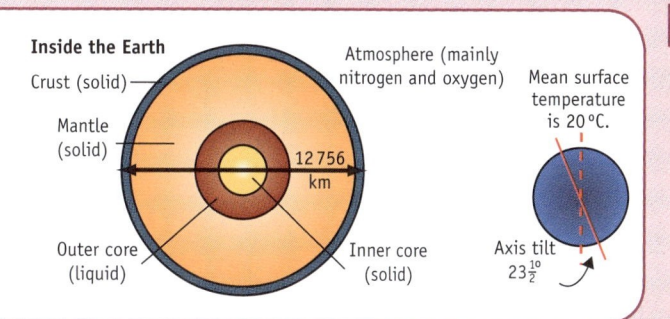

Inside the Earth
Crust (solid)
Mantle (solid)
12 756 km
Outer core (liquid)
Inner core (solid)
Atmosphere (mainly nitrogen and oxygen)
Mean surface temperature is 20 °C.
Axis tilt $23\frac{1}{2}°$

Earth history

begins 4600 million years ago, when the Earth started as a molten body.
- 4600–570 million years ago: The Earth cooled and became solid. The *crust*, *mantle* and *core* formed, followed by oceans and *atmosphere*. Movement and crashing of plates making up the *lithosphere* caused *earthquakes* and volcanic activity. Glaciation and mountain building occurred and *minerals* formed.
- 570–225 million years ago: A supercontinent (Pangaea) formed and sedimentation occurred in shallow seas, forming *sedimentary rocks* (e.g. limestone, sandstone and coal).
- 225–65 million years ago: Sea floor spreading and continental drift occurred. Lowlands and inland seas formed and more sedimentation occurred. Uplifting of continents occurred.
- 65–1.6 million years ago: Sea floor spreading moved the continents to their present positions. There was mountain-building volcanic activity and erosion.
- 1.6–present: Glaciation (the Ice Age) caused the sea level to fall. Continental shelves were exposed and eroded. Ice melted causing flooding, forming estuaries and fiords (flooded glacial valleys).
- Present: Crust is still changing due to plate movements, earthquakes, volcanoes, new crust forming, uplift forming mountains, flooding, erosion and sedimentation.

Earth, Sun and Moon

vary in their revolution. The *Earth* rotates once on its axis every 24 hours. It revolves around the *Sun* in an elliptical (oval) *orbit* in 365 days. The *Moon* revolves around the Earth in an elliptical orbit in 28 days. It also takes 28 days to rotate on its axis. As a result one side of the Moon always faces the Earth.

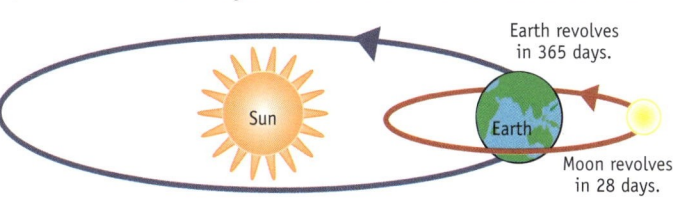

Earth revolves in 365 days.
Sun
Earth
Moon revolves in 28 days.

Excel Illustrated Science Dictionary Years 5–8

earthquake zones

earthquake zones

are areas in which *earthquakes* occur. Most volcanic activity also occurs in these zones. See **volcano**.

— Earthquake zones

Earthquakes follow the crustal plate margins. Most volcanic activity also occurs in these zones.

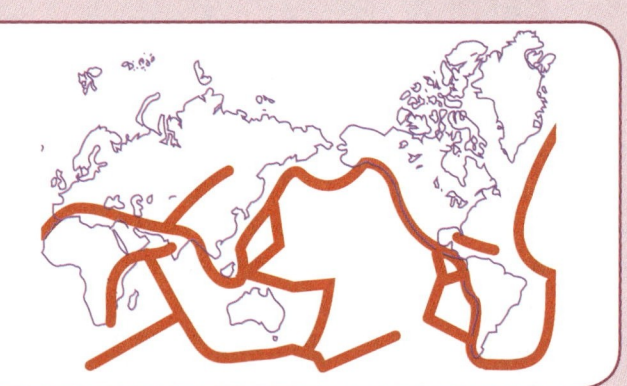

earthquakes

are vibrations in the Earth's *crust* caused by *Earth* movements below the surface. They may cause buildings and bridges to collapse, and create small cliffs and landslides. Fires can begin as a result of broken gas pipelines and electrical wiring. Earthquakes are measured with *seismographs*. See **earthquake zones**.

echo

occurs when *sound* bounces off hard objects and is heard a split second later. Bats and dolphins use sound waves and echoes to find their way around. Ships use echoes to find the depth of the water.

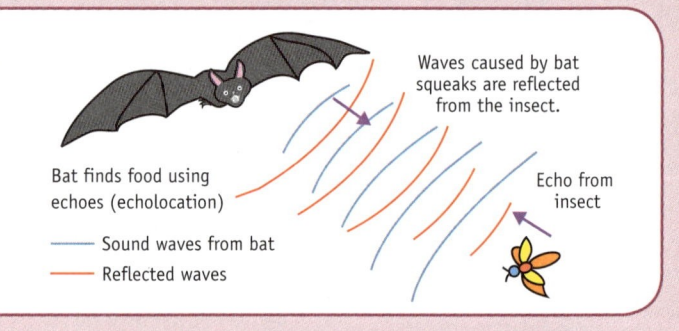

Bat finds food using echoes (echolocation)
Waves caused by bat squeaks are reflected from the insect.
Echo from insect
— Sound waves from bat
— Reflected waves

eclipse

occurs when one body in the sky hides another. See **eclipse of the Sun; eclipse of the Moon**.

eclipse of the Moon

is known as a lunar eclipse. This occurs when the *Earth* is between the *Sun* and the Moon, blocking the Sun's rays. The Moon does not shine because light from the Sun does not reach it.

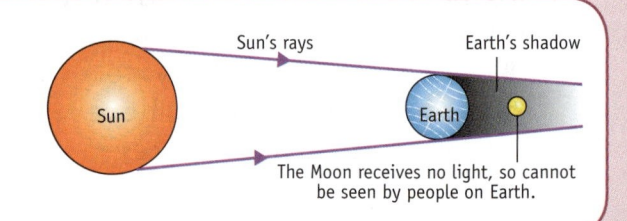

Sun's rays   Earth's shadow
Sun   Earth
The Moon receives no light, so cannot be seen by people on Earth.

Excel Illustrated Science Dictionary Years 5–8

eclipse of the Sun

is known as a solar eclipse. This occurs when the *Moon* passes between the *Sun* and the *Earth*, blocking the Sun from view.

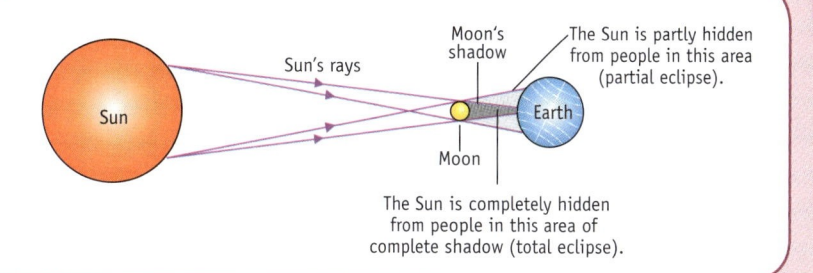

The Sun is partly hidden from people in this area (partial eclipse).

The Sun is completely hidden from people in this area of complete shadow (total eclipse).

ecosystem

is a place containing *living things* that interact with each other and their surroundings (*environment*). It is made up of living and non-living features. A pond is an example of an ecosystem. See **ecosystem interactions**.

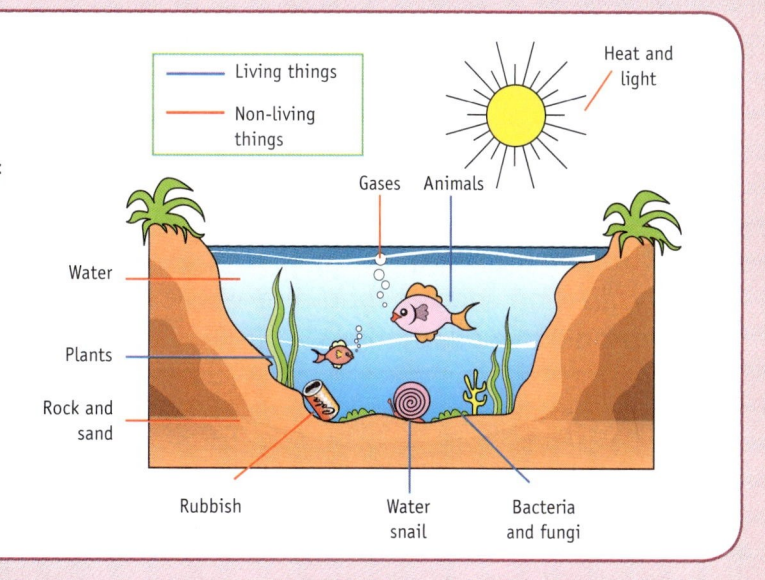

ecosystem interactions

occur when *organisms* in an *ecosystem* affect each other.

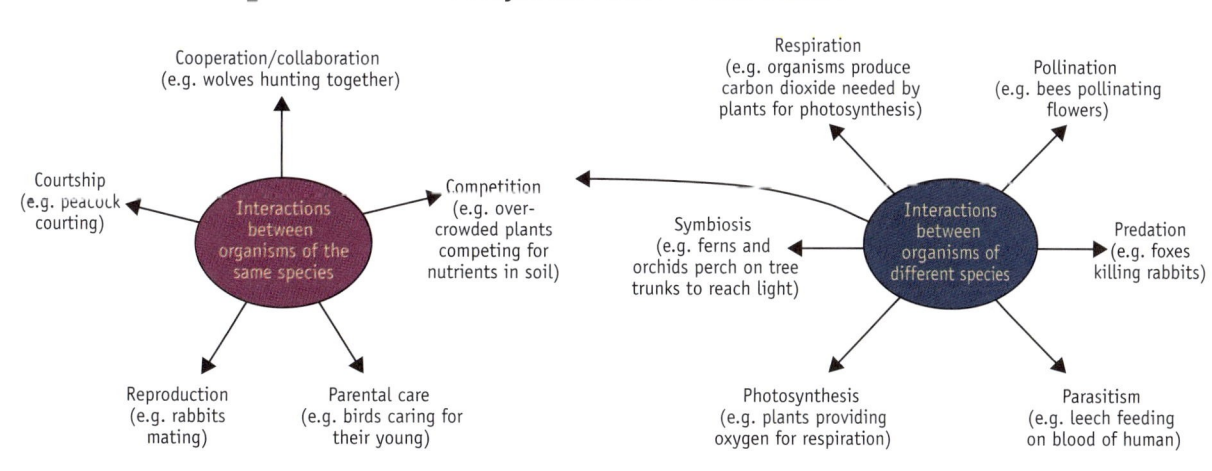

Interactions between organisms of the same species
- Cooperation/collaboration (e.g. wolves hunting together)
- Courtship (e.g. peacock courting)
- Competition (e.g. over-crowded plants competing for nutrients in soil)
- Reproduction (e.g. rabbits mating)
- Parental care (e.g. birds caring for their young)

Interactions between organisms of different species
- Respiration (e.g. organisms produce carbon dioxide needed by plants for photosynthesis)
- Pollination (e.g. bees pollinating flowers)
- Symbiosis (e.g. ferns and orchids perch on tree trunks to reach light)
- Predation (e.g. foxes killing rabbits)
- Photosynthesis (e.g. plants providing oxygen for respiration)
- Parasitism (e.g. leech feeding on blood of human)

Excel Illustrated Science Dictionary Years 5–8

efficiency of a machine

is a measure of how well it uses *energy*. The energy (or *work*) we get from a *machine* is generally less than the energy (or work) we put into it. This is because *friction* changes some of the original energy to *heat* energy.

$$\text{efficiency of a machine} = \frac{\text{work done by the machine}}{\text{work put into the machine}} \times 100$$

See **mechanical advantage**.

The boy's energy is transferred to the bike and moves it up the hill.

Some of the energy is converted to heat energy because of friction.

egg (ovum)

is the female reproductive or sex *cell*. In some *animal*s it is enclosed in a shell after *fertilisation* and has *food* reserves. It is produced by the ovary. See **fertilisation; reproductive adaptations**.

El Niño

is a weather pattern that occurs every three to seven years when the *wind* and *ocean currents* in the Pacific Ocean change. This alters the *climate* and causes *natural disasters*, such as *droughts*, floods and severe storms.

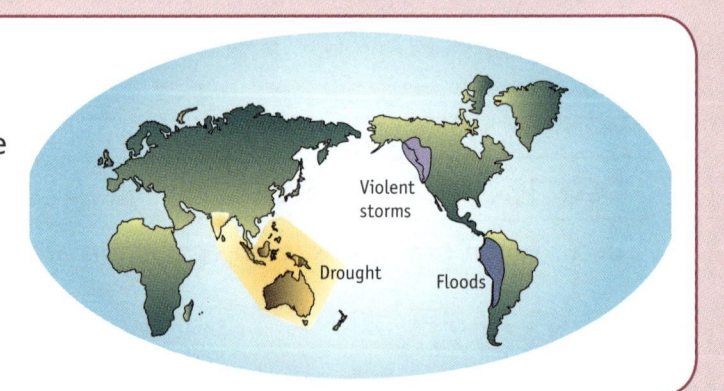

elastic material

is material that will return to its original shape after it has been stretched, twisted or bent (e.g. rubber). The material possesses elasticity. See **potential energy**.

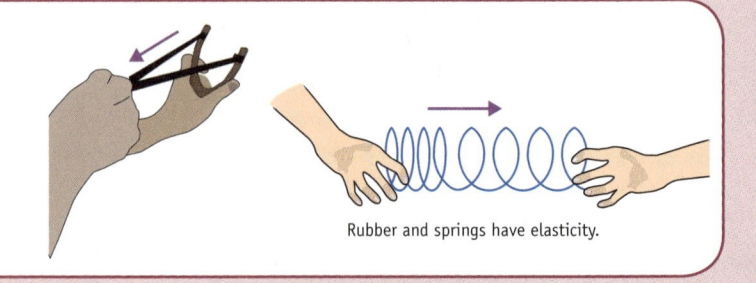

Rubber and springs have elasticity.

electric cells

are used to make up a *battery*. *Chemical reaction*s produce a positive *charge* on the carbon rod and a negative charge on the zinc casing.

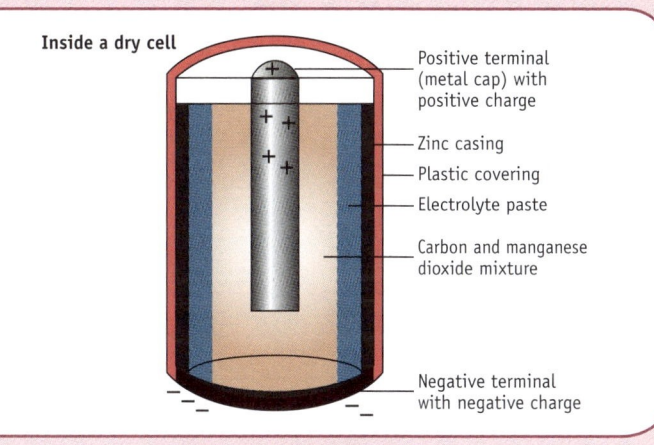

Inside a dry cell
- Positive terminal (metal cap) with positive charge
- Zinc casing
- Plastic covering
- Electrolyte paste
- Carbon and manganese dioxide mixture
- Negative terminal with negative charge

electric circuit

See **circuit**.

electric current

is a flow of *electricity* or moving negative *charge*. Electricity will move along a wire if there is a difference in electrical pressure or *voltage*. Current can be increased by increasing the voltage. See **direct current (DC)**; **alternating current (AC)**.

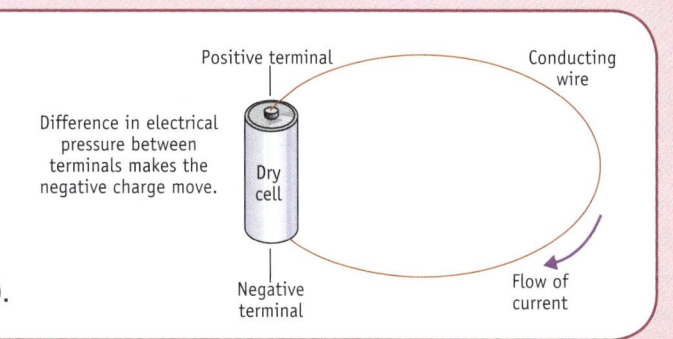

Difference in electrical pressure between terminals makes the negative charge move.
Positive terminal — Conducting wire — Dry cell — Negative terminal — Flow of current

electrical energy

or *electricity* is *energy* involving *charges*. The charges may be moving to produce *current electricity* or stationary to produce *static electricity*.

electrical energy used by an appliance

The watts shown on an appliance indicate how much *power* it draws from the *electricity* supply. The amount of *energy* used (in kilowatt hours) = electricity it draws (in kilowatts) × time it is in use (in hours).

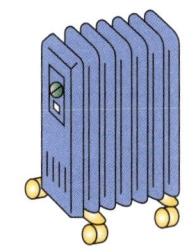

What does a 3000 watt radiator cost to run for 2 hours?

Power = 3000 watts = 3 kilowatts
Energy used = Power × time (in use)
= 3 × 2
= 6 kilowatt hours (kWh)
If 1 kWh of energy costs 10 cents, then 6 kWh will cost 60 cents.

Excel Illustrated Science Dictionary Years 5–8

E

electrical symbols

electrical symbols

are used to show components (parts) of a *circuit*.

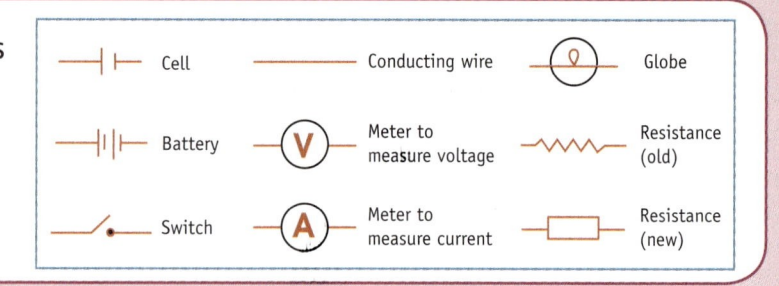

—⊢⊢— Cell	——— Conducting wire	—Ⓠ— Globe
—⊢⊩⊢— Battery	—Ⓥ— Meter to measure voltage	—⋀⋁⋀— Resistance (old)
—/•— Switch	—Ⓐ— Meter to measure current	—▭— Resistance (new)

electricity

is a form of energy, as it can bring about a change in things. See **electrical energy**.

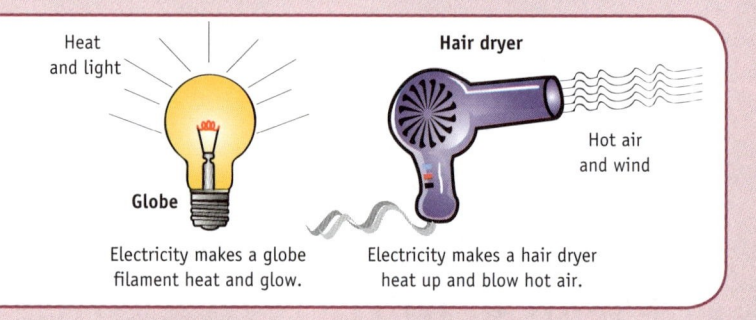

Heat and light

Globe
Electricity makes a globe filament heat and glow.

Hair dryer

Hot air and wind
Electricity makes a hair dryer heat up and blow hot air.

electricity generation

can be achieved by a variety of energy sources:
- *fossil fuels* (non-renewable)
- flowing water (i.e. *hydroelectricity*)
- wave energy
- tidal energy
- solar energy
- wind energy
- geothermal energy
- nuclear energy (non-renewable).

electromagnet

is a *magnet* that can be switched on and off. Electromagnets are made by passing a *current* through a coil of wire wrapped around a piece of iron. Electromagnets are used in motors, speakers and electric bells, and on cranes to pick up and transfer large pieces of steel and scrap iron.

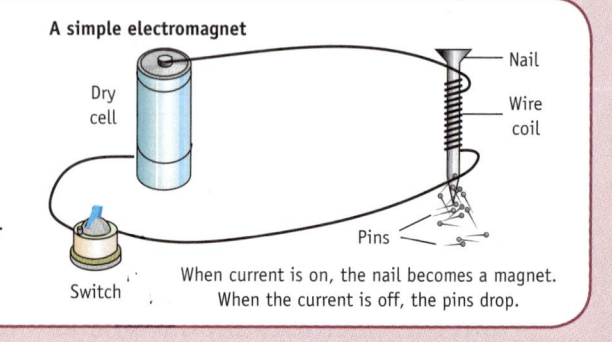

A simple electromagnet

Dry cell

Nail

Wire coil

Pins

Switch

When current is on, the nail becomes a magnet. When the current is off, the pins drop.

electrostatic charge

See **charge; charging an object**.

42

Excel Illustrated Science Dictionary Years 5–8

electrostatic field

electrostatic (electric) field

is the area around a charged object where it exerts a force. See **charge**; **static electricity**; **electrostatic force**.

electrostatic force

is the pull or push exerted by a charged object. For example, nylon clothes become charged in a dryer and cling to other clothes. Unlike charges attract each other. Like charges repel each other. See **static electricity**; **charge**; **charging an object**.

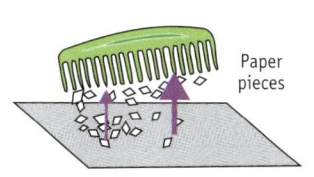

Paper pieces

Comb and paper have opposite charges. The paper is attracted to the comb.

Charged hairs repel each other.

Each hair has the same charge.

element

is a pure substance made up of one type of particle or *atom* (e.g. the element carbon is composed only of carbon particles). It cannot be converted to a simpler substance. There are 92 naturally occurring elements. Scientists have made more by artificial means (e.g. plutonium and einsteinium). Most elements exist as solids but some are liquids or gases. Elements exist as *metals* or *non-metals*. A small number of elements have *properties* between metals and non-metals (e.g. silicon, Si). See **chemical element symbols**; **periodic table**.

element symbols

See **chemical element symbols**.

emulsion

is a *colloid* in which a *liquid* is spread through another liquid. For example, homogenised milk has tiny globules of butterfat spread through it.

Emulsions are found commonly in foods.

Excel Illustrated Science Dictionary Years 5–8

energy

energy

of an object is its ability to do things and to cause change (*work*). Energy can be transferred or transmitted (moved) and can be changed (transformed) into another form. See **energy sources**; **energy types**; **energy transfer**; **energy transformation**.

1. Electrical energy is transferred to the toaster.
2. Electrical energy is changed to heat energy.
3. Heat energy toasts the bread (does the work).

energy conservation

See **conservation of energy**.

energy sources

used by early civilisations for fuel were wood, charcoal and oil (from *plants* and seeping from the ground). In the 19th and 20th centuries oil, *gas*, *electricity* and nuclear power techniques were developed. See **renewable energy sources**; **non-renewable energy sources**; **electricity generation**.

energy transfer

occurs when *energy* is passed on from one object to another. For example, vibrations from an *earthquake* travel through the ground and *air* and can be felt in distant places. See **echo**; **energy transfer in living things**.

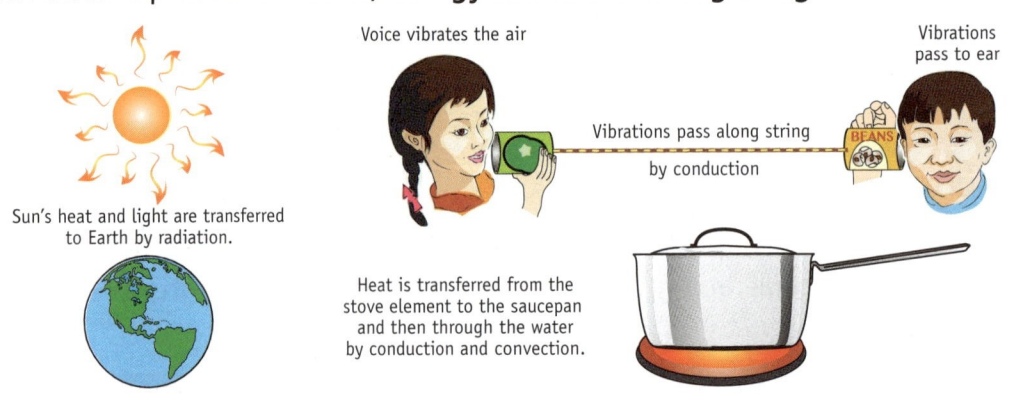

Sun's heat and light are transferred to Earth by radiation.

Voice vibrates the air
Vibrations pass along string by conduction
Vibrations pass to ear

Heat is transferred from the stove element to the saucepan and then through the water by conduction and convection.

energy transfer in living things

occurs when *food* is passed along a *food chain* from one *living thing* to another.

energy transformation

energy transformation

is when *energy* is changed into a different form. No energy is lost. See **energy transformation in living things**.

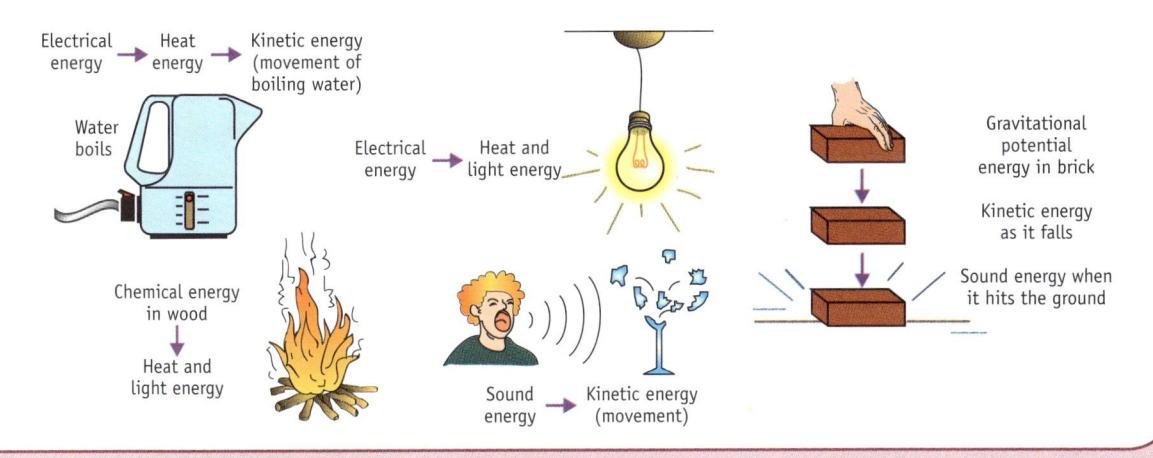

energy transformation in living things

is when one form of *energy* is changed into another. *Light* energy from the Sun is converted to *chemical energy* by *plants* during *photosynthesis*. *Organisms* convert the chemical energy stored in *food* to other forms, such as *movement energy* and *heat* energy. See **energy used in human activities; solar energy**.

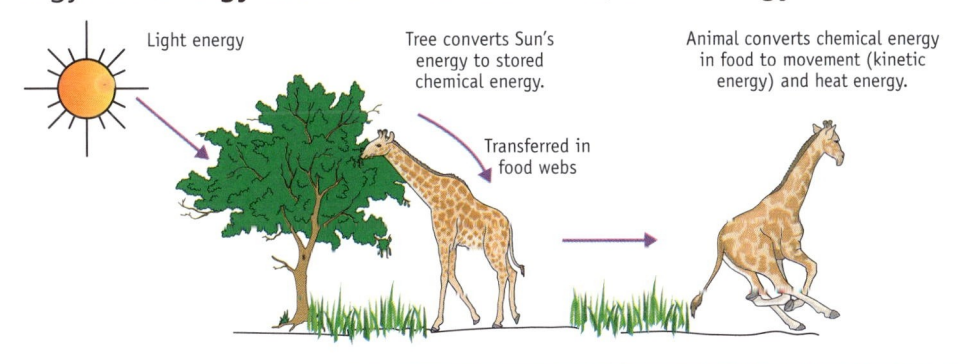

energy transmission

See **energy transfer**.

energy types

include movement, *heat*, *light*, *sound*, *electrical*, *chemical* and *nuclear*. Energy may be grouped as *kinetic* or *potential*. See **solar energy; radiant energy; energy sources**.

Excel Illustrated Science Dictionary Years 5–8

energy used in Australia

comes mostly from oil (petrol) and *coal*. Oil and petrol are used mainly for transport. Coal is used to produce *electricity* and *gas*. *Uranium*, a source of *nuclear energy*, is exported and is not used to produce electricity in Australia. In Australia, approximately 84% of electricity is produced from coal. The rest is from *renewable resources*, mainly *hydroelectricity*.

energy used in human activities

depends on the size and age of the person, and different activities require different amounts of *energy*.

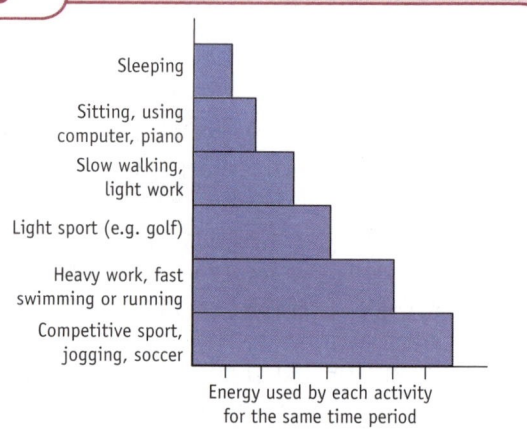

Sleeping
Sitting, using computer, piano
Slow walking, light work
Light sport (e.g. golf)
Heavy work, fast swimming or running
Competitive sport, jogging, soccer

Energy used by each activity for the same time period

environment

is an *organism's* surroundings. It includes *living things* (*plants*, *animals*, *bacteria* and *fungi*) as well as non-living things such as *rocks*, *air*, moisture, *temperature* and *light*. Changes in the environment may affect *ecosystem interactions*. See **terrestrial; aquatic; environmental changes**.

environmental changes

affect growth and survival of living things (e.g. adding fertiliser to a plant helps it grow). Changes may also alter the interactions in the *ecosystem*. *Drought*, *bushfires* and *floods*, as well as humans, change the environment. Activities of humans, such as agriculture, removing forests, building, *mining*, polluting and introducing new *species* may result in changes that cannot be reversed. See **ecosystem interactions; environmental changes caused by humans; balance of nature**.

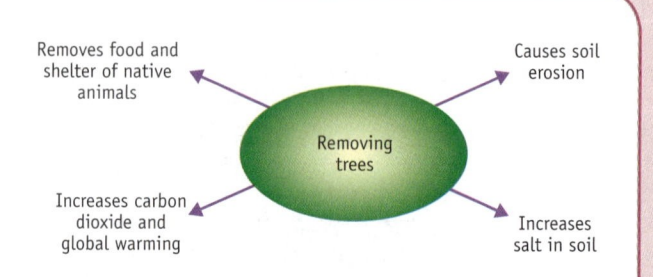

Removing trees
- Removes food and shelter of native animals
- Causes soil erosion
- Increases carbon dioxide and global warming
- Increases salt in soil

environmental changes caused by humans

environmental changes caused by humans

are many and varied. Some can be reversed but many others cannot.

Human activities have had a major impact on the environment. These activities include deforestation, *mining*, agriculture and *pollution*. As a result, *habitats* and food supplies are destroyed and *species* are threatened. For example, in Borneo and Sumatra rainforests are being removed for oil palm plantations. This is destroying the habitats of orangutans who are threatened with *extinction*.

Many Australian *plants* are stimulated by fire to grow and release their seeds. Aboriginal and Torres Strait Islander peoples modified the environment by using fire during hunting. This promoted new growth that formed woodlands and grasslands and attracted herbivores. Humans introduced cane toads to Queensland to control the sugar cane beetle, which was a pest. The toads rapidly multiplied and spread. This has caused native species to decline, mainly due to the poison from the toads. The toad also carries disease and competes with native wildlife for food and shelter. See **ecosystem interactions; soaps and detergents; waste disposal**.

enzyme

is a chemical that increases the speed of a *chemical reaction* but is not used up in the reaction. Enzymes are in saliva, digestive juices made by the stomach and intestine wall, and the pancreas. They are important in chemical *digestion*, as well as *respiration* and *photosynthesis*. See **catalyst; digestion, chemical**.

erosion

is the wearing away of the land. *Rocks* are *weathered* and the rock fragments formed are carried to another place where they are deposited to form *sediments* and may eventually develop into *sedimentary rocks*. See **erosion from water; erosion from wind; erosion from moving ice; soil erosion**.

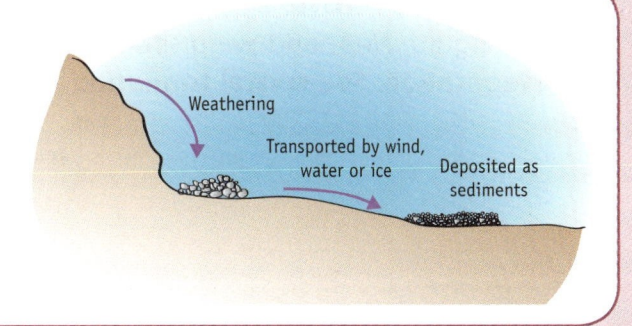

erosion from moving ice

is caused by glaciers. A *glacier* is a large mass of ice slowly moving down a valley. The moving ice carries stones that grind into the valley, wearing down the land. When the ice *melt*s, the stones are deposited. See **corrasion**.

erosion from water

occurs because rivers and ocean waves often carry rock fragments and sand. These particles have an abrasive effect and grind into riverbeds and cliff faces. When the water slows, the particles are deposited. See **corrasion**.

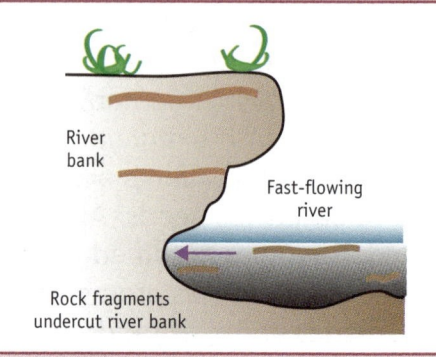

River bank
Fast-flowing river
Rock fragments undercut river bank

erosion from wind

occurs because strong winds often carry weathered rock particles (e.g. sand). The particles have an abrasive effect and wear down the surrounding landscape. As the *wind* slows down, the particles are deposited. See **corrasion**.

Sand blown by wind shapes rock

evaporation

occurs when a *liquid* is converted to a *vapour* or *gas*. It is used to recover a *solid* that has been *dissolved* in a liquid. *Heat* and *wind* speed up evaporation. See **crystal formation**.

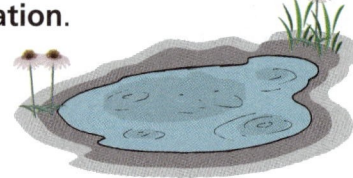

Water evaporates slowly from the puddle and it eventually dries up.

Water evaporates quickly from the kettle as the water boils.

evolution

is a series of gradual changes in *organisms* and the development of new varieties and *species* over a long period of time. See **fossil**.

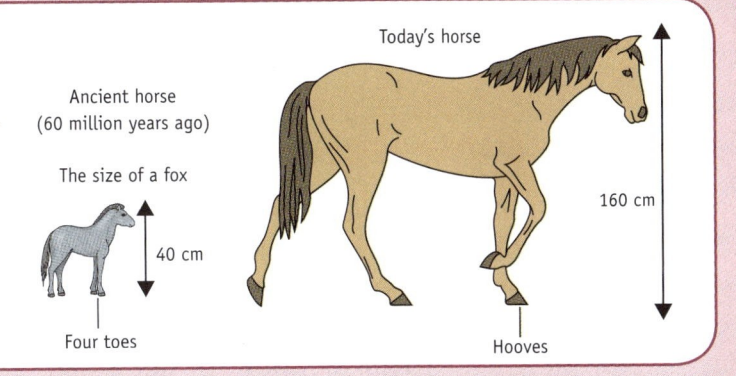

Today's horse

Ancient horse (60 million years ago)

The size of a fox

40 cm

160 cm

Four toes

Hooves

excretion

is the removal of wastes that have formed in *cells* during chemical reactions. Wastes are removed by the kidneys and bladder as urine and by the skin as perspiration. *Carbon dioxide* is removed by the lungs. See **excretory system; respiratory system in humans**.

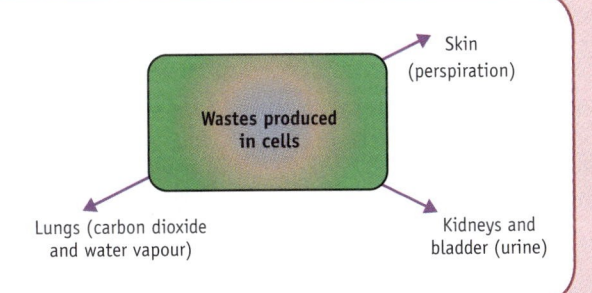

Wastes produced in cells

Skin (perspiration)

Lungs (carbon dioxide and water vapour)

Kidneys and bladder (urine)

excretory system

consists of kidneys, ureters, bladder and urethra. Chemical wastes from *cells* are taken by the blood to the excretory system, where they are removed from the body. The lungs and the skin are also excretory *organs*. See **respiratory system in humans**.

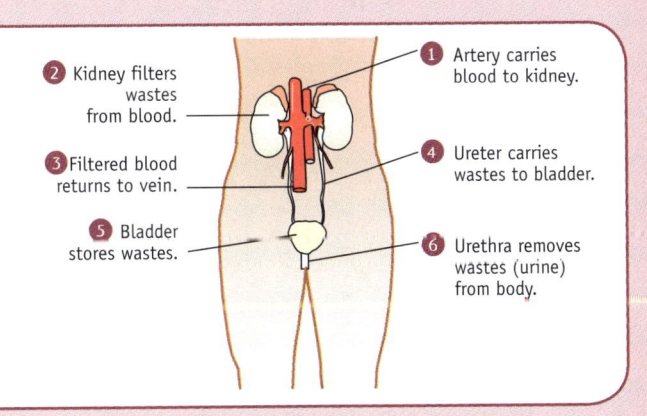

1. Artery carries blood to kidney.
2. Kidney filters wastes from blood.
3. Filtered blood returns to vein.
4. Ureter carries wastes to bladder.
5. Bladder stores wastes.
6. Urethra removes wastes (urine) from body.

expansion of matter

occurs when *matter* is heated. Heating makes the particles move more and spread out, taking up more space. Compare **contraction of matter**. See **particle theory of matter**.

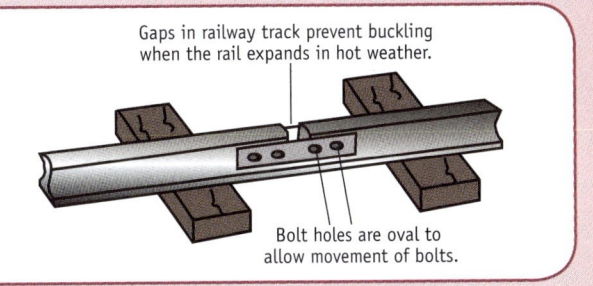

Gaps in railway track prevent buckling when the rail expands in hot weather.

Bolt holes are oval to allow movement of bolts.

experiment

See **scientific method (fair test)**.

extinction

is when *organisms* disappear from the *Earth* because of changes in the *environment* (e.g. *climate*) and human activities (e.g. land clearing and introducing other *animals*). The Tasmanian wolf or 'tiger' (thylacine) has not been seen since the early 1930s. See **megafauna**.

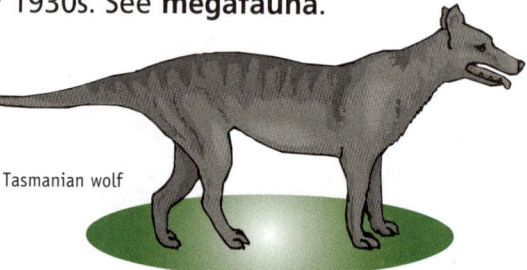

Tasmanian wolf

Dodo

fair test

fair test
See **scientific method (fair test)**.

fats and oils
are organic *nutrients*. They provide an *energy* store and an *insulating* layer under the skin and around *organs* to keep the body and organs warm. See **organic compound**.

fault
is a crack or join in the rock where there has been movement on one side relative to the other. Mountains and valleys form when a block of land moves between two faults. Faulting and folding is important in the formation of *minerals* and *fossil fuel resources*.

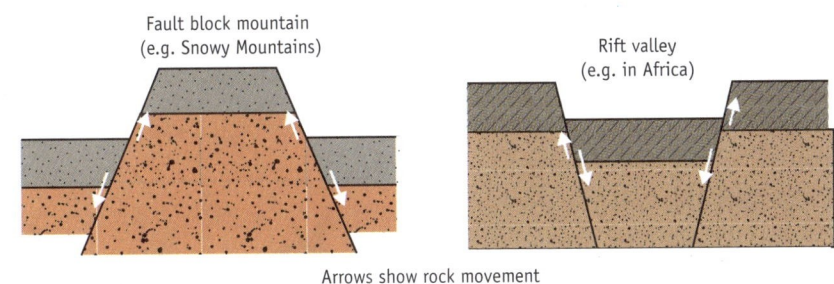

Fault block mountain (e.g. Snowy Mountains)

Rift valley (e.g. in Africa)

Arrows show rock movement

feedback and feed forward systems
are *systems* the *organs* use to send or 'feed' messages to the brain, to keep the body working properly.

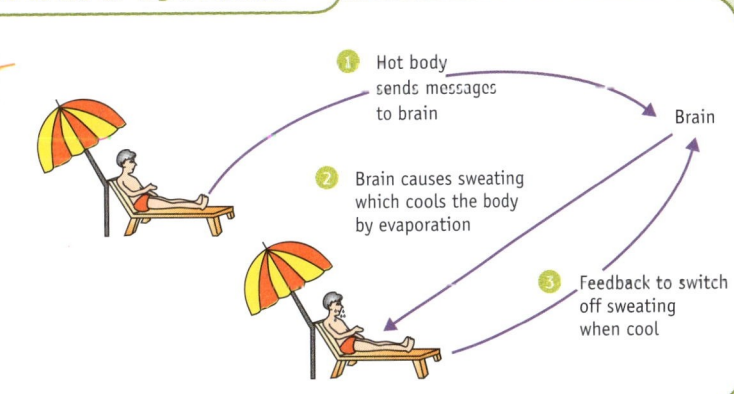

1. Hot body sends messages to brain → Brain
2. Brain causes sweating which cools the body by evaporation
3. Feedback to switch off sweating when cool

feeding relationships
See **food chain; predation; parasitism**.

Excel Illustrated Science Dictionary Years 5–8

F

feral

refers to *plants* and *animals* that are wild but not in their native *habitat* (e.g. feral cats). They compete with or *prey* on native *organisms*.

fertilisation

is the joining of *egg* (ovum) and *sperm* during *sexual reproduction*. The fertilised egg grows and develops to form a new individual similar to its parents. See **reproductive adaptations**.

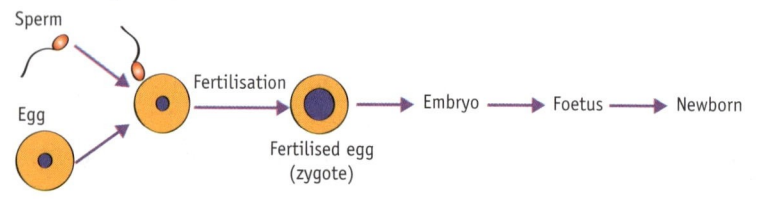

Sperm → Fertilisation → Fertilised egg (zygote) → Embryo → Foetus → Newborn
Egg

fibres

are threads that make up fabrics and ropes. Cotton, wool, linen (from flax) and silk are natural fibres. Nylon, polyester and acrylics are man-made, or *synthetic*, products. Most synthetic fibres are made from *petroleum*.

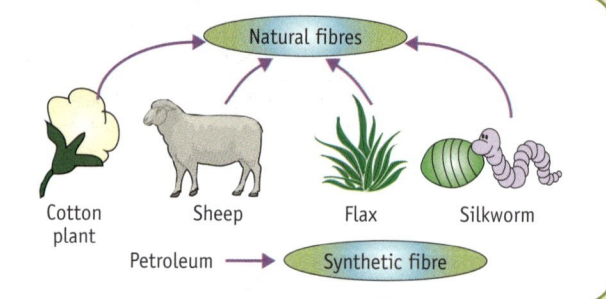

Natural fibres: Cotton plant, Sheep, Flax, Silkworm
Petroleum → Synthetic fibre

field

is an area in which a body experiences a force from another body. See **magnetic field**; **electrostatic (electric) field**.

filtration

is used to separate solid particles using a filter. For example, when muddy salt water is filtered, the mud is collected on the filter and the salt water passes through it. Peas are separated from cooking water using a sieve. Rocks and sand are separated using mesh. See **sieving**.

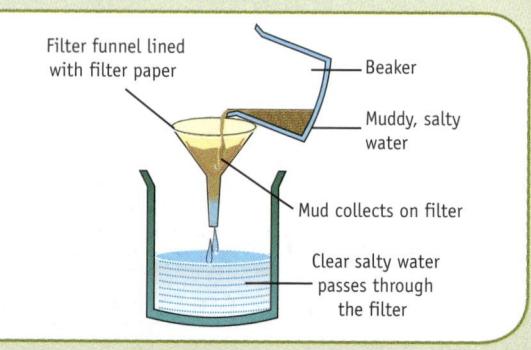

Filter funnel lined with filter paper — Beaker
Muddy, salty water
Mud collects on filter
Clear salty water passes through the filter

float

means to stay on the surface of or be suspended in a fluid. An object will float if its *weight* and the upward *force* (or *upthrust*) are equal. An object that is light for its size will float. Its *density* is less than the density of the surrounding fluid. See **sink**; **buoyancy**.

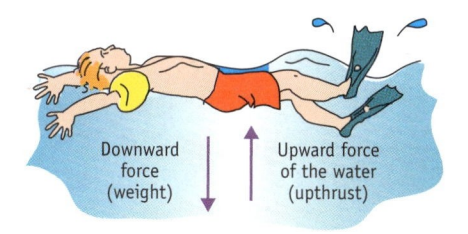

flower

is a *plant structure* in which *sexual reproduction* occurs. The anthers make pollen, which contains the male sex *cells*. The ovary makes female sex cells or *eggs*. See **reproduction in flowering plants**.

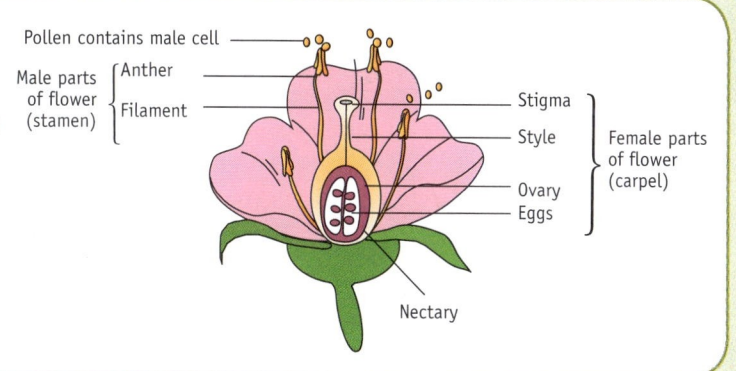

flowering plants

have *flowers*, and produce *seeds* and *fruit*. See **plant structure**; **life cycle of a flowering plant**.

fluorescent globe

is a tube that contains a *gas* (e.g. mercury vapour). A discharge causes a stream of electrons to move from one electrode to the other. They bump the mercury atoms causing them to emit ultraviolet radiation. The ultraviolet light is converted to visible light by a fluorescent coating on the inside of the tube. Compact fluorescent lamps (CFL) save energy and are designed to replace incandescent globes as they use less *power* and have a longer life. They contain a circuit board and work electronically. Compare **incandescent globe**.

(cont.)

Excel Illustrated Science Dictionary Years 5–8

fluorescent globe (cont.)

fluorescent globe (cont.)

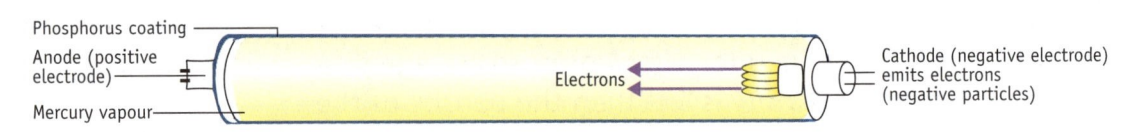

Phosphorus coating
Anode (positive electrode)
Mercury vapour
Electrons
Cathode (negative electrode) emits electrons (negative particles)

food

See **nutrients**.

food chain

shows the feeding relationships in an *ecosystem*. Each food chain starts with a *producer* (plant), which is eaten by a *consumer* (animal). The arrows show the direction of flow of *nutrients* and *energy* in the ecosystem. See **food web**.

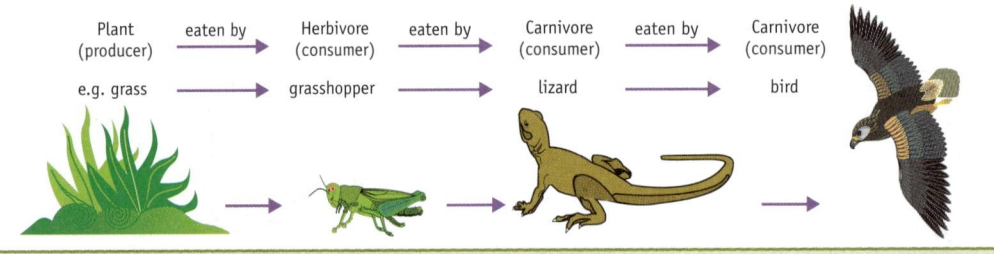

Plant (producer) — eaten by → Herbivore (consumer) — eaten by → Carnivore (consumer) — eaten by → Carnivore (consumer)

e.g. grass → grasshopper → lizard → bird

food preservation

is when the *chemical reactions* of *microorganisms* in *food* are stopped. These *chemical reactions* cause *decomposition*. Food can be preserved by:
- killing and/or preventing the entry of microorganisms (e.g. *vacuum* sealing, salting, smoking, irradiating)
- slowing or stopping the chemical reactions by freezing or drying.

food pyramid

(e.g. pyramid of numbers) can be used to illustrate a *food chain*, with the *producers* at the base and then *herbivores* and *carnivores* as they occur in the food chain.

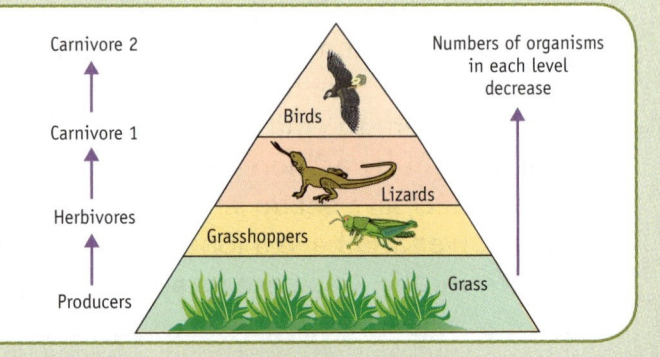

Carnivore 2 — Birds
Carnivore 1 — Lizards
Herbivores — Grasshoppers
Producers — Grass

Numbers of organisms in each level decrease

food web

shows feeding relationships in an *ecosystem*. In nature many *food chains* combine to form a complex food web. See **food chain**.

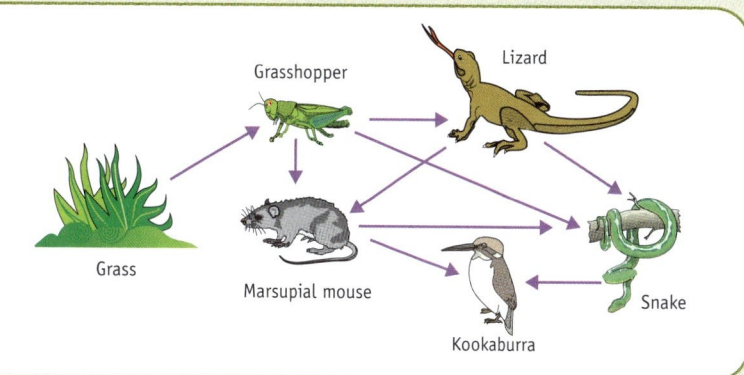

force

is a push or a pull. It is measured in newtons (N).

A force is needed to start an object moving or to *speed* its movement.

A force is needed to slow down or stop movement.

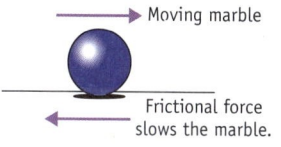

A force is needed to change the direction of movement.

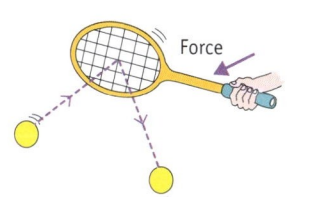

A force is needed to change shape.

See **balanced and unbalanced forces**; **gravity**; **electrostatic force**; **magnetic force**; **tension and compression**; **bridges**; **acceleration**.

forces between particles in matter

See **bonds**.

fossil

is a remain or trace (e.g. bone, footprint) of ancient life. Fossils show us what life in the past was like. For example, archaeopteryx is a fossil that has some bird and some reptile features. See **dinosaurs**; **fossil fuel**; **rock age**.

(cont.)

Excel Illustrated Science Dictionary Years 5–8

fossil (cont.)

fossil (cont.)

Archaeopteryx — Mouth with teeth, Scales on head, 3 clawed fingers (1 2 3), Feathered wing, Clawed toes, Scales, Long tail with feathers

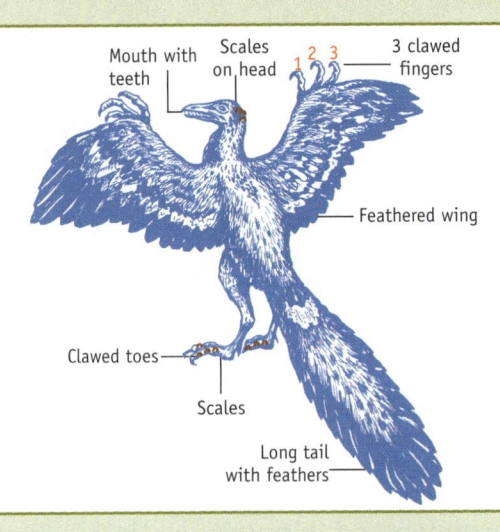

fossil fuel

is obtained from the *Earth* and was made from *plants* or *animals* millions of years ago. *Coal*, *petroleum* and natural gas are *fossil* fuels. They are *non-renewable resources*. See **fossil fuel use; conservation of non-renewable resources**.

fossil fuel use

provides about 90% of the world's *energy*. Humans use fossil fuels for heating, cooling and cooking, and in industry. Once used, these fuels cannot be replaced. See **petroleum**.

Products from petroleum

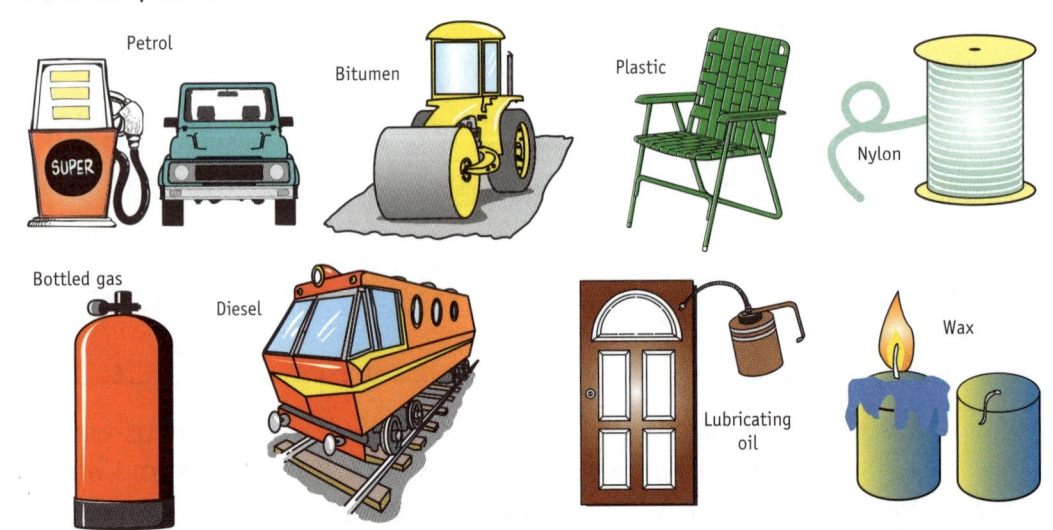

Petrol, Bitumen, Plastic, Nylon, Bottled gas, Diesel, Lubricating oil, Wax

Excel Illustrated Science Dictionary Years 5–8

freezing point

F

freezing point

is the *temperature* at which a *liquid* turns into a *solid*. Different substances have different freezing points, but it is always the same as the *melting point* of the substance. Compare **boiling point**.

frequency of a wave

is the number of waves that pass in a second. See **pitch of a sound**.

friction

is a *force* that tries to slow or stop the movement between surfaces. Friction is less between smooth or slippery surfaces. See **friction reduction**.

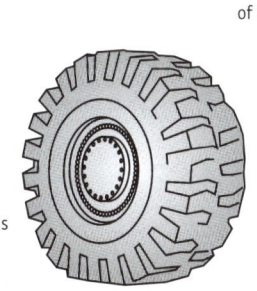

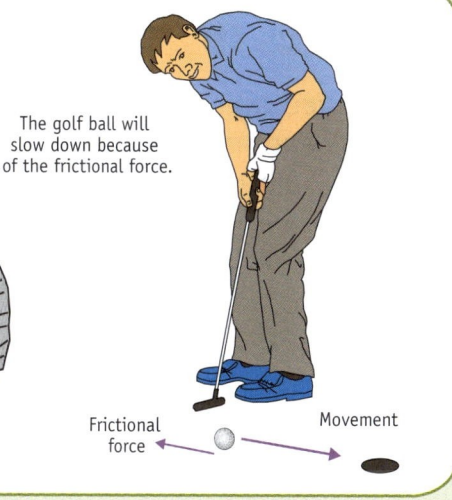

The golf ball will slow down because of the frictional force.

Tyres have deep treads to increase friction and stop skidding.

Frictional force ← → Movement

friction reduction

Is achieved by oiling, sanding or waxing a surface, or streamlining an object.

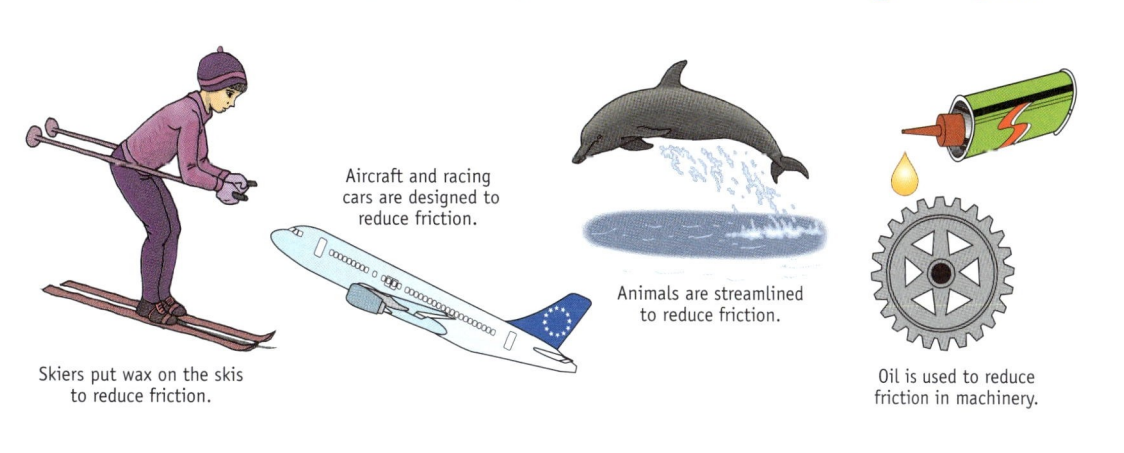

Skiers put wax on the skis to reduce friction.

Aircraft and racing cars are designed to reduce friction.

Animals are streamlined to reduce friction.

Oil is used to reduce friction in machinery.

Excel Illustrated Science Dictionary Years 5–8

57

fruit

fruit

may be fleshy (e.g. peach or tomato), woody (e.g. gumnut), a dry capsule (e.g. poppy) or a dry pod (e.g. pea pod). A fruit encloses *seeds*.

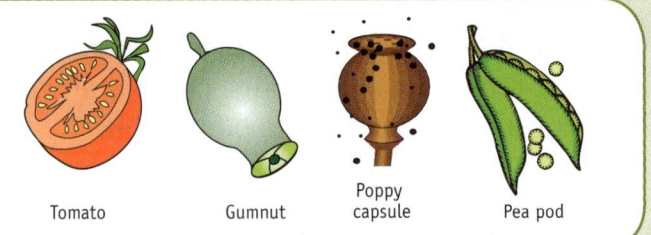

Tomato   Gumnut   Poppy capsule   Pea pod

fuel

is a source of *energy*. See **energy sources; fossil fuel**.

fungus (plural: fungi)

is a *decomposer*. The fungus *kingdom* includes mushrooms, yeast, mould, and rusts and smuts that cause disease in *plants*. Fungi have plant-like *cells*, but no chloroplasts. See **microorganisms**.

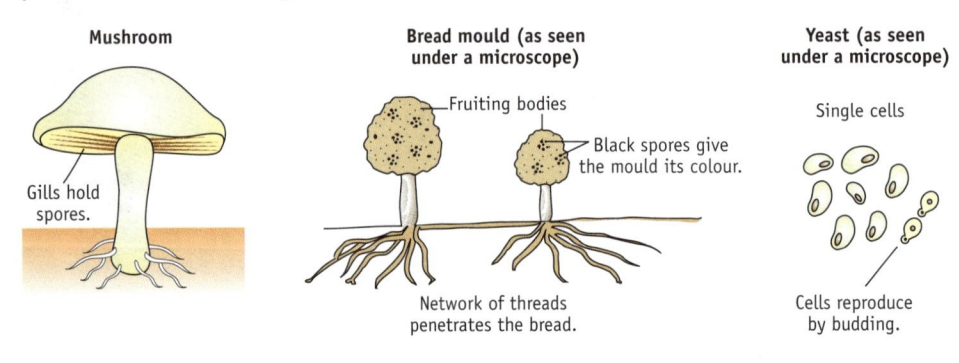

Mushroom
Gills hold spores.

Bread mould (as seen under a microscope)
Fruiting bodies
Black spores give the mould its colour.
Network of threads penetrates the bread.

Yeast (as seen under a microscope)
Single cells
Cells reproduce by budding.

Excel Illustrated Science Dictionary Years 5–8

galaxy

is a huge cluster of *stars*. There are millions of galaxies moving around the *universe*. Our galaxy is a rotating spiral made up of billions of stars, dust and *gases*. The band of stars seen across the sky is part of our galaxy and is called the Milky Way.

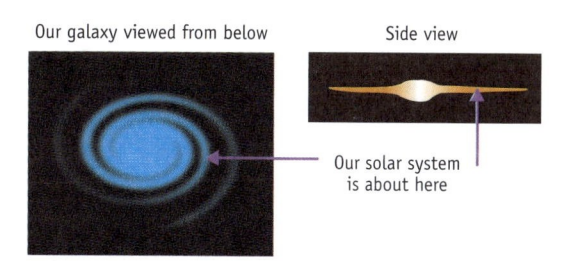

Our galaxy viewed from below

Side view

Our solar system is about here

galvanise

See **rust proofing**.

gas

is one of the *states of matter*. Gases have *mass* but no definite size (*volume*). They spread out to fill a container and take its shape. See **particle theory of matter**.

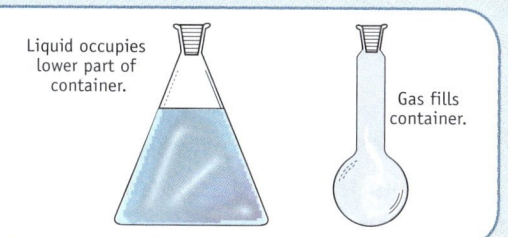

Liquid occupies lower part of container.

Gas fills container.

gears

are simple *machines* made of wheels with teeth (cogs). When one wheel turns, it transfers its motion and *energy* to another wheel. Gears are found in bikes, clocks and many more complex machines.

1. Gear wheels that are the same size change the direction of movement.

   Direction changes

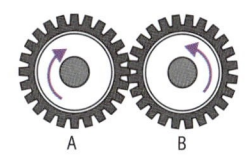

   A   B
   1 turn in A produces 1 turn in B

2. A small gear wheel will make a large wheel exert more *force*.

   Force magnifies

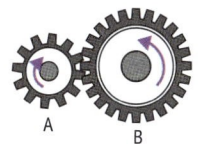

   A   B
   1 turn in A produces a $\frac{1}{2}$ turn in B

3. A large gear wheel turning slowly will make a small wheel rotate fast.

   Speed magnifies

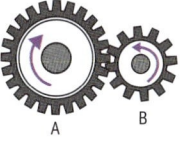

   A   B
   1 turn in A produces 2 turns in B

Excel Illustrated Science Dictionary Years 5–8

generator

generator

is a *machine* that produces an *electric current*. A generator consists of a coil of wire next to a *magnet*. The coil is rotated by steam (usually produced by burning coal) or by a *turbine*. It changes *kinetic energy* (e.g. steam, wind or moving water) to *electrical energy*. See **turbine**; **geothermal energy**; **hydroelectricity**.

genes

are composed of DNA and found in the nucleus of *cells*. They control the way *organisms* develop. Genes are passed on from one generation to the next. See **genetic engineering**.

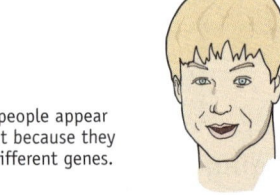

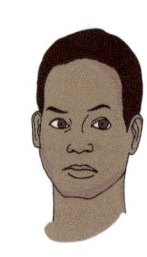

These people appear different because they have different genes.

genetic engineering

is the process of altering *genes* present in an *organism*. Scientists have separated useful genes and transferred them to other organisms.

Cotton plants can be given a gene that makes them resistant to caterpillars.

Potato plants can be given a gene that helps them resist virus attack.

Tomato plants can be given a gene to stop them squashing.

geothermal energy

comes from *heat* in underground water and *rocks* in volcanic areas. It is brought to the surface as steam. The steam turns *turbines*, which drive *generators* and produce *electricity*. See **renewable energy sources**.

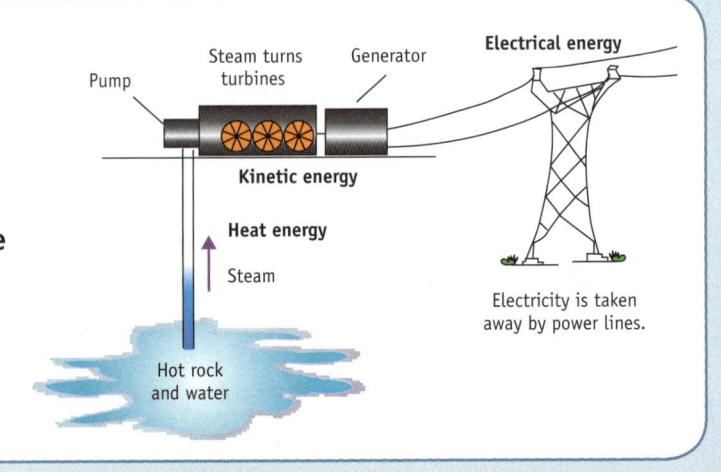

Pump — Steam turns turbines — Generator — Electrical energy

Kinetic energy

Heat energy

Steam

Hot rock and water

Electricity is taken away by power lines.

germination

germination

occurs when the small *plant* (embryo) inside a *seed* begins to grow. Seeds need water, moisture and warmth. Some seeds (e.g. wattles) germinate better after fire.

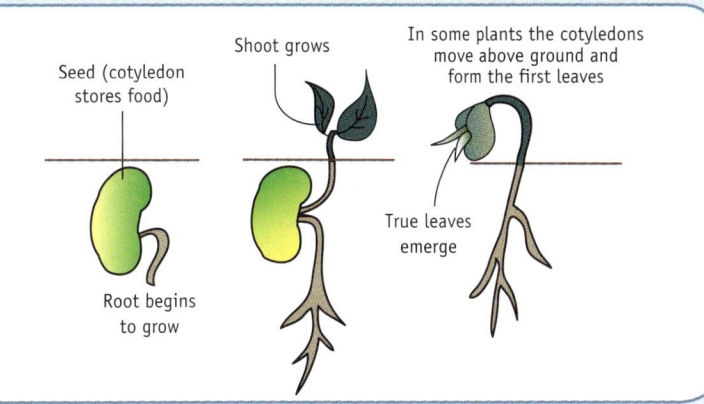

glacier

is a mass of ice slowly moving down a mountainside or off the edges of a polar ice-cap. See **erosion from moving ice**.

global air currents

occur when *air* moves along the *Earth's* surface from the poles towards the equator. The hot ground at the equator heats the *air* causing it to rise. This warm air moves above the ground, back to the poles. The air currents curve to the west because of the Earth's rotation. See **convection in the atmosphere**.

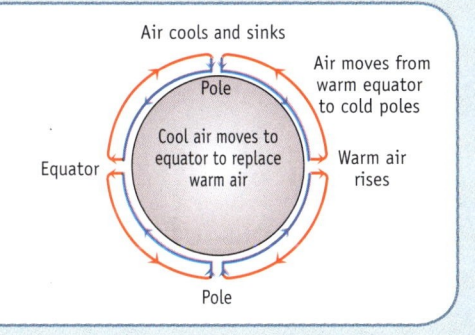

global ocean currents

occur in the surface water of the oceans. They are caused by *wind* circulation, *convection* and the *Earth's* rotation. The *Sun* heats the oceans and currents carry this *heat* to other places. This affects the *weather* and *climate* around the Earth. See **El Niño**; **ocean currents**.

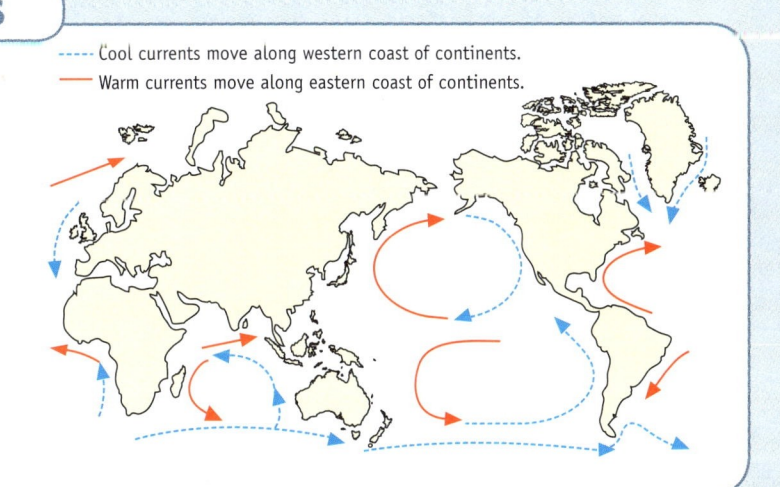

Excel Illustrated Science Dictionary Years 5–8

global warming

global warming

is the increase in the Earth's *temperatures* as a result of excess *carbon dioxide* in the *air*. Carbon dioxide has increased because of overuse of *fossil fuels* and the removal of forests (trees remove carbon dioxide from the air). Pollutants, such as fluorocarbons from aerosol cans and refrigerants, also trap *heat*. See **greenhouse effect**.

Greenhouse gases trap heat and increase global warming.

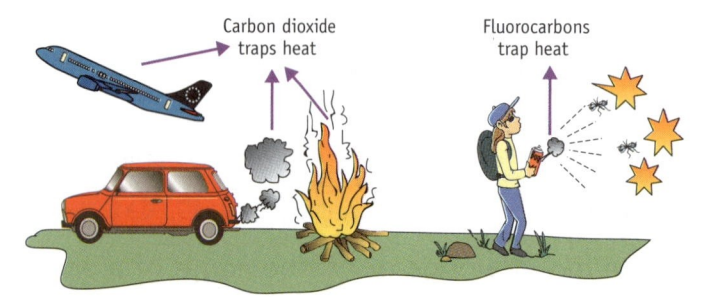

Carbon dioxide traps heat

Fluorocarbons trap heat

Destroying plants increases global warming.

These trees removed carbon dioxide when they were alive.

globe

See **fluorescent globe; incandescent globe**.

granite

See **igneous rocks**.

gravity

is a *force* of attraction that exists between all *matter* in the *universe*. The *Earth* has a gravitational force that pulls things towards its centre and makes them fall. This force is the object's *weight*. See **gravity and mass; gravity and distance; orbit and gravity**.

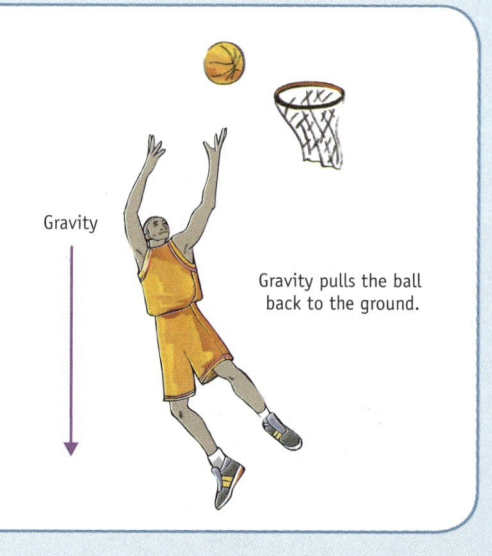

Gravity

Gravity pulls the ball back to the ground.

gravity and distance

are connected. *Gravity* becomes less when objects are further apart.

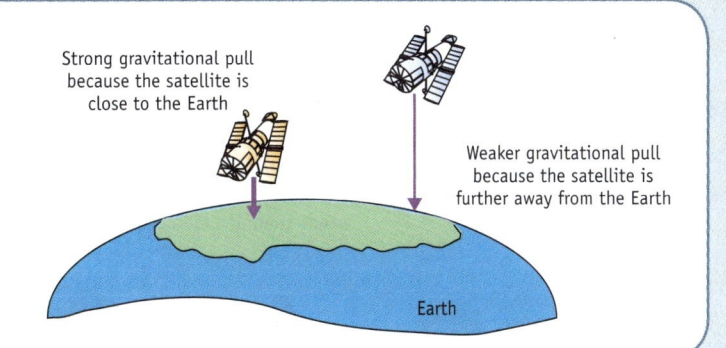

Strong gravitational pull because the satellite is close to the Earth

Weaker gravitational pull because the satellite is further away from the Earth

Earth

gravity and mass

are connected. Objects with large *mass* (that contain a large amount of *matter*) have a greater gravitational *force* than objects with small mass. For example, the *Earth's* pull of *gravity* on an object is greater than the *Moon's* pull on the same object. See **weight**.

greenhouse effect

describes how *carbon dioxide* and other greenhouse gases in the *atmosphere* trap *heat* that is radiated from the *Earth's* surface. These gases keep the outer surface of the Earth warm in a similar way to the glass roof of a plant greenhouse. See **global warming**.

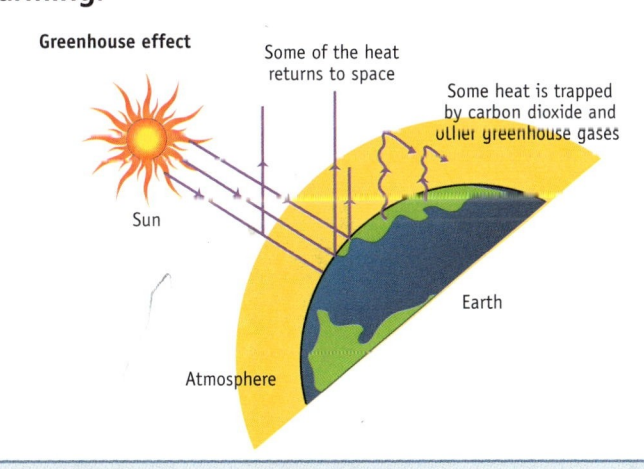

Greenhouse effect

Some of the heat returns to space

Some heat is trapped by carbon dioxide and other greenhouse gases

Sun

Earth

Atmosphere

Excel Illustrated Science Dictionary Years 5–8

habitat

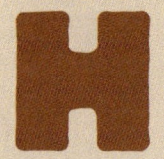

habitat

is the place where an *organism* lives (e.g. creek, bushland or desert). *Plants* and *animals* have features or *adaptations* to help them survive in their habitat. See **aquatic**; **terrestrial**.

Adaptation for aquatic habitat

Shells prevent animals drying out at low tide

Adaptation for a dry/hot habitat

Australian grass tree
- Leaves channel water to roots
- Leaves have fewer stomates to reduce water loss
- Becomes dormant during drought

heat

makes things hot. It makes the particles in a substance vibrate more and move apart so that the object expands. *Heat* is detected by a *thermometer* and is measured in degrees Celsius (°C). Heat is often produced as a by-product when *energy* is transferred or transformed. For example, when brakes on a car are applied, *kinetic energy* is involved and heat is also produced. When *electricity* in a *globe* passes through the filament to produce *light* energy, heat is also produced. See **heat movement; energy transfer; energy transformation; state of matter, change**.

heat absorption

is how objects take in *heat* from warmer surroundings. Dark objects absorb heat more rapidly than light-coloured objects. Compare **heat radiation**.

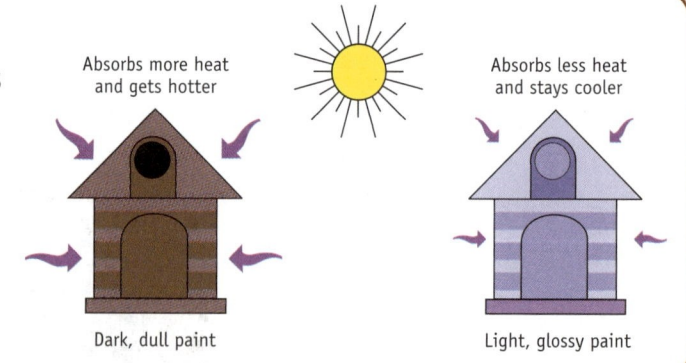

Absorbs more heat and gets hotter — Dark, dull paint

Absorbs less heat and stays cooler — Light, glossy paint

heat movement

is when *heat* moves from a hot place to a cooler place. It can be moved or transferred from one place to another by *conduction*, *convection*, *radiation* and *reflection*. See **thermos flask**.

heat radiation

is one way *heat* energy can travel. The heat travels in beams or rays (infra-red rays). This is *radiant energy* and does not need particles to travel; it can pass through a *vacuum*. Compare **conduction of heat**; **convection**.

Dark objects radiate more heat than a shiny, light-coloured ones

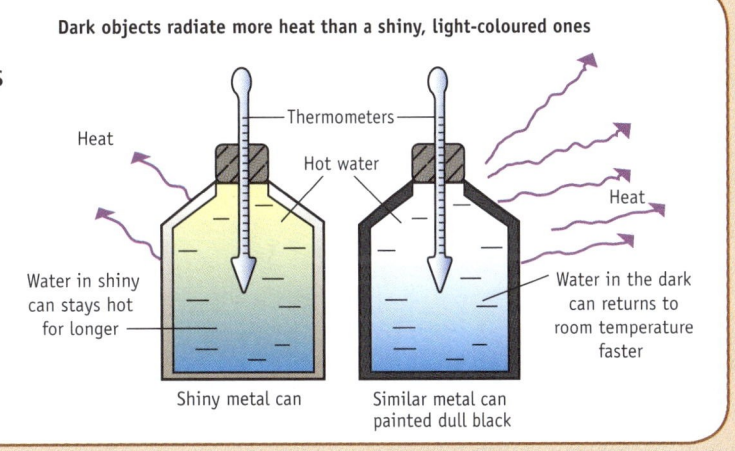

Thermometers — Hot water — Heat — Water in shiny can stays hot for longer — Shiny metal can — Water in the dark can returns to room temperature faster — Similar metal can painted dull black

heavy metal

is *metal* made up of large particles. Some of these metals (e.g. lead and mercury) are poisonous and can pollute the *environment*. See **waste disposal**.

herbivore

is an *animal* that eats *plants* (e.g. kangaroo, rabbit). Herbivores have teeth adapted for grinding plants. The digestive system has a very large pouch called the caecum and an appendix between the small intestine and the colon. The caecum contains *bacteria* which break down cellulose in plant food. Compare **digestive system in humans**. See **food chain**.

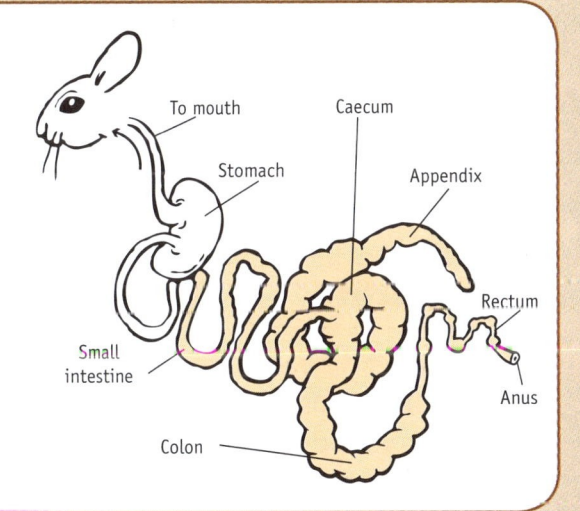

To mouth — Caecum — Stomach — Appendix — Rectum — Small intestine — Anus — Colon

hibernate

is what some *animals* (e.g. bats) do to conserve *energy* when *food* is scarce. During winter they become inactive and their heart rate and *breathing* become very slow. *Carnivores* such as bears do not actually hibernate but may sleep for long periods of time.

Excel Illustrated Science Dictionary Years 5–8

high pressure system

often brings calm, fine *weather*. In the southern hemisphere, the *air* moves away from an area of high *air pressure* in an anticlockwise direction. Compare **low pressure system**. See **wind**.

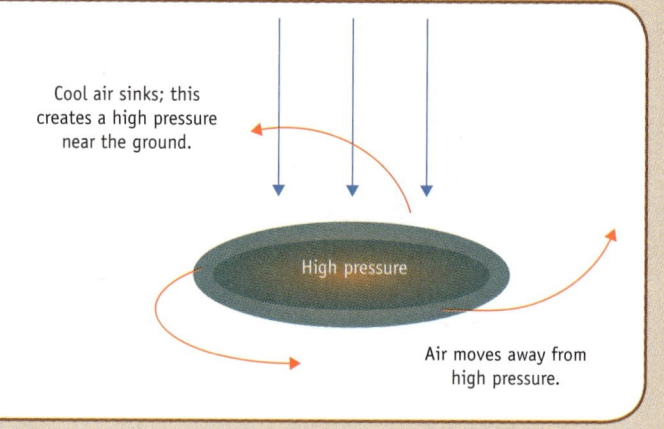

Cool air sinks; this creates a high pressure near the ground.

High pressure

Air moves away from high pressure.

Hubble Space Telescope

was launched in 1990 and was designed to see into outer *space* while it is in *orbit*. It operates outside the *Earth's atmosphere* and so produces images that are not distorted by the atmosphere. See **optical telescope; radio telescope**.

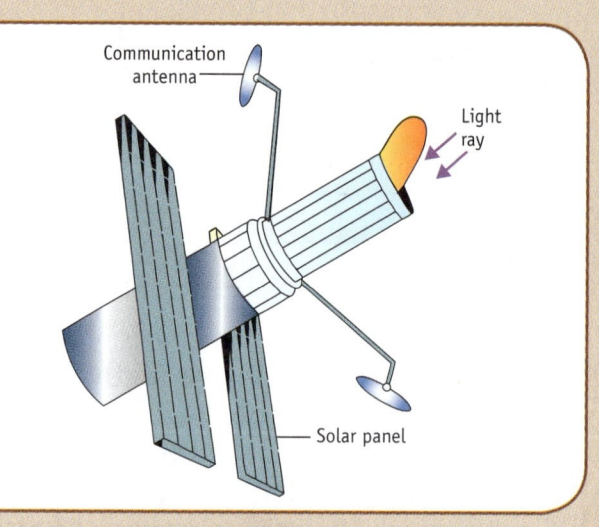

Communication antenna

Light ray

Solar panel

humidity

is the water *vapour* or moisture in the *air*. As air cools, some of the water vapour condenses to form *liquid* water. This produces *clouds*, fog and dew. Humidity is measured by a wet-and-dry-bulb thermometer.

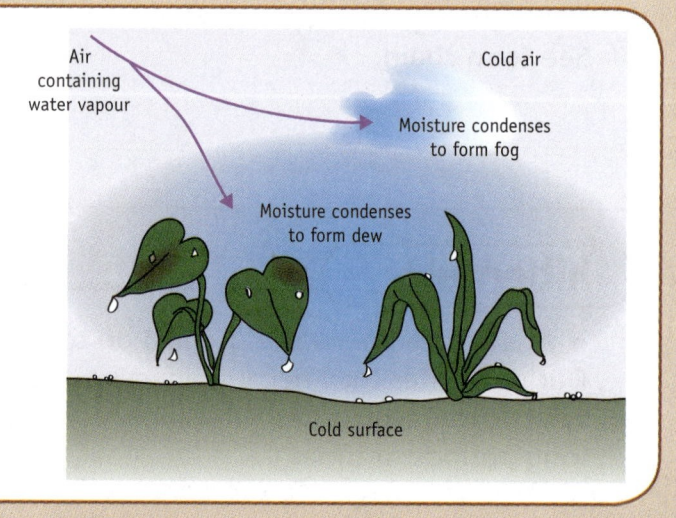

Air containing water vapour

Cold air

Moisture condenses to form fog

Moisture condenses to form dew

Cold surface

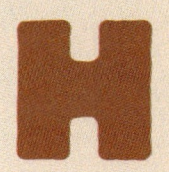

hydroelectricity

is *electrical energy* produced by *generators* driven by flowing water. The flowing water is commonly provided by dams built in mountainous areas. Compare **tidal energy; wave energy**. See **renewable energy sources**.

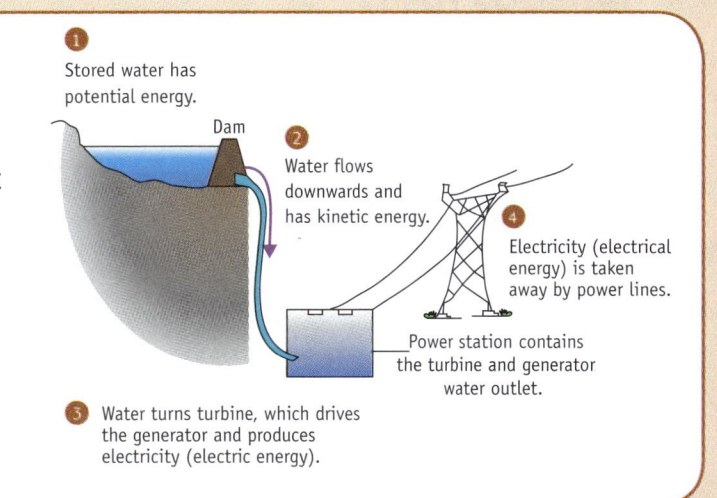

① Stored water has potential energy.
② Water flows downwards and has kinetic energy.
③ Water turns turbine, which drives the generator and produces electricity (electric energy).
④ Electricity (electrical energy) is taken away by power lines.

Power station contains the turbine and generator water outlet.

Dam

hydrosphere

is the water on and around the *Earth*, including seas, oceans, moisture and *vapour* in the *atmosphere*, as well as ice and snow. Compare **lithosphere**.

igneous rocks

igneous rocks

are formed deep inside the *Earth* from *magma* (molten or melted rock) or on the surface from *lava* from volcanoes. As the molten rock cools, it forms interlocking *crystal*s. See **crystal formation; pumice**.

Diagram of a volcano showing:
- Lava
- Rocks formed here cool quickly and have *small* crystals, (e.g. basalt).
- Rocks formed here cool slowly and have *large* crystals (e.g. granite).
- Magma

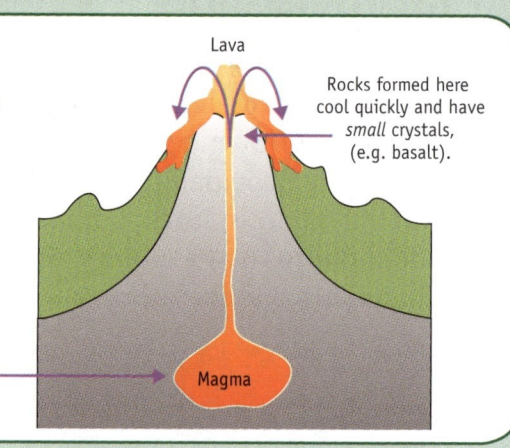

impact

describes the effects human activities and natural disasters have on the *environment* and *Earth*. The impact may be helpful and/or harmful (e.g. the use of *fossil fuels* provides *energy* but also pollutes and uses *non-renewable resources*). See **conservation; extinction; global warming**.

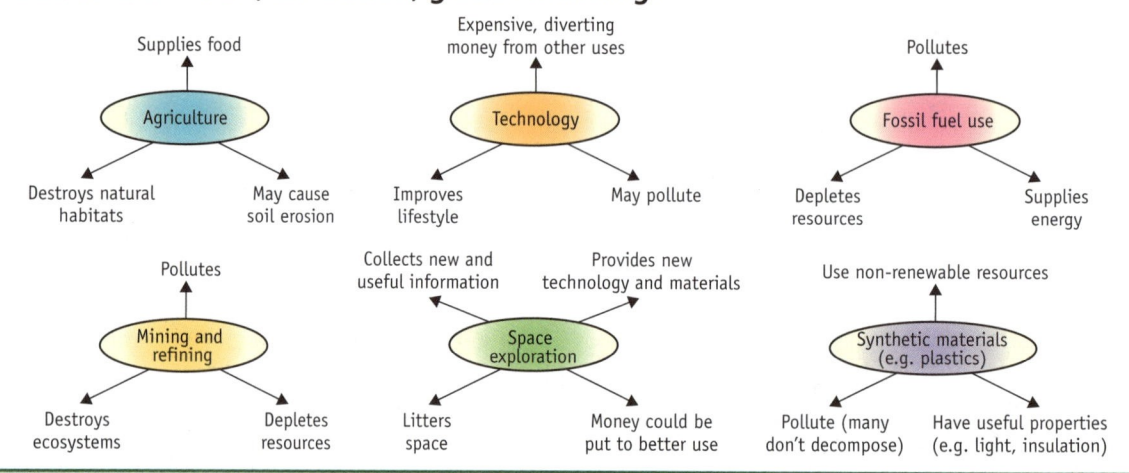

Concept map showing:

Agriculture: Supplies food; Destroys natural habitats; May cause soil erosion

Technology: Expensive, diverting money from other uses; Improves lifestyle; May pollute

Fossil fuel use: Pollutes; Depletes resources; Supplies energy

Mining and refining: Pollutes; Destroys ecosystems; Depletes resources

Space exploration: Collects new and useful information; Provides new technology and materials; Litters space; Money could be put to better use

Synthetic materials (e.g. plastics): Use non-renewable resources; Pollute (many don't decompose); Have useful properties (e.g. light, insulation)

incandescent globe

is an ordinary glass bulb containing a tungsten filament or wire and an unreactive *gas*, such as argon. An *electric current* flowing through the filament heats it to white-hot causing it to produce light. Compare **fluorescent globe**. See **power**.

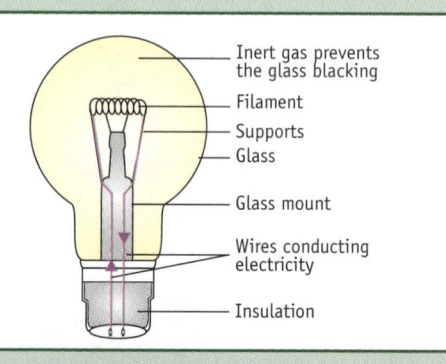

Diagram of a light bulb labelled:
- Inert gas prevents the glass blacking
- Filament
- Supports
- Glass
- Glass mount
- Wires conducting electricity
- Insulation

Excel Illustrated Science Dictionary Years 5–8

inorganic nutrients

inorganic nutrients

are *minerals* and water that are needed for growth and *chemical reactions* in *living things*. *Animals* obtain inorganic *nutrients* from their *food*. *Plants* obtain minerals and water from the *soil* and *carbon dioxide* from the *air*. Compare **organic compounds**.

insoluble

describes a substance that will not *dissolve*. Compare **soluble**.

insulators of electricity

are poor *conductors* and stop the flow of a *current*. They prevent electric shock and short circuits. Electrical wires are usually coated with an insulator such as *plastic* or rubber.

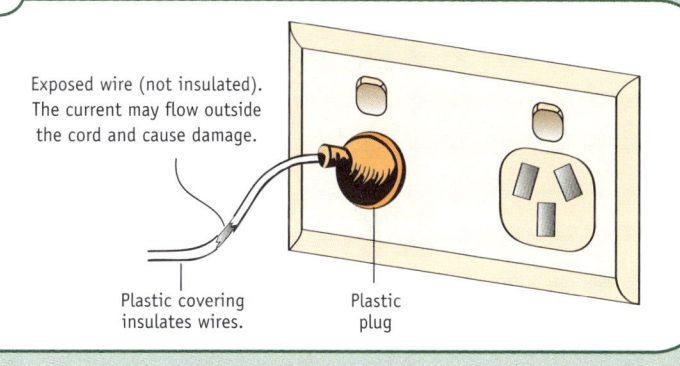

Exposed wire (not insulated). The current may flow outside the cord and cause damage.

Plastic covering insulates wires.

Plastic plug

insulators of heat

are poor *conductors* and reduce the flow of *heat* from a hot area to a cold one. *Materials* such as wood, *plastic*, glass, rubber and *air* are insulators. They are often used to control movement of *heat*. See **conduction of heat**.

Plastic handle stops heat flowing into hand

Bird fluffs up its feathers to trap air and stop heat loss

Foam or polystyrene cups slow down heat loss

interdependent relationships in ecosystems

See **ecosystem interactions**.

invertebrates

invertebrates

are animals that do not have a backbone. The main groups are shown in the diagram.

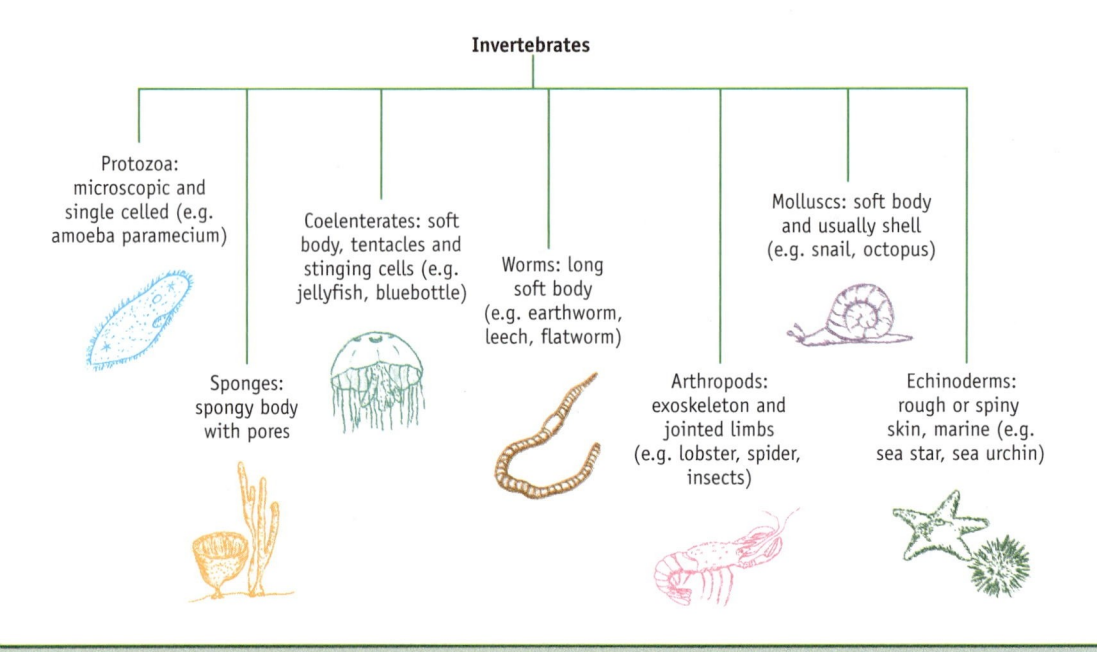

Invertebrates:
- Protozoa: microscopic and single celled (e.g. amoeba paramecium)
- Sponges: spongy body with pores
- Coelenterates: soft body, tentacles and stinging cells (e.g. jellyfish, bluebottle)
- Worms: long soft body (e.g. earthworm, leech, flatworm)
- Arthropods: exoskeleton and jointed limbs (e.g. lobster, spider, insects)
- Molluscs: soft body and usually shell (e.g. snail, octopus)
- Echinoderms: rough or spiny skin, marine (e.g. sea star, sea urchin)

iron ore

See **refining**.

Excel Illustrated Science Dictionary Years 5–8

Jupiter

is the largest *planet* in our solar system and is mainly *gas*. The outer layers show coloured, banded clouds with ovals and spots caused by storms. One storm area, called the Great Red Spot, is three times the size of *Earth*. Jupiter has four large *moons* and many tiny moons. The total number of moons discovered is currently 67.

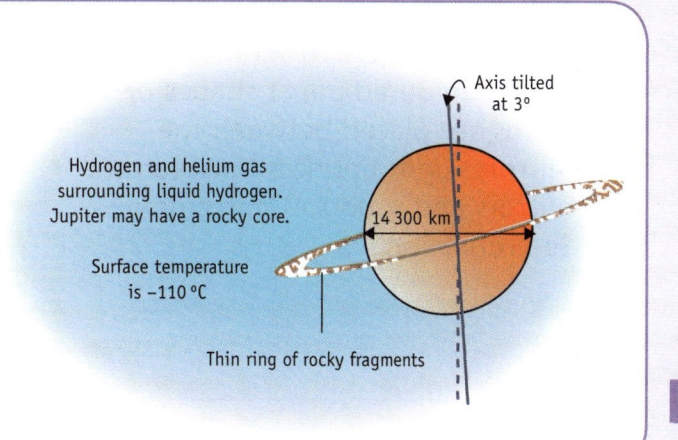

Hydrogen and helium gas surrounding liquid hydrogen. Jupiter may have a rocky core.

Surface temperature is −110 °C

14 300 km

Axis tilted at 3°

Thin ring of rocky fragments

kaleidoscope

kaleidoscope

is made up of *mirrors* joined at an angle. Coloured paper shapes or beads are placed between the mirrors. *Light* bounces between the mirrors and produces patterns. See **reflection**.

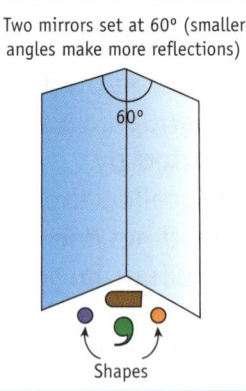

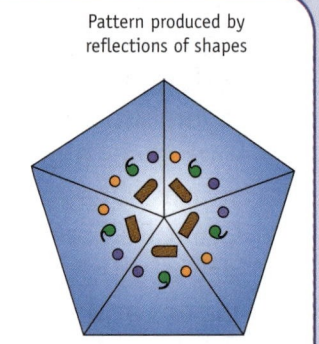

Two mirrors set at 60° (smaller angles make more reflections)

Pattern produced by reflections of shapes

Shapes

keys

are used to identify and classify *living things*. A key divides or branches into two sections at each step and so is called a dichotomous key (di = two, chotomous = branch). The diagram shows a simple key to identify *animals* with a backbone:

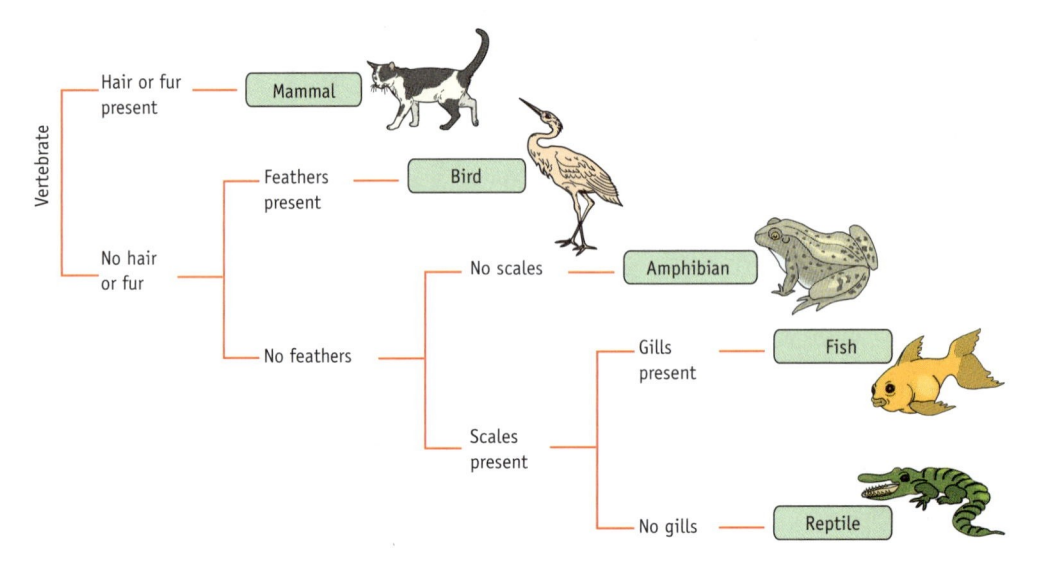

Vertebrate
- Hair or fur present → Mammal
- No hair or fur
  - Feathers present → Bird
  - No feathers
    - No scales → Amphibian
    - Scales present
      - Gills present → Fish
      - No gills → Reptile

This same key may be written as follows. Select (a) or (b) at each step.
1. (a) hair or fur present ⟶ mammal
   (b) no hair or fur ⟶ go to 2
2. (a) feathers present ⟶ bird
   (b) no feathers ⟶ go to 3
3. (a) scales present ⟶ go to 4
   (b) no scales present ⟶ amphibian
4. (a) gills present ⟶ fish
   (b) no gills ⟶ reptile

kinetic energy

kinetic energy

is the *energy* in a moving object such as *wind*, flowing water, a falling rock, a swinging axe or a moving car. All these are capable of changing an object they hit. The faster an object is moving, the more kinetic energy it has. Compare **potential energy**.

Moving axe has kinetic energy

Moving arrow has kinetic energy

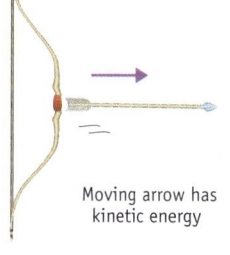

kingdoms

are the first level in the *classification of living things*. A five-kingdom system is commonly used. It places all living things into one of five kingdoms: *plants, animals, fungi,* protists (including single-celled plants and animals) and Monera (including *bacteria*). See **classification of living things; classification groups**.

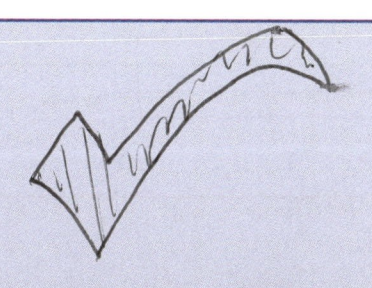

Plants

Animals

Protists (single-celled organisms)

Monera (bacteria)

Fungi

Excel Illustrated Science Dictionary Years 5–8

land management

See **resource management**.

larva

is the young immature stage of some *animals*. It hatches from the egg and is unlike the adult in appearance. Examples include a maggot (fly larva), caterpillar (butterfly or moth larva) and tadpole (frog larva). See **metamorphosis**; **life cycle**.

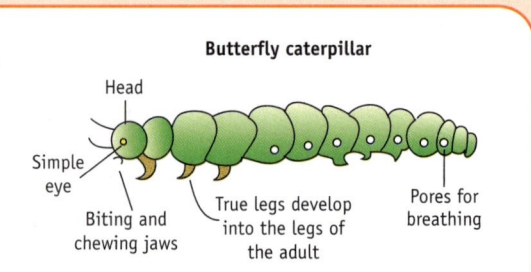

Butterfly caterpillar
Head — Simple eye — Biting and chewing jaws — True legs develop into the legs of the adult — Pores for breathing

lava

is molten or *liquid* rock which rises to the *Earth's* surface and flows over it. Compare **magma**. See **igneous rocks**; **volcano**.

leaves

make *food* for the *plant* by the process of *photosynthesis*. They transpire and this draws water up the plant. The water cools the plant and carries minerals to *cells*. See **transpiration**; **stomates**.

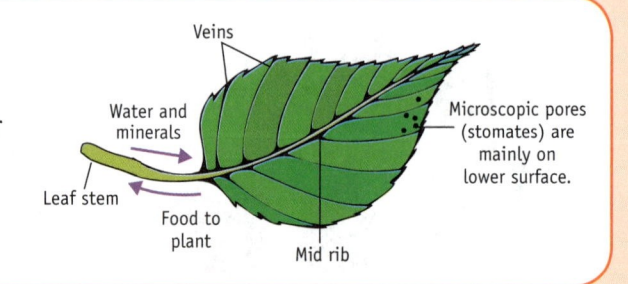

Veins — Water and minerals — Leaf stem — Food to plant — Mid rib — Microscopic pores (stomates) are mainly on lower surface.

lens

is a disc made of a clear material with one or both surfaces curved (e.g. magnifying glass). Lenses are found in the eye, cameras, spectacles, *telescopes* and microscopes. *Light* bends as it passes through a lens. See **vision**; **refraction**.

Diverging lens (thin at centre) spreads light rays

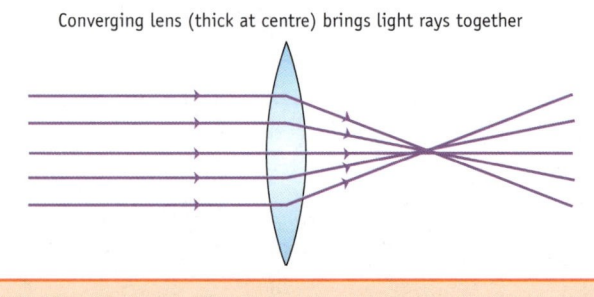

Converging lens (thick at centre) brings light rays together

lever

lever

is a simple *machine*. It is a rigid bar that can move about a pivot called a fulcrum. The effort *force* applied at one end of the lever can be used to move a load. See **lever types**; **levers in the human body**.

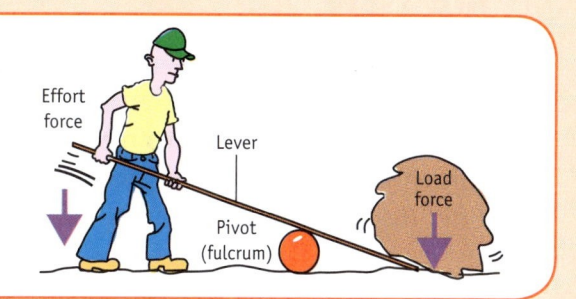

lever types

There are three types of levers.

1. **First-class lever** has the pivot between the effort and the load. These levers will increase the size of the *force* if the pivot is close to the load. They will increase the movement of the load if the pivot is close to the effort.

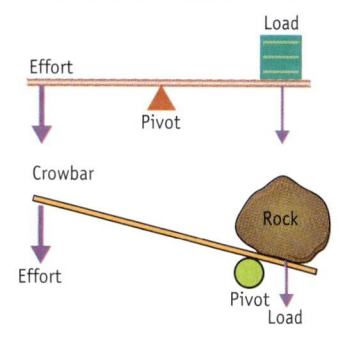

2. **Second-class lever** has the load between the effort and the pivot. These levers all increase force.

3. **Third-class lever** has the effort between the pivot and the load. These levers increase movement.

See **levers in the human body**.

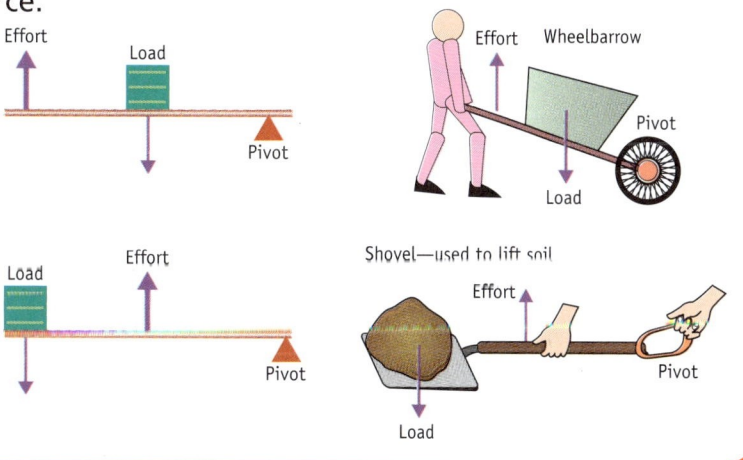

levers in the human body

are the lever systems (simple *machines*) formed by the muscles and bones.

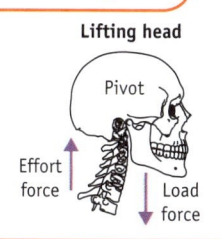

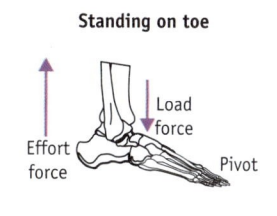

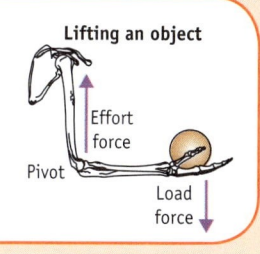

Excel Illustrated Science Dictionary Years 5–8

life cycle

life cycle

is the stages through which *living things* pass as they develop. A young *organism* grows and develops into a mature organism, which reproduces to create more young. See **life cycle of a flowering plant**.

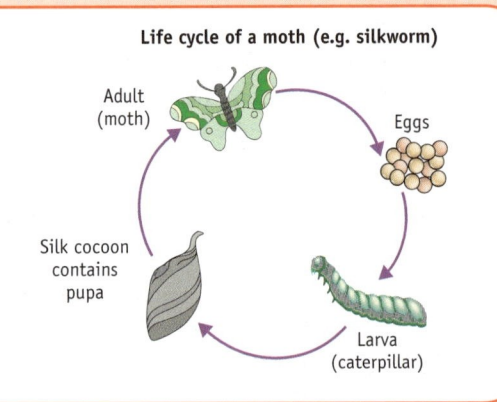

Life cycle of a moth (e.g. silkworm)
- Adult (moth)
- Eggs
- Larva (caterpillar)
- Silk cocoon contains pupa

life cycle of a flowering plant

occurs when a *seed* germinates and grows into a mature plant. This plant produces *flowers* where *fertilisation* occurs. As a result, new seeds develop.

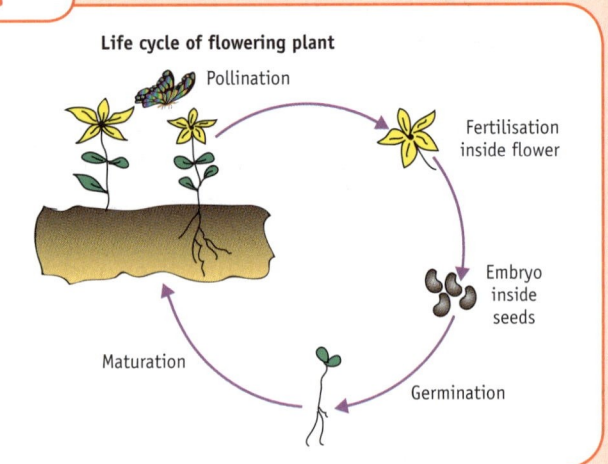

Life cycle of flowering plant
- Pollination
- Fertilisation inside flower
- Embryo inside seeds
- Germination
- Maturation

life processes

are activities that occur in *living things* (e.g. *digestion*, *photosynthesis*, *respiration*, absorption).

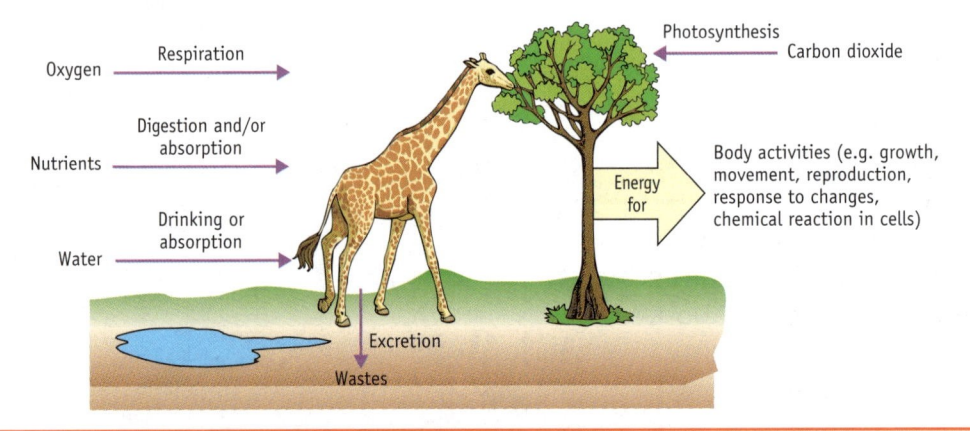

- Oxygen — Respiration
- Nutrients — Digestion and/or absorption
- Water — Drinking or absorption
- Photosynthesis — Carbon dioxide
- Energy for — Body activities (e.g. growth, movement, reproduction, response to changes, chemical reaction in cells)
- Excretion — Wastes

Excel Illustrated Science Dictionary Years 5–8

light

light

is a form of *energy* as it can bring about a change. It is a type of wave, and does not need particles (*matter*) to be transferred. It can travel through a *vacuum*. Light rays travel in straight lines. See **mirrors; lens; light filters; shadows; colours; vision.**

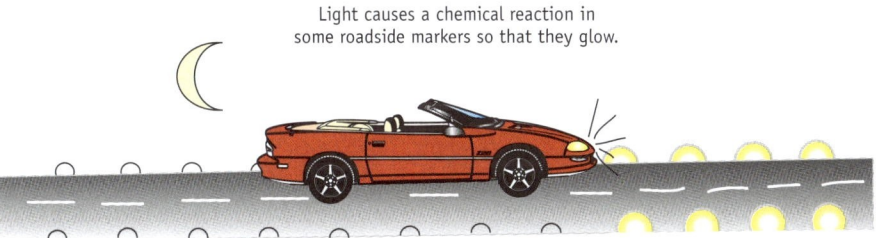

Light causes a chemical reaction in some roadside markers so that they glow.

light filter

is a screen that separates the different colours in *light* by only allowing specific colours to pass through.

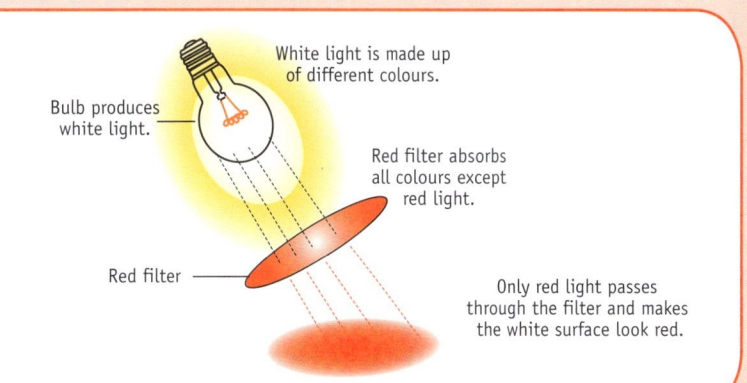

White light is made up of different colours.
Bulb produces white light.
Red filter absorbs all colours except red light.
Red filter
Only red light passes through the filter and makes the white surface look red.

light globe

See **fluorescent globe; incandescent globe**

light year

is the distance *light* travels in one *year*. Light travels at 300 000 km/s. In one year it travels about 9 500 000 000 000 km. Light takes eight minutes to reach *Earth* from the *Sun* (our nearest star). It takes 4.3 years to reach us from the next nearest star.

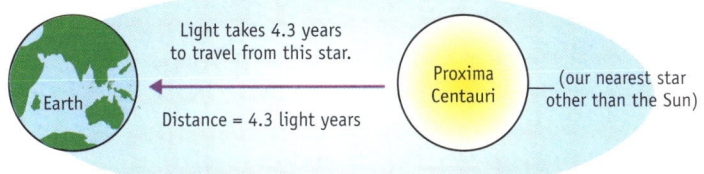

Light takes 4.3 years to travel from this star.
Earth
Distance = 4.3 light years
Proxima Centauri (our nearest star other than the Sun)

Excel **Illustrated Science Dictionary Years 5–8**

liquid

liquid

is one of the three *states of matter*. The particles in a *liquid* can slide over each other so a liquid can flow into a container of any shape. Liquids have a definite *volume*. See **particle theory of matter**.

lithosphere

is the *rock* in the *Earth's crust* and part of the upper *mantle*. Its depth varies from 40 km to 250 km. The lithosphere is divided into plates that rub and cause *earthquakes* and *volcano*es, and collide to produce mountains and trenches. Compare **hydrosphere**; **atmosphere**. See **asthenosphere**.

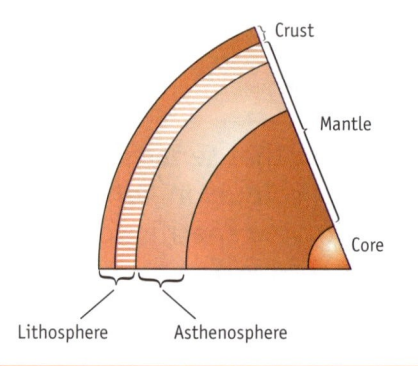

living things

are called *organisms*. They are made of one or more *cells* and carry out *life processes* (e.g. growing and reproducing). *Animals*, *plants*, *fungi* and *bacteria* are living things. See **classification of living things**; **invertebrates**; **vertebrates**.

loudness (volume of a sound)

is caused by the size of the vibrations causing the sound. A large vibration causes a loud sound and a small vibration produces a soft sound. Loudness is measured in decibels (dB). See **sound**.

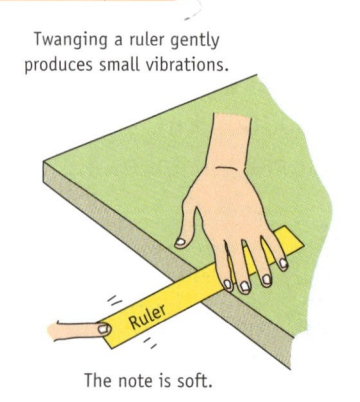

Twanging a ruler gently produces small vibrations. The note is soft.

Twanging strongly produces large vibrations. The note is loud.

low pressure system

low pressure system often indicates unsettled *weather*, *rain* and storms. In the southern hemisphere, *air* moves into an area of low *pressure* in a clockwise direction. Compare **high pressure system**. See **wind**.

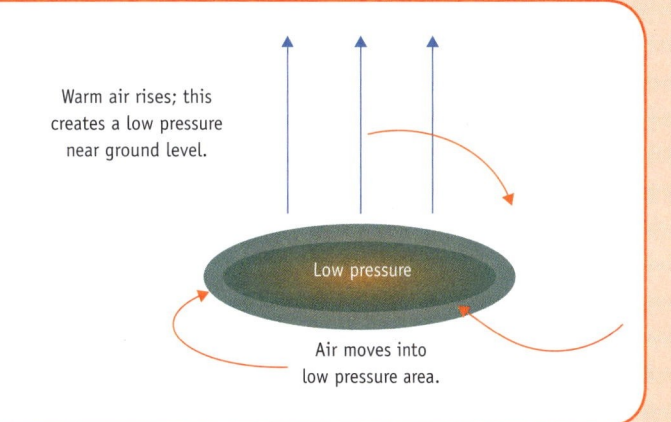

Warm air rises; this creates a low pressure near ground level.

Low pressure

Air moves into low pressure area.

machines

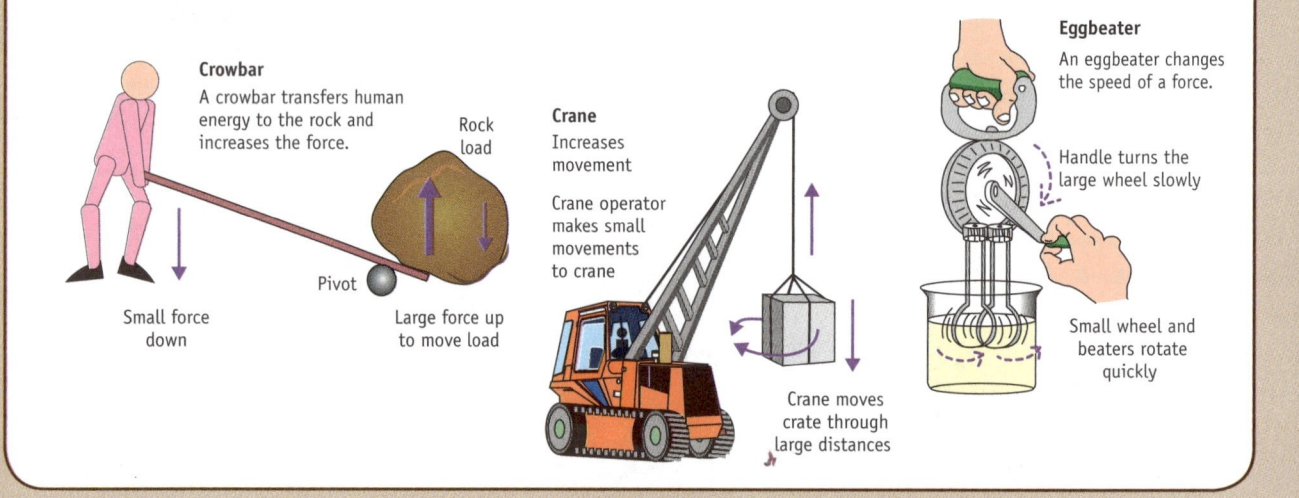

make *work* easier because they can move *energy* to where it is needed, change the direction of a *force* and increase a force. Simple machines can also change a small movement into a large movement and change the *speed* of a force. Ramps, *levers*, *pulleys*, *gears* and hydraulic machines are examples of simple machines. See **mechanical advantage**; **efficiency of a machine**.

Crowbar
A crowbar transfers human energy to the rock and increases the force.
Rock load
Small force down
Pivot
Large force up to move load

Crane
Increases movement
Crane operator makes small movements to crane
Crane moves crate through large distances

Eggbeater
An eggbeater changes the speed of a force.
Handle turns the large wheel slowly
Small wheel and beaters rotate quickly

macro-

means large, or visible to the naked eye. Compare **micro-**.

magma

is molten or *liquid rock* found deep inside the *Earth*. Compare **lava**.

magnet

is a piece of *metal* (e.g. iron, steel) that attracts iron and a few other metals. When a magnet is hanging freely it will line itself up in a north-south direction. See **magnetic field**; **magnetic force**.

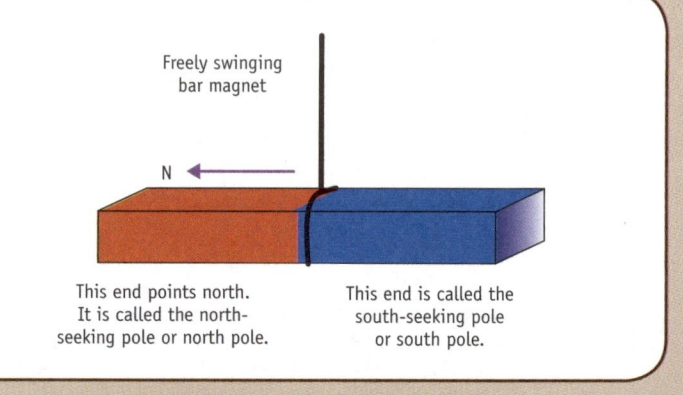

Freely swinging bar magnet

This end points north. It is called the north-seeking pole or north pole.

This end is called the south-seeking pole or south pole.

magnet making

is possible by:
- stroking a piece of iron in one direction with one pole of a magnet
- passing a *current* through a coil with a piece of iron or steel inside the coil.

See **electromagnet**.

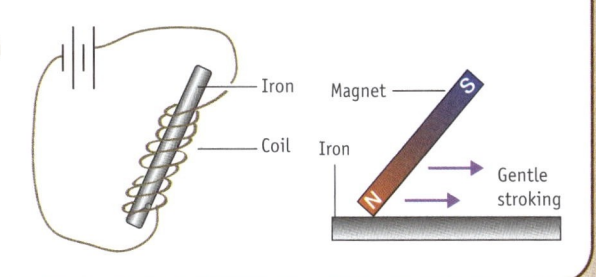

magnet uses

are many. They are used in:
- motors and many household appliances
- compasses for navigation (a compass is a freely swinging *magnet*)
- *generator*s in power stations to make *electricity*
- *mining*.

See **magnetic separation**.

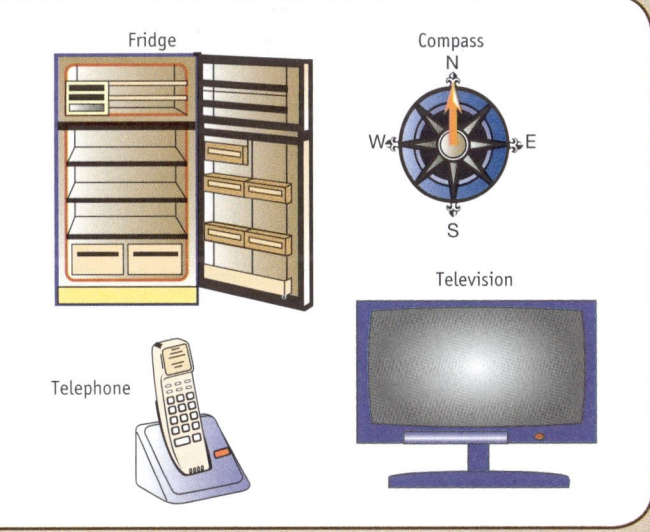

magnetic energy

is the *energy* stored in a *magnet*. It enables the magnet to pick up iron and to attract and repel other magnets. See **magnetic separation**; **magnetic force**.

magnetic field

exists around a *magnet*. It is the area where *magnetic forces* of attraction or repulsion exist.

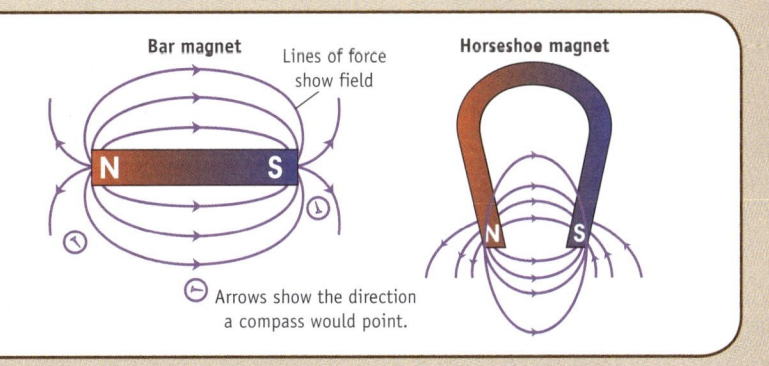

Arrows show the direction a compass would point.

Excel Illustrated Science Dictionary Years 5–8

magnetic force

magnetic force

is the *force* the poles of a *magnet* exert on each other.

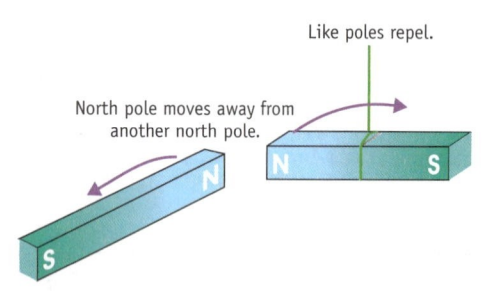

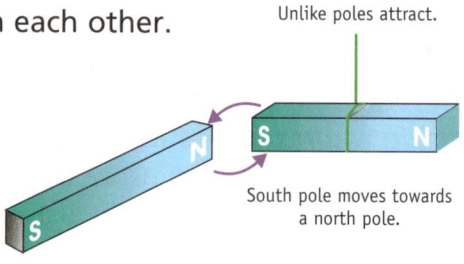

Like poles repel.
North pole moves away from another north pole.

Unlike poles attract.
South pole moves towards a north pole.

magnetic separation

is when *magnets* are used to separate iron from a *mixture*. Magnetic separation is commonly used in *mining* to separate iron from *rocks* and to remove iron impurities from *ores*.

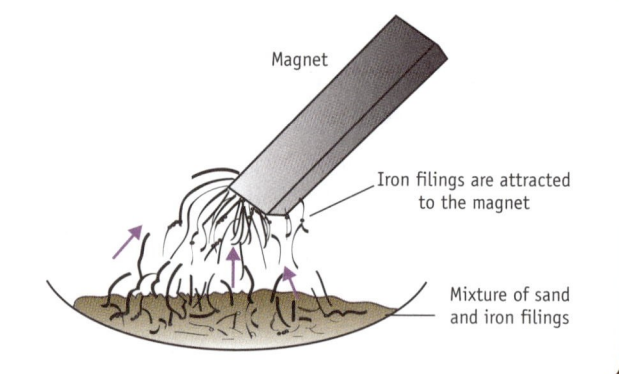

Magnet
Iron filings are attracted to the magnet
Mixture of sand and iron filings

mantle

is the layer of the *Earth* between the *crust* and the *core*. The upper mantle is known as the *asthenosphere*.

manufacture

is the process of making things and *materials* with particular *properties* and for specific purposes. See **plastics**.

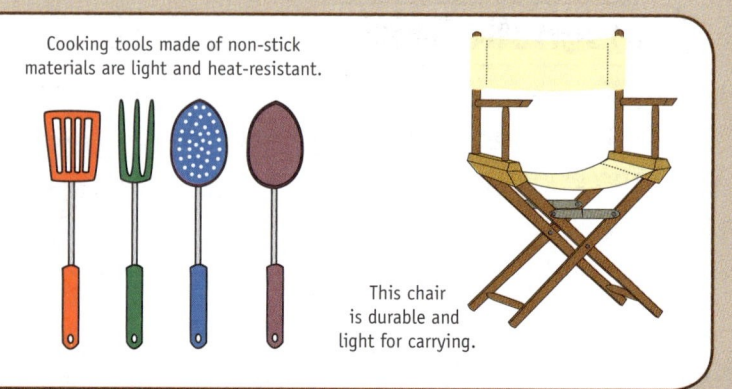

Cooking tools made of non-stick materials are light and heat-resistant.

This chair is durable and light for carrying.

marble

marble

is a *metamorphic rock* formed by the recrystallisation of limestone. It often has patterns (veins) and is used for ornamental work and monuments. White marble with fine grain is used for sculpture.

Mars

(the 'red planet') is a rocky *planet* with craters, extinct volcanoes and dried-up river beds. The surface is covered with fine red soil, which is blown into the *atmosphere* forming dust storms. Mars has two *moons*.

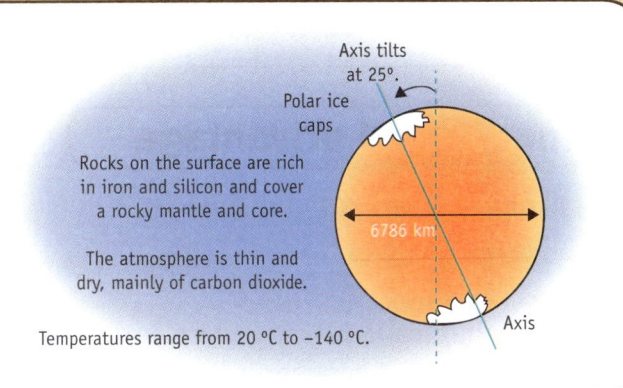

Axis tilts at 25°.
Polar ice caps
Rocks on the surface are rich in iron and silicon and cover a rocky mantle and core.
6786 km
The atmosphere is thin and dry, mainly of carbon dioxide.
Temperatures range from 20 °C to −140 °C.
Axis

mass

is the amount of *matter* in an object or substance. It is measured in grams (g) and kilograms (kg). Compare **weight**.

materials

are the substances that make up things. The *properties* of materials make them suitable for a particular use. Humans can modify or process materials to make them more useful. See **natural materials; synthetic materials; processed materials; resources**.

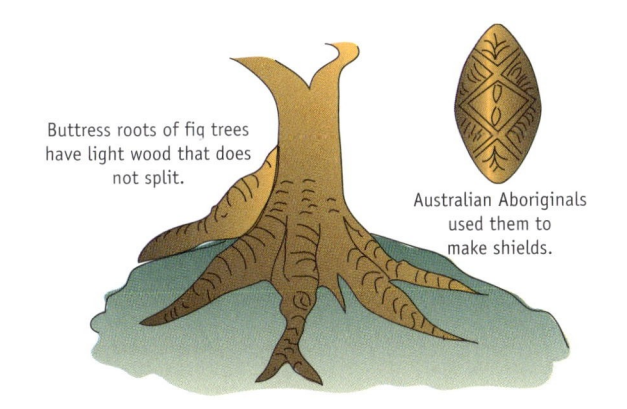

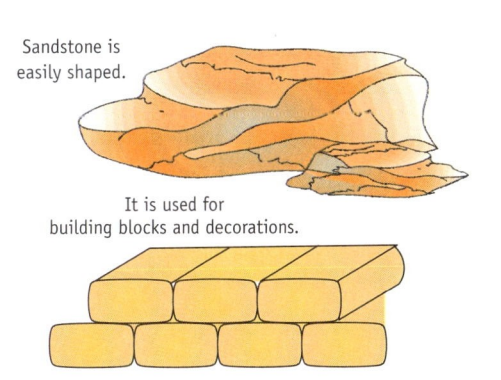

Buttress roots of fig trees have light wood that does not split.

Australian Aboriginals used them to make shields.

Sandstone is easily shaped.

It is used for building blocks and decorations.

Excel Illustrated Science Dictionary Years 5–8

matter

is the material from which things are made. The amount of matter present is the object's *mass*. Matter takes up space and exists as *solid*, *liquid* or *gas*. Solids, liquids and gases occur as *element*s, *mixture*s or *compound*s. See **state of matter; particle theory of matter; bonds; expansion of matter; contraction of matter; compression of matter**.

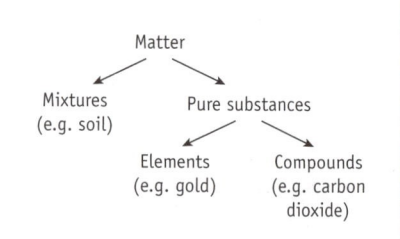

```
              Matter
            ↙       ↘
      Mixtures    Pure substances
      (e.g. soil)   ↙       ↘
              Elements    Compounds
              (e.g. gold)  (e.g. carbon
                            dioxide)
```

mechanical advantage

of a *machine* compares the load to be lifted with the effort applied to the machine.

$$\text{mechanical advantage} = \frac{\text{load } force}{\text{effort } force}$$

A mechanical advantage larger than 1 indicates the machine is efficient and makes work easier. A mechanical advantage of 1 or less indicates the machine is not very efficient. See **efficiency of a machine**.

megafauna

in Australia lived about a million years ago and included the giant kangaroo and diprotodon, known as the giant wombat. Diprotodon is the largest pouched *animal* known. It was the size of a modern hippopotamus and weighed 2800 kg. Most of these large animals died out about 15000 years ago, probably because of change in *climate* and vegetation and hunting. See **extinction**.

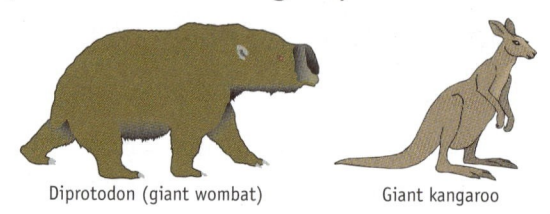

Diprotodon (giant wombat)   Giant kangaroo

melting

is a *change of state* from *solid* to *liquid*. During melting, the solid absorbs heat and its particles begin to move more and slide over each other. See **melting point**.

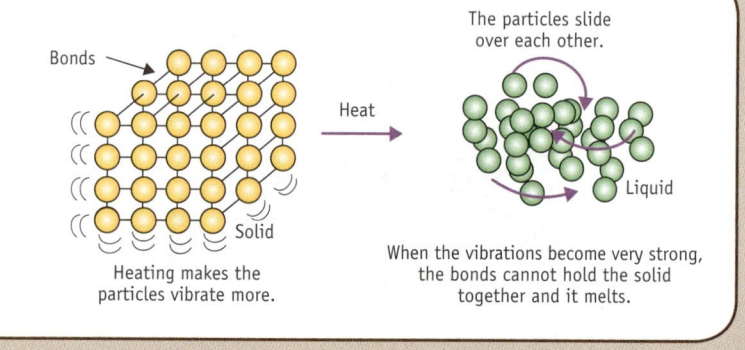

Bonds → Solid
Heating makes the particles vibrate more.

Heat →

The particles slide over each other.
Liquid
When the vibrations become very strong, the bonds cannot hold the solid together and it melts.

Excel Illustrated Science Dictionary Years 5–8

melting point

melting point

is the *temperature* at which a *solid* substance turns to *liquid*. A solid with strong *bonds* between its particles (e.g. iron) has a high melting point. A solid with weak bonds has a low melting point (e.g. ice melts at 0°C). Compare **boiling point**; **freezing point**.

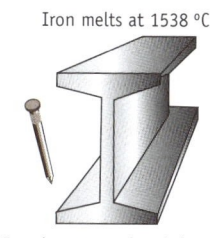

Iron melts at 1538 °C

Iron has strong bonds between its particles. It needs a lot of heat to break them.

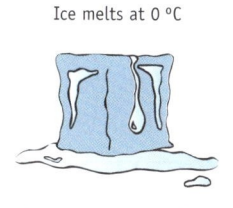

Ice melts at 0 °C

Ice has weak bonds between its particles. It needs little heat to break them.

Mercury

is the closest *planet* to the *Sun*. Its surface is similar to that of the *Moon*. It has craters, plains, cliffs and hills. Mercury is the most iron-rich planet in the *solar system*. It has no moons.

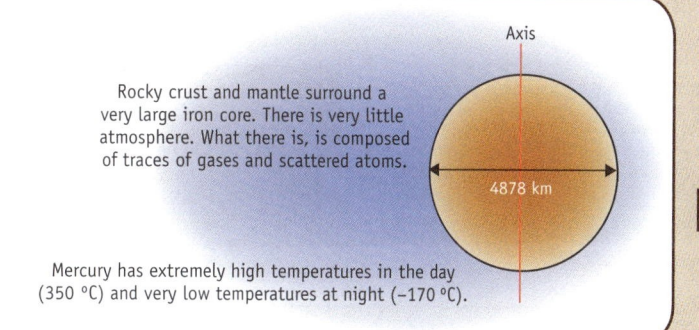

Axis

Rocky crust and mantle surround a very large iron core. There is very little atmosphere. What there is, is composed of traces of gases and scattered atoms.

4878 km

Mercury has extremely high temperatures in the day (350 °C) and very low temperatures at night (−170 °C).

metal

is strong, shiny (has lustre), can be beaten into a shape and bends without snapping (is malleable). Metals are good *conductors* of *heat* and *electricity*. See **element symbols**; **alloys**; **metal reactivity**; **metal properties**.

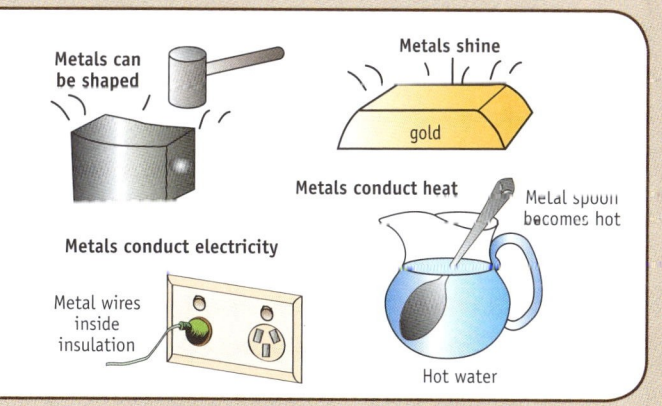

Metals can be shaped

Metals shine — gold

Metals conduct heat — Metal spoon becomes hot — Hot water

Metals conduct electricity — Metal wires inside insulation

metal properties

are the qualities of the *metal*. Metals have different *properties* and so have different uses. For instance, gold does not corrode; it is soft and easy to shape. It is not abundant and is used for jewellery, coins and ornaments. Aluminium is light, easily shaped, not corrosive and abundant. It is used in aircraft and buildings. See **metal reactivity**.

Excel **Illustrated Science Dictionary Years 5–8**

metal reactivity

refers to the different abilities *metals* have to react with other substances. For example, gold is unreactive, while sodium is very reactive. Unreactive metals may be found in the *Earth's crust* in pure form. Reactive metals exist as *compounds* called *ores* or *minerals*.

metamorphic rocks

have formed from other *rocks* that have been altered by *pressure* and/or *heat*. *Earth* movements create massive pressure and heat (from *friction*) and may also alter rocks. See **marble; slate**.

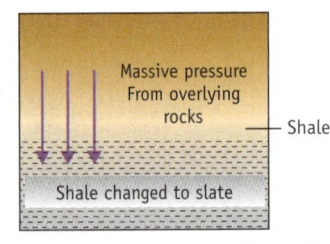

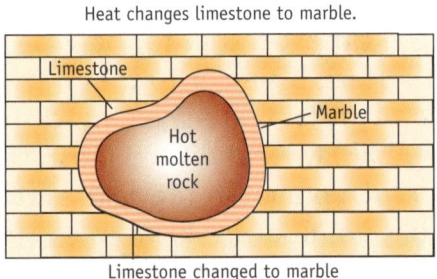

metamorphosis

is the change of form of an *organism* during its *life cycle*. Some insects change from *larva* to *pupa* to adult. Adult frogs develop from tadpoles. See **life cycle**.

meteorites

are lumps of *rock* or *metal* that come from space and hit the *Earth*. Compare **meteors**.

meteorology

meteorology

is the study of the *atmosphere* in relation to *weather* and *climate*.

meteors

or 'shooting stars' are small fragments of *matter* attracted to the *Earth* from space. As they enter the *atmosphere*, *heat* from *friction* causes them to burn. Compare **meteorites**.

micro-

means small and often refers to structures that cannot be seen with the naked eye (e.g. *microorganism*).

microbe

See **microorganisms**.

microorganisms

are microscopic *living things* such as *unicellular organisms*, *bacteria* and some *fungi*. Many microorganisms are useful; however, some are harmful and cause disease. For example, tinea is a fungal disease and pneumonia is a bacterial disease. See **virus**.

Useful microorganisms

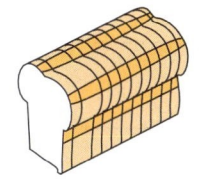

The fungus, yeast, is used to bake bread.

Bacteria in the gut of herbivores digest plant food.

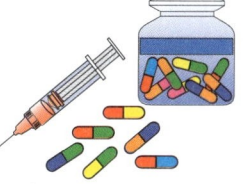

Microorganisms are used to make vaccines and antibiotics which help control disease.

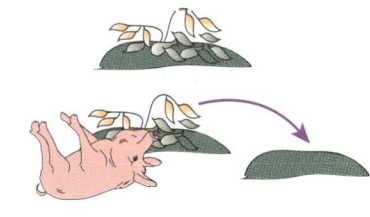

Microorganisms decompose dead organisms and recycle nutrients to the soil.

Excel Illustrated Science Dictionary Years 5–8

microscope

microscope

is a tool used to magnify very small objects. Microscopes were developed in 1590 by the Janssen brothers in Holland. They experimented with lenses in a tube (known as a compound microscope) and magnified objects up to 9×. In the 17th century a number of scientists, including Galileo and Leeuwenhoek, further developed the microscope. Anthony van Leeuwenhoek, a Dutch scientist, made microscopes which consisted of a convex *lens* attached to a metal plate. They were focused by a screw. He viewed bacteria, yeast and blood cells, and microorganisms in water.

The compound microscope uses multiple lenses. The image magnified by one lens was then magnified again. English scientist Robert Hooke used a three-lens microscope. He discovered the cell.

Recent technology has improved microscopes, with a screen replacing the eyepieces and the ability to enlarge the image to 100 mm (the traditional microscope enlarges the image to 3 mm). An electron microscope uses electrons instead of light to produce a magnified image. The first electron microscope was built in 1931 by Ernst Ruska, a German engineer.

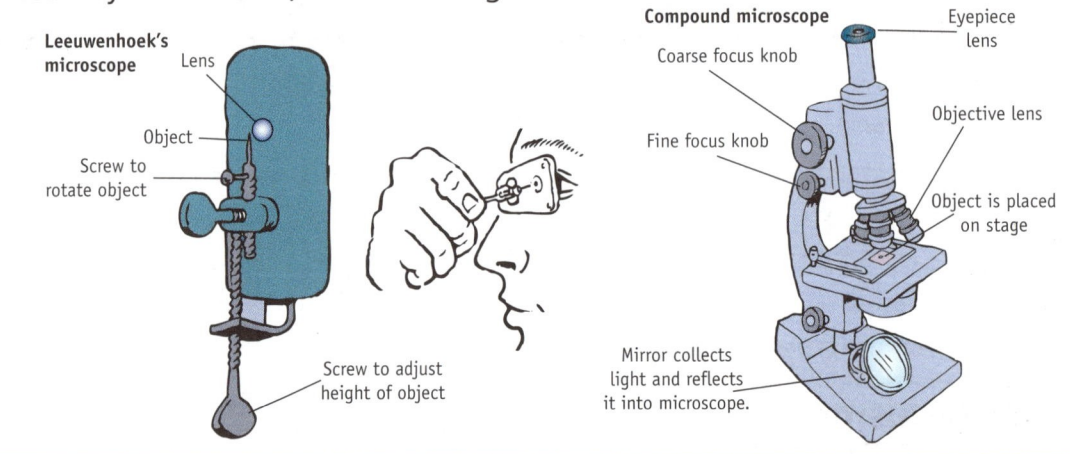

Leeuwenhoek's microscope
- Lens
- Object
- Screw to rotate object
- Screw to adjust height of object

Compound microscope
- Eyepiece lens
- Coarse focus knob
- Fine focus knob
- Objective lens
- Object is placed on stage
- Mirror collects light and reflects it into microscope.

migration

is the movement of populations of animals from one area to another. It is usually related to *seasons* and *temperature*. For example, humpback whales migrate from the Antarctic to the Australian coast for winter.

mineral

is a *compound* found in the *Earth* in *rocks*. Common minerals are quartz, feldspar and calcite. See **mineral properties; mineral uses; mineral nutrients; rock minerals; ore minerals; mining.**

mineral nutrients

are needed for tissue growth and body functioning (e.g. *animals* need iron to make blood and *plants* need nitrates to make *protein*). Plants obtain *minerals* from the *soil* and animals obtain them from their *food* (i.e. plants or animals).

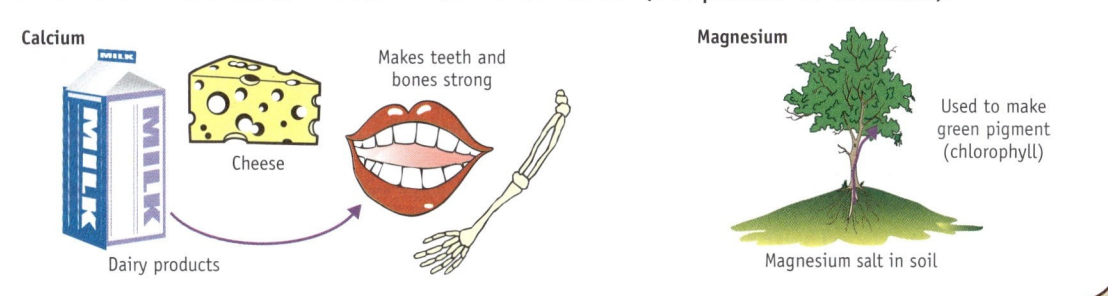

Calcium — Dairy products (Milk, Cheese) — Makes teeth and bones strong

Magnesium — Magnesium salt in soil — Used to make green pigment (chlorophyll)

mineral properties

allow *minerals* to be identified. The *properties* are their distinct *crystal* shape (which may be microscopic), colour, colour of their streak (powder), hardness, lustre or sheen, and cleavage (the way they split).

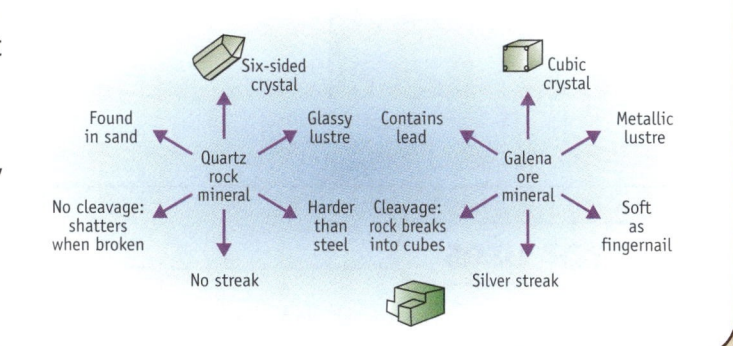

Quartz rock mineral: Found in sand, Six-sided crystal, Glassy lustre, No cleavage: shatters when broken, No streak

Galena ore mineral: Contains lead, Cubic crystal, Metallic lustre, Cleavage: rock breaks into cubes, Harder than steel, Soft as fingernail, Silver streak

mineral uses

are related to their *properties*.

Mineral	Property	Use
quartz	hard	sandpaper
ruby	attractive	jewellery
haematite	coloured	pigment and dye
mica and asbestos	heat-resistant	insulators

mining

is used to extract *minerals* and *ores* and other useful substances, such as *coal*, from the *Earth*. Mining destroys small areas of natural land and *ecosystems*. See **non-renewable resources**.

Excel Illustrated Science Dictionary Years 5–8

M mirror

mirror

is a reflecting surface. A mirror may be flat (plane) or curved. See **mirror reflections**; **mirror uses**.

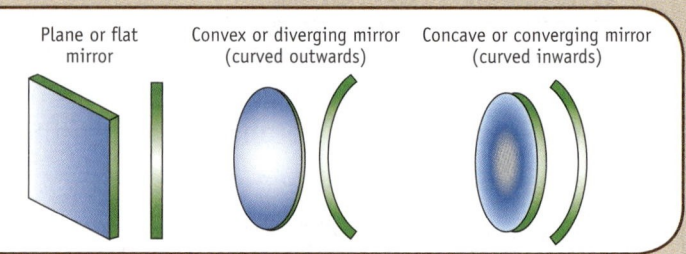

Plane or flat mirror

Convex or diverging mirror (curved outwards)

Concave or converging mirror (curved inwards)

mirror reflections

occur when *light* hits a *mirror*. The light is reflected (bounces off) in a regular way. See **kaleidoscope**.

Plane mirror: a beam of light perpendicular to the mirror is reflected back along the path.

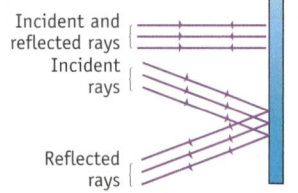

Incident and reflected rays
Incident rays
Reflected rays

A beam hitting the mirror at an angle is reflected at the same angle but in the opposite direction.

Convex mirror: a beam of light spreads out (diverges) when reflected.

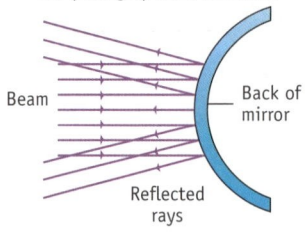

Beam
Back of mirror
Reflected rays

Concave mirror: a beam of light comes to a point (converges) when reflected.

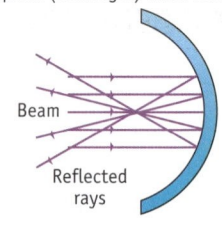

Beam
Reflected rays

mirror uses

depend on the shape of the mirror. With plane (flat) mirrors the image is undistorted, reversed sideways and is the same size as the object (e.g. bathroom mirror). With convex mirrors the image is smaller than the object and there is a wide field of view. They are sometimes used for rear vision mirrors on cars. With concave mirrors the image is larger than the object so these mirrors are often used for shaving or make-up. They are also used in *telescopes*, reflectors for solar furnaces and in search lights and torches. See **mirror**; **mirror reflections**.

mixture

is made of two or more substances mixed or blended together without a chemical change (e.g. sea water, *soil*, *air*). *Solutions*, *suspensions*, *colloids* and *emulsions* are mixtures. The substances in a mixture may be separated because of their different *properties*. Compare **element**; **compound**. See **separation methods**; **colloid**.

Ingredients are mixed to make a cake

Mixture of flour sugar and butter

molecule

molecule

is a group of *atoms* held together by *forces* or *bonds*. The atoms in the molecule may be the same or different. See **compound**.

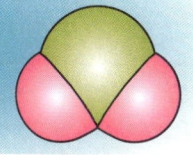

A hydrogen molecule (H₂) is made up of two hydrogen atoms.

A water molecule (H₂O) is made up of two hydrogen atoms and one oxygen atom.

moon

is a large natural body or *satellite orbiting* a *planet*. Our Moon is about one-quarter the size of the *Earth*. It has no atmosphere and no water, is rocky and covered with soil, and the surface is made up of craters, plains ('seas'), mountains and valleys. The side facing the *Sun* reflects the Sun's *light* rays. This causes it to glow. See **phases of the moon**; **eclipse of the moon**.

Earth's Moon

moulting

is the shedding of skin (reptiles) or exoskeleton (insects) to enable the *animal* to grow, or the shedding of feathers (birds) or hair (mammals) to allow new growth.

movement (motion)

See **force**; **balanced and unbalanced forces**.

movement energy

See **kinetic energy**.

multicellular organisms

are made up of many different *cells*, which are usually grouped into *tissues* and *organs*. Compare **unicellular organisms**.

Excel Illustrated Science Dictionary Years 5–8

N natural disasters

natural disasters

may destroy the *environment* and property, and kill people. See **drought**; **bushfires and floods**; **cyclone**; **earthquakes**; **volcano**; **tsunami**.

natural materials

come from *living things*, the *Earth*, *air* or water (e.g. *food*, *ores*, *oxygen*, wood). Many natural *materials* are modified to make them more useful (e.g. raw wool and cotton are converted to useful fibres). Humans use natural materials to make new materials (e.g. *plastics*, *detergents*, fibreglass). See **materials**; **resources**; **processed materials**; **synthetic materials**.

nebulae

are large clouds of dust and glowing *gas* in space. The Crab Nebula is a huge cloud of expanding gas formed by an exploding *star* (supernova). The Orion Nebula glows because of newly formed stars embedded in the gas.

Neptune

is a very distant *planet* in our *solar system*. It is made of *gas* and has distinctive cloud features and very strong winds. It had a large spot, called the Great Dark Spot, and two smaller ones caused by storms. There are eight known *moons* orbiting Neptune.

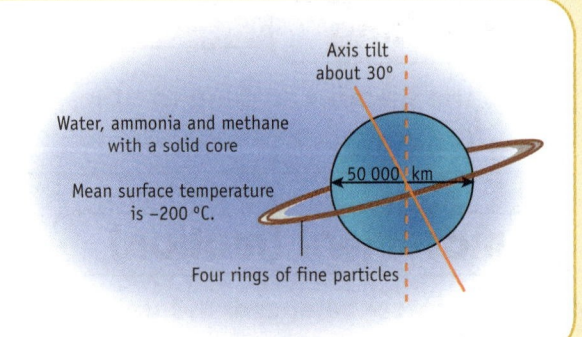

Axis tilt about 30°
Water, ammonia and methane with a solid core
Mean surface temperature is −200 °C.
50 000 km
Four rings of fine particles

nocturnal

describes *animals* that move around at night (e.g. owls, possums). The darkness provides protection from predators and the *heat* of the day. Compare **diurnal**.

non-metals

are generally light, do not have lustre (sheen) and are not malleable (cannot be beaten into a shape). They do not conduct *electricity* or *heat*. About one-sixth of the *elements* are non-metals. Compare **metal**. See **element symbols**.

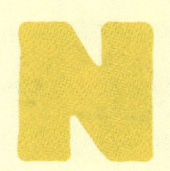

non-renewable energy sources

include *fossil fuels* (*coal*, oil, natural gas). They are used to produce *electricity* and provide petrol and other fuels. *Nuclear energy* obtained from *uranium* metal is also used to generate electricity. Compare **renewable energy sources**. See **non-renewable resources**.

non-renewable resources

are substances that cannot be replaced once they are used (e.g. *fossil fuels*, *minerals*, *rock*, *metals*). They were formed millions of years ago, over long periods of time. Compare **renewable resources**. See **energy sources, non-renewable energy sources; conservation of non-renewable resources**.

nuclear energy

is released from radioactive substances, such as *uranium*. In nuclear power plants, nuclear energy is used to make *electricity* and products important for medical *science*.

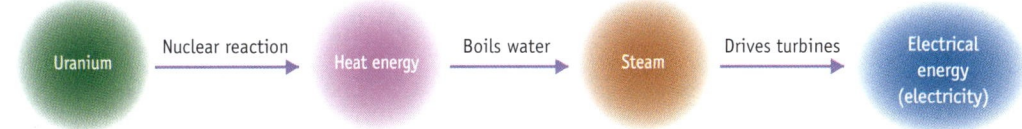

Uranium → Nuclear reaction → Heat energy → Boils water → Steam → Drives turbines → Electrical energy (electricity)

nutrients

are the *food* substances an *organism* requires to function correctly and to maintain health. There are five main groups: *proteins*, *carbohydrates* (sugars), *fats*, *vitamins* and *minerals*. See **organic compounds; inorganic nutrients; photosynthesis**.

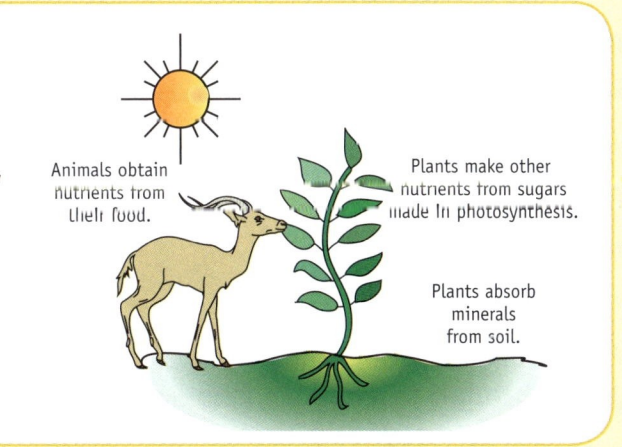

Animals obtain nutrients from their food.

Plants make other nutrients from sugars made in photosynthesis.

Plants absorb minerals from soil.

nutrition

is the process by which *organisms* absorb substances (*nutrients*) needed for maintenance, growth and repair of *tissues* and functioning of the body.

Excel Illustrated Science Dictionary Years 5–8

ocean currents

are the movements of water in the ocean caused by *winds* and different water densities. The *density* of the water changes as it heats or cools and as the salt content changes. See **global ocean currents**.

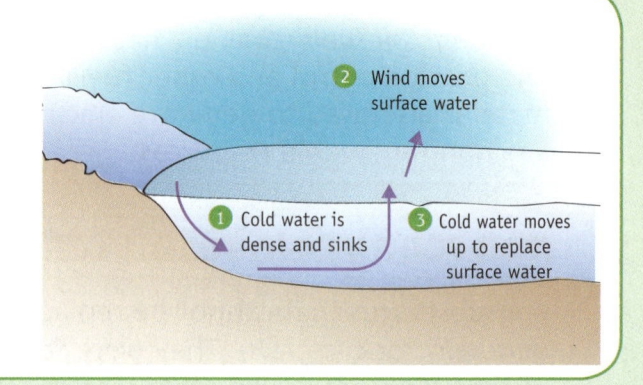

ocean depth

affects the conditions present. *Animals* living in the depths of the ocean have *adaptations* that enable them to survive without *light* or *plants*, in low *temperatures* and under high *pressures*.

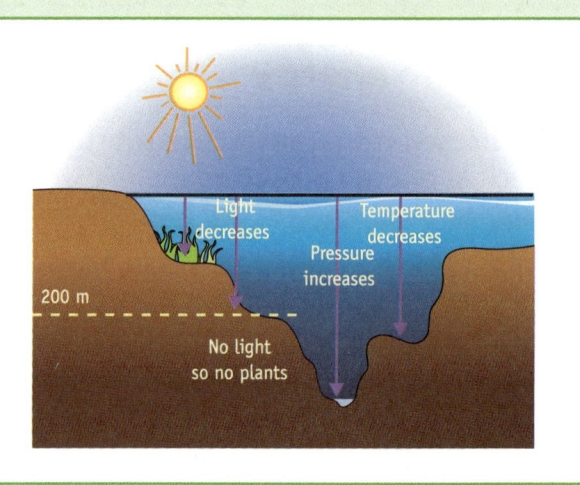

oceans and weather

are connected. The ocean waters cool or warm the *air* and add moisture to it. They influence the *weather* and *climate*. See **global ocean currents**; **El Niño**.

opaque

describes something *light* cannot pass through (e.g. wood). The light bounces off (is *reflected*) or is absorbed. When light hits an opaque object, a *shadow* may be formed. Compare **transparent**; **translucent**.

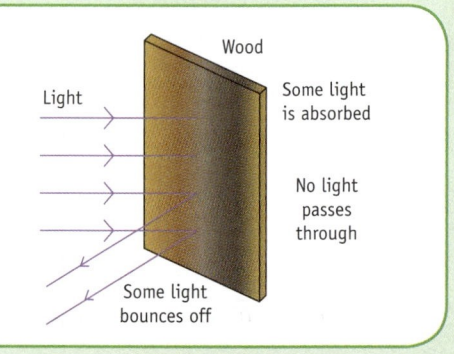

optical telescope

optical telescope

is used to observe objects in *space*. It can magnify objects and also collect *light* from very faint objects. Reflecting telescopes collect light with *mirrors* and refracting telescopes collect light with *lenses*. See **radio telescope**; **Hubble Space Telescope**.

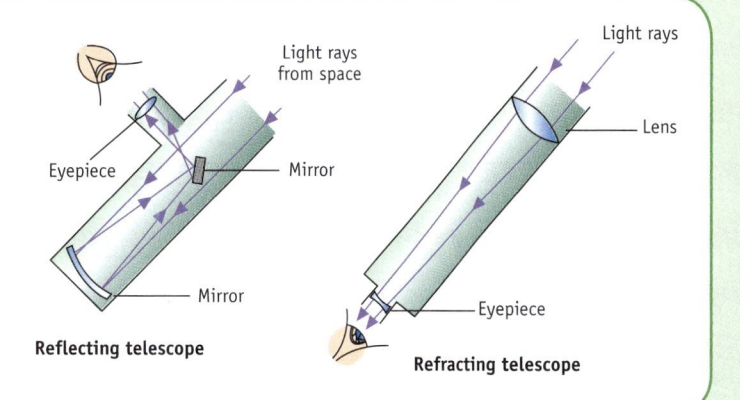

Reflecting telescope — Light rays from space, Eyepiece, Mirror, Mirror

Refracting telescope — Light rays, Lens, Eyepiece

orbit

is the regular path of one object around another (e.g. *planets* and *satellites* are in orbit). The planets move around the *Sun* in elongated orbits (ellipses), in the same direction and almost the same plane. The dwarf planet Pluto has a completely different orbit. See **year**.

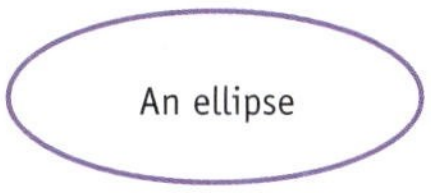

An ellipse

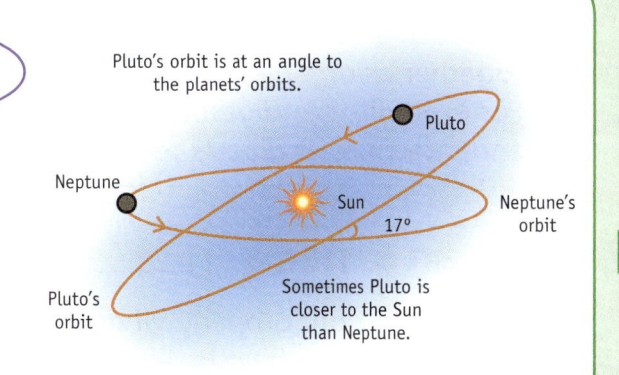

Pluto's orbit is at an angle to the planets' orbits.
Neptune, Pluto, Sun 17°, Neptune's orbit, Pluto's orbit
Sometimes Pluto is closer to the Sun than Neptune.

orbit and gravity

is similar to whirling a weight on a rope. The Sun's *gravity* keeps the *planets* in a circular motion or orbit.

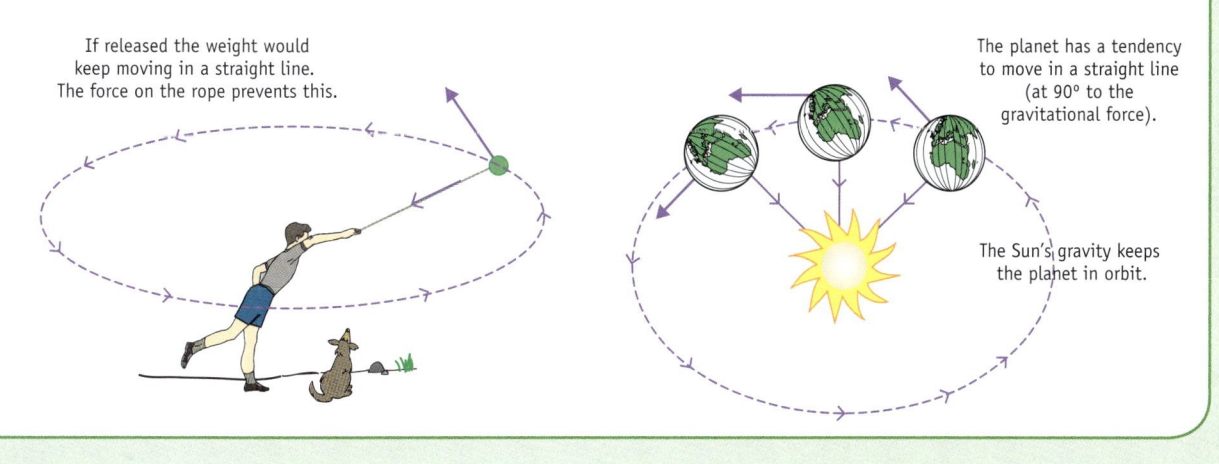

If released the weight would keep moving in a straight line. The force on the rope prevents this.

The planet has a tendency to move in a straight line (at 90° to the gravitational force).

The Sun's gravity keeps the planet in orbit.

Excel Illustrated Science Dictionary Years 5–8

95

O ore

ore

is a concentrated mass of useful *minerals* mixed with unwanted *materials* and found in the *Earth's crust*. Haematite is an ore containing iron. Bauxite contains aluminium. See **mining**; **refining**.

ore minerals

are *minerals* found in *ores*. They are *metals* and other substances useful to humans. For example, aluminium is found in bauxite and iron in haematite. Titanium is obtained from the ore rutile and copper from chalcopyrite.

organ

is part of a living body made up of one or more *tissues*. Different organs work together as *organ systems*. Each organ system has a specialised job (function). For example, the *digestive system* is made up of organs such as the stomach and intestines. It digests food so that it can pass into the bloodstream.

organ systems

in humans work properly when the person has a healthy lifestyle (a well-balanced diet, exercise and rest). *Organ* systems in *plants* include *stems*, *roots* and *leaves*. See **plant structure**.

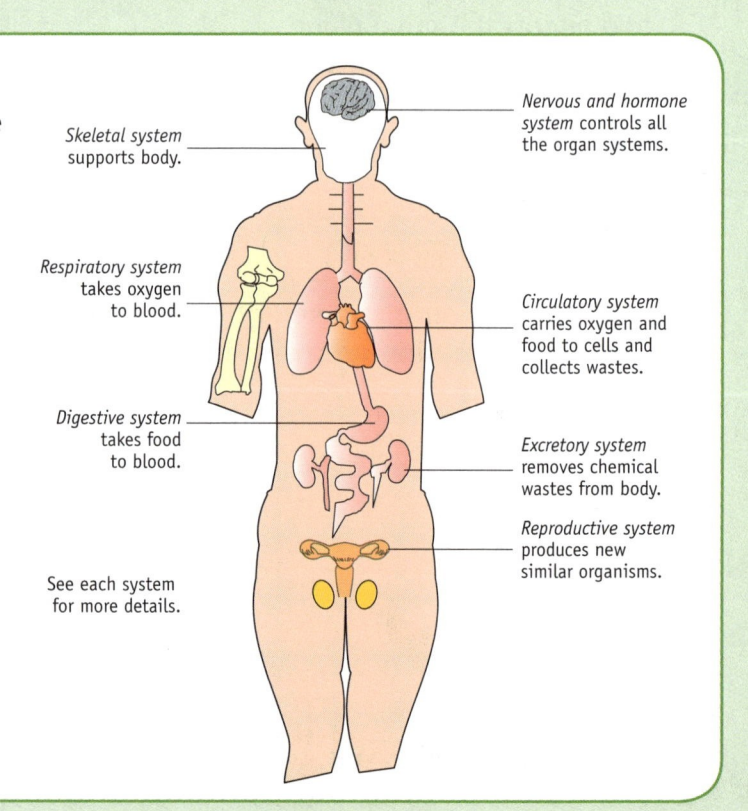

Skeletal system supports body.

Respiratory system takes oxygen to blood.

Digestive system takes food to blood.

See each system for more details.

Nervous and hormone system controls all the organ systems.

Circulatory system carries oxygen and food to cells and collects wastes.

Excretory system removes chemical wastes from body.

Reproductive system produces new similar organisms.

organic compounds

contain carbon and hydrogen and many have a long chain structure. They make up living *tissues* and are found in *materials* from *living things* (e.g. wood, petrol, cotton, wool, leather). *Proteins*, *carbohydrates* (sugars), *fats* and *vitamins* are organic *nutrients*. Compare **inorganic nutrients**.

organism

is a *living thing*. See **multicellular organisms; unicellular organisms**.

ovum (plural: ova)

See **egg**.

oxygen (O$_2$)

is a *gas* found in the *atmosphere*. It is used by *plants* and *animals* for *respiration*, and to burn substances.

Burning produces heat energy

Photosynthesis

Respiration provides energy

ozone (O$_3$)

is a form of *oxygen* that exists in a layer in the upper *atmosphere*. The ozone layer is helpful to life as it shields the surface of the *Earth* from excessive *ultraviolet* (UV) radiation from the *Sun*.

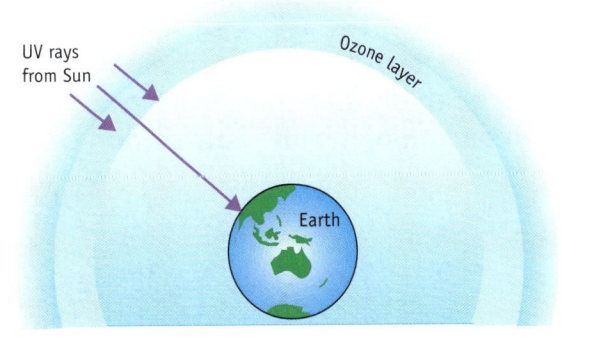

UV rays from Sun

Ozone layer

Earth

Some pollutants (CFCs) reduce the ozone layer and allow more UV to reach the Earth.

Excel Illustrated Science Dictionary Years 5–8

parasite

See **parasitism**.

parasitism

occurs when one *organism* lives on or in another and feeds from it.

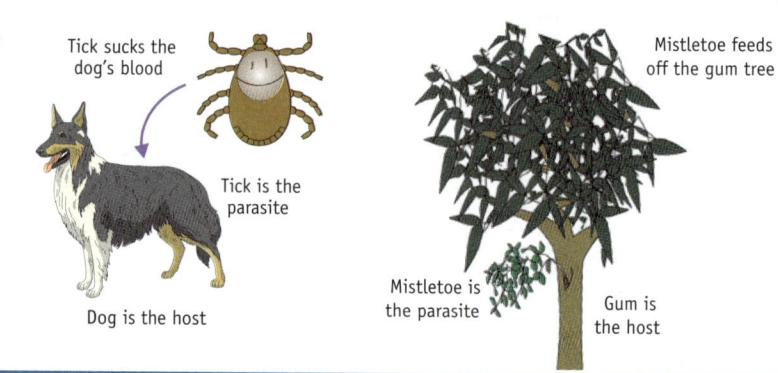

Tick sucks the dog's blood
Tick is the parasite
Dog is the host

Mistletoe feeds off the gum tree
Mistletoe is the parasite
Gum is the host

parental care

is the care mammals, birds and some reptiles give their young after birth so they have a high survival rate. Fish and amphibians do not care for their young and so the young have a high death rate. These creatures produce large numbers of offspring to ensure some survive.

particle theory of matter

explains the behaviour of substances. This theory describes *matter* as small, moving particles (*atoms* or *molecules*). Heating matter makes the particles move more rapidly and cooling it slows their movement. See **state of matter, change; expansion of matter; contraction of matter**.

Solid: particles are closely held together and vibrating.

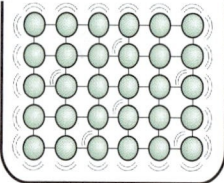

Liquid: particles are close together and slide over each other.

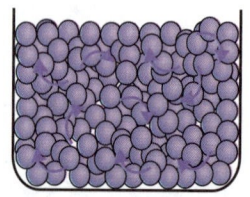

Gas: particles are far apart and moving freely.

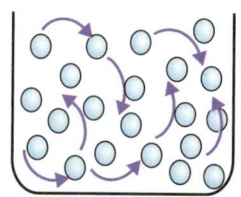

periodic table

periodic table

is a chart of the *elements* showing relationships. Elements with similar properties are placed in columns called groups. For example, all the elements in the first group are *metals* while those in the right-hand group are inactive *gases* known as noble gases. Properties change gradually across the rows called periods, from metals on the left-hand side through to non-metals on the right.

A portion of the periodic table showing some common elements

- Metals
- Non-metals
- Transition metals
- Properties between metals and non-metals

HYDROGEN H																	HELIUM He
LITHIUM Li	BERYLLIUM Be											BORON B	CARBON C	NITROGEN N	OXYGEN O	FLUORINE F	NEON Ne
SODIUM Na	MAGNESIUM Mg											ALUMINIUM Al	SILICON Si	PHOSPHOROUS P	SULPHUR S	CHLORINE Cl	ARGON Ar
POTASSIUM K	CALCIUM C			CHROMIUM Cr	MANGANESE Mn	IRON Fe	COBALT Co	NICKEL Ni	COPPER Cu	ZINC Zn				ARSENIC As		BROMINE Br	KRYPTON Kr
								SILVER Ag	CADMIUM Cd		TIN Sn				IODINE I		
					Table continues down												

petroleum

is a *fossil fuel*. It is refined to obtain petrol and many other useful substances. See **fossil fuel uses**.

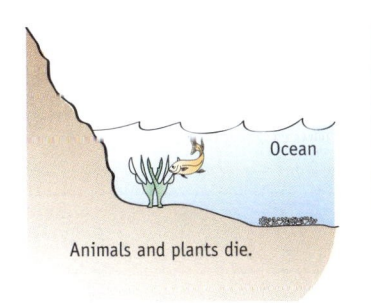

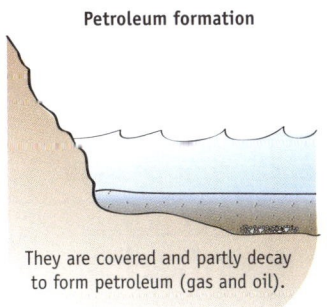

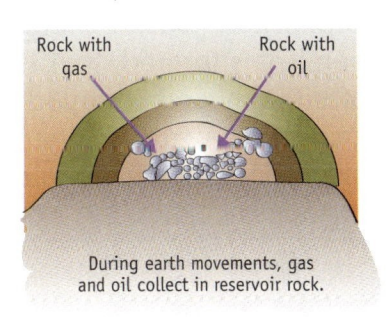

Petroleum formation

Animals and plants die. (Ocean)

They are covered and partly decay to form petroleum (gas and oil).

During earth movements, gas and oil collect in reservoir rock.

Rock with gas — Rock with oil

phases of the Moon

refers to its different shapes (e.g. full moon, new moon). The side of the *Moon* facing the *Sun* reflects light (i.e. is lit up). As the Moon revolves around the *Earth*, we see different portions of the Moon reflecting light to the Earth.

(cont.)

Excel Illustrated Science Dictionary Years 5–8

phases of the Moon (cont.)

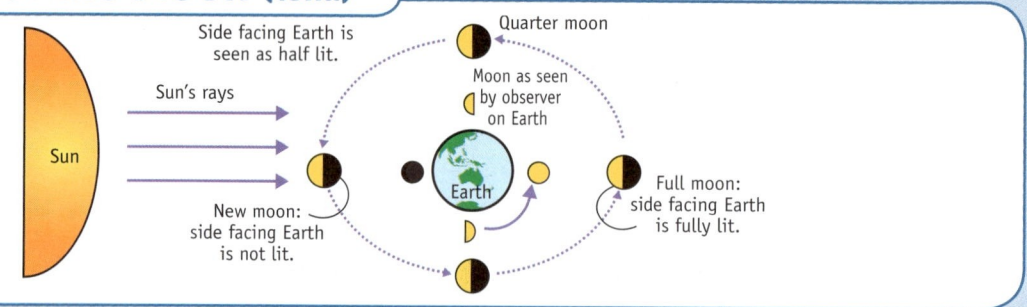

phloem

tissue carries the *food* made in the leaves of *plants* to *cells* and *organs* for use or storage (e.g. sugars are stored in *fruits*). See **transport systems in plants**.

photosynthesis

is the process *plants* use to make their own *food*. In this process, the plants use sunlight to convert *carbon dioxide* and water to sugars (food). At the same time, *oxygen* and water are formed. See **chloroplast**.

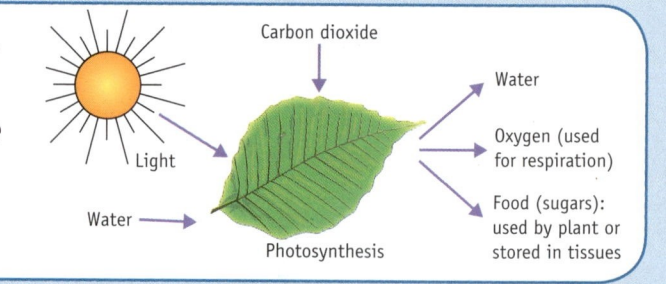

physical change

occurs when *matter* changes but no new chemical is formed, that is, there is a *change of state* (e.g. wood chopped into pieces, sugar *dissolved* in water). Generally it can be readily reversed. Compare **chemical reaction or change**.

physical (mechanical) weathering

is caused by several processes.
1. Abrasion by particles carried by *wind*, water or *glaciers* wear down the rock. See **corrasion**.
2. *Temperature* changes make *rocks* expand and contract, weakening them so that they crumble. Water freezing in cracks in rocks also splits them.
3. The roots of *plants* grow into cracks.

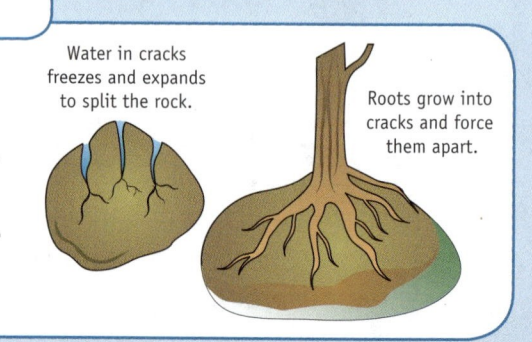

Excel **Illustrated Science Dictionary Years 5–8**

pitch of a sound

is its highness or lowness. A rapid vibration produces a high note and a slow vibration produces a low note. The number of vibrations in a second is called the frequency. See **sound**; **frequency**.

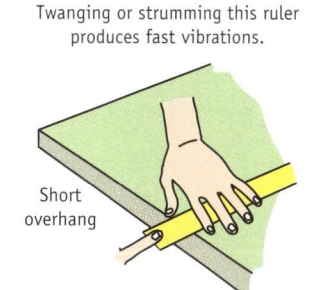

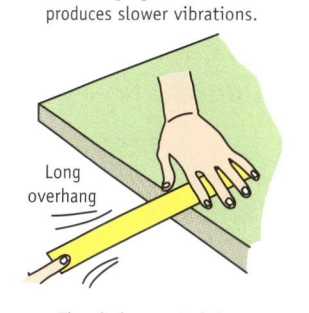

Twanging or strumming this ruler produces fast vibrations.

Short overhang

The pitch or note is high.

Twanging this ruler produces slower vibrations.

Long overhang

The pitch or note is low.

planet

is a body revolving around a *star*. In the *solar system* eight planets *orbit* the *Sun*. The planets, in order from the Sun, are *Mercury*, *Venus*, *Earth*, *Mars*, *Jupiter*, *Saturn*, *Uranus*, *Neptune* and *Pluto* (dwarf planet). Each rotates on its axis and most have *moon*s. Until August 2006 Pluto was also classed as a planet. It is now reclassified as a dwarf planet. See **planet sizes**; **planet distances from the Sun**.

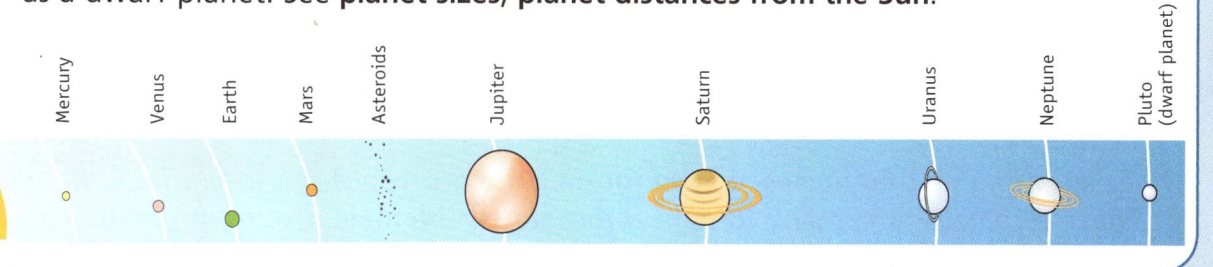

Mercury | Venus | Earth | Mars | Asteroids | Jupiter | Saturn | Uranus | Neptune | Pluto (dwarf planet)

planet distances from the Sun

are immense. The distance between *Pluto* and the *Sun* is 5900 million km. If we call this distance 100 mm (10 cm), then the distance of each *planet* from the Sun is as shown in the table below.

Planet	Distance
Mercury	1 mm
Venus	2 mm
Earth	2.5 mm
Mars	4 mm
Jupiter	13 mm

Planet	Distance
Saturn	24 mm
Uranus	50 mm
Neptune	77 mm
Pluto (dwarf planet)	100 mm

See **light year**.

Excel Illustrated Science Dictionary Years 5–8

planet revolutions

around the Sun follow an elliptical (oval) *orbit*. The *planets* are all in the same plane called the ecliptic (except for the dwarf planet, *Pluto*). The time it takes for one revolution is the planet's year. See **light year; year**.

planet sizes

can range from small to large. The diameter of the *Sun* is 1 400 000 km. If we imagine the Sun is the size of a large rockmelon, then the *planets* would be about these sizes:

Planet	Size
Mercury	salt grain
Venus	peppercorn
Earth	peppercorn
Mars	salt grain
Jupiter	walnut

Planet	Size
Saturn	large grape
Uranus	pea
Neptune	small pea
Pluto (dwarf planet)	salt grain

plant

is an *organism* that makes its own *food* by the process of *photosynthesis*. Its *cells* have a cell wall and many contain *chloroplasts*. The main groups of plants are algae (mainly water weed), mosses and liverworts, ferns, cone plants or conifers, and *flowering plants*.

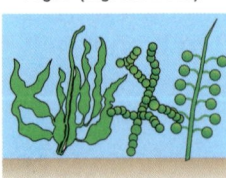

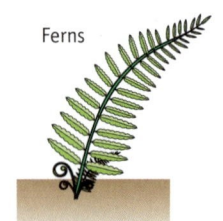

Algae (e.g. seaweed) Ferns Mosses and liverworts Conifers (e.g. pine) Flowering plants

plant growth and survival

is affected by changing environments. For example, a shade-dwelling fern may stop growing and die if placed in hot sun. Different plant species have different soil and fertiliser requirements. Camellias grow well in slightly acid soil while boxwoods need alkaline soil.

plant structure

plant structure (flowering plant)

consists of *leaves*, *stems*, *roots* and *flowers*. These plant *organ*s provide the plant with *nutrition* and enable it to reproduce and function (*work*).

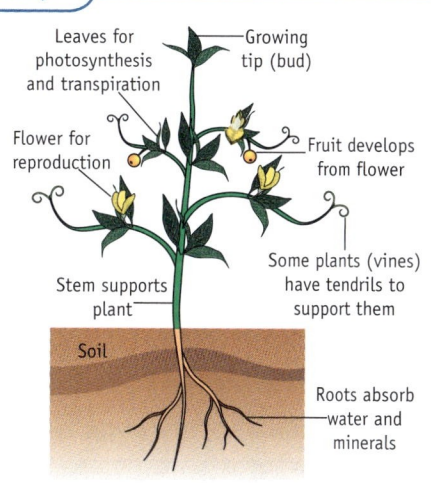

- Leaves for photosynthesis and transpiration
- Growing tip (bud)
- Flower for reproduction
- Fruit develops from flower
- Some plants (vines) have tendrils to support them
- Stem supports plant
- Soil
- Roots absorb water and minerals

plastics

are made by humans (so are *synthetic materials*) and most are made from *petroleum*. They are organic and generally have very large *molecules*. There are many different types and they have many uses.

Plastic	Properties	Use
PVC	hard-wearing, strong	floor and upholstery coverings, guttering
polystyrene	can be made into light foam	packaging, insulation
nylon	light, strong; can be made into threads	ropes, clothing, fishing lines
PTFE	heat-resistant; resists chemicals	non-stick lining on frying pans
polythene (polyethylene)	tough, flexible; resists chemicals	food wrapping, shopping bags

Pluto

is a dwarf *planet* orbiting the *Sun* beyond *Neptune*. It is tiny and too far away from *Earth* to see surface details. Pluto has a very large, close *moon* and together they *orbit* the Sun on a plane different from that of the planets.

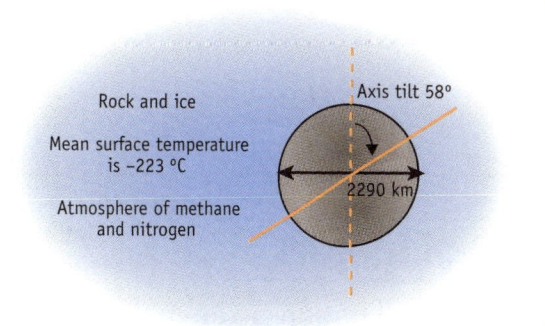

- Rock and ice
- Mean surface temperature is −223 °C
- Atmosphere of methane and nitrogen
- Axis tilt 58°
- 2290 km

Excel Illustrated Science Dictionary Years 5–8

103

pollination

pollination

is the transfer of pollen, which contains the male sex *cell*, to the female part of the *flower* (the stigma). Pollination enables *plants* to reproduce. See **pollination by animals**; **pollination by wind**.

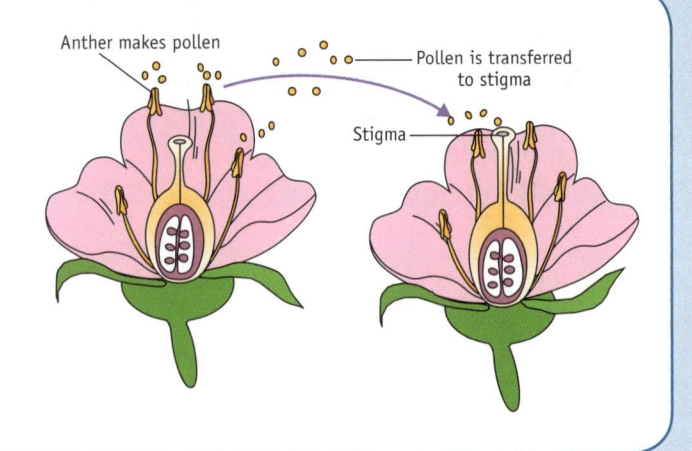

pollination by animals

occurs when birds, insects and other *animals* transfer pollen while they are foraging for nectar. The *flowers* of *plants* pollinated by animals are often brightly coloured and/or have strong perfume to attract pollinators. Compare **pollination by wind**. See **pollination**.

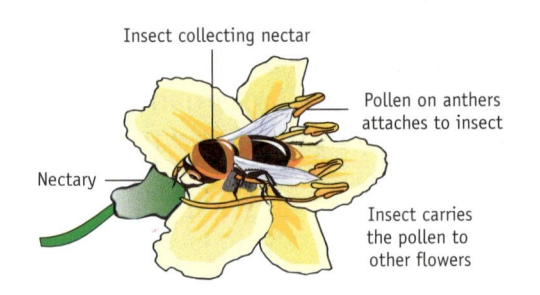

pollination by wind

is used by some *plants* (e.g. grasses). Their *flowers* tend to be small and plain but well exposed to catch air-borne pollen. Compare **pollination by animals**. See **pollination**.

pollinators

See **pollination by animals**.

pollution

pollution

is the spreading of harmful substances (e.g. fumes from cars, smoke from factories and refineries, garbage, sewage, pesticides and fertilisers) into the *environment* and the use of *materials* that are not *biodegradable* (e.g. many *plastic*s). See **global warming**; **waste disposal**.

population

is a group of similar *organisms* living in an area (e.g. the rabbit population in a paddock, koala population in a national park). *Environmental changes* may cause the numbers in the population to change. See **population numbers**.

population numbers

may change if new *species* are introduced into the area. These new *organisms* may *prey* on or compete with the original *population* so that their numbers drop, or they may provide *food* for the original population so that population numbers increase. See **predation**; **environmental changes caused by humans**.

porous

means full of small holes or openings (e.g. a sponge). Sandy *soils* are porous and water drains through them rapidly. Less porous soils (e.g. clay soils) hold or retain more water. See **soil water retention**.

potential energy

is stored *energy*. The following are some examples of potential energy: a rock on a cliff has gravitational potential energy; a wound-up spring or a stretched elastic band has elastic potential energy; and the chemicals in *batteries*, *fuel* and firecrackers have chemical potential energy. See **energy transformation**.

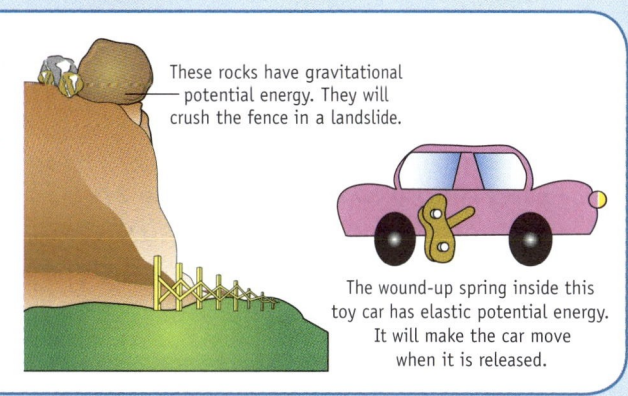

These rocks have gravitational potential energy. They will crush the fence in a landslide.

The wound-up spring inside this toy car has elastic potential energy. It will make the car move when it is released.

Excel Illustrated Science Dictionary Years 5–8

P power

power

is the amount of *electrical energy* used in a second. It is measured in *watts* (W). LED globes use less power and have less heat build-up. See **electrical energy used by an appliance**.

A 40 watt globe uses less power, heats little and glows dimly.

A 100 watt globe uses more power, heats up a lot and glows brightly.

predation

occurs when one *animal* (the *predator*) hunts and kills another (the *prey*) for *food*. Predation will affect the *population numbers* of both the predators and the prey, as shown in the graph.
1. Prey numbers increase, providing more food for the predators.
2. Predators have plenty of food so their numbers increase.
3. Prey are eaten so their numbers drop.
4. Predators now have less food, so they die and their numbers decrease.

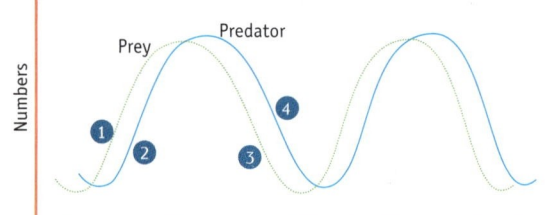

predator

is an *animal* that hunts and kills another. See **predation**.

pressure

is the *force* acting on a certain area of a surface.

$$\text{pressure} = \frac{\text{force}}{\text{area}}$$

Spreading a force over a large area decreases the pressure. See **air pressure; pressure and the particle theory**.

A brick standing on its end applies more pressure to the surface.

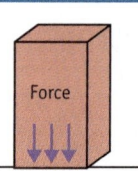

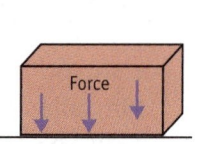

Brick pushing down on a small area

Brick pushing on a large area

Snow shoes spread the person's weight over a large area and stop them sinking in the snow.

pressure and the particle theory

suggests *pressure* of a *gas* is a measure of collisions of particles with the walls of a container. See **compression**.

A flat tyre has low pressure.
Small number of particles hit the inside wall.

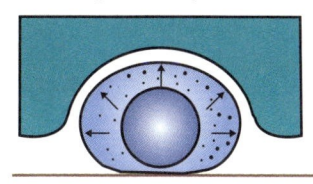

An inflated tyre has high pressure.
Many particles hit the walls.

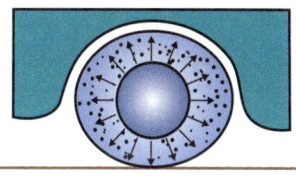

prey

is an **animal** which is killed and eaten by another animal. See **predation**.

processed materials

are natural *materials* that are modified to make them more useful. For instance, wood is converted to timber for building, and *ores* are processed or refined to obtain *metals*. Compare **synthetic materials**. See **processing**.

Examples of processed materials

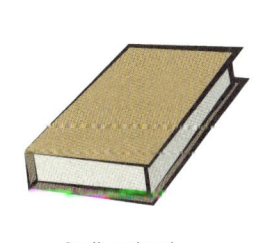

Cardboard and paper from plants

Timber from trees

Glass from sand

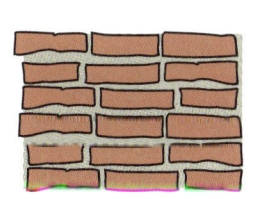

Bricks and cement from the Earth

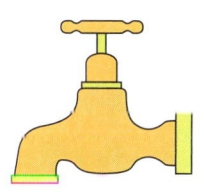

Metal from ores

processing

is how humans change the *properties* of *materials* to produce items for a particular purpose. Australian Aboriginals made water bags from possum skins, which were strengthened and preserved with tannin from wattle bark. See **processed materials; food preservation; rust proofing; refining.**

P producers

producers

are *organisms* that can make their own *food* by a process such as *photosynthesis*. *Plants* are producers. Producers are at the start of *food chains* and at the base of *food pyramids*.

properties

are the characteristics of a substance that make it suitable for a particular use. Properties include appearance, strength, flexibility, elasticity, conductivity, *melting* and *boiling points*, *density*, *buoyancy* and solubility. See **property changes; mineral uses; rock use; metal properties**.

Sugar (clear sweet crystals) sinks and dissolves in water.

Sponge is spongy, porous and flexible.

Rubber is flexible and does not conduct electricity or heat.

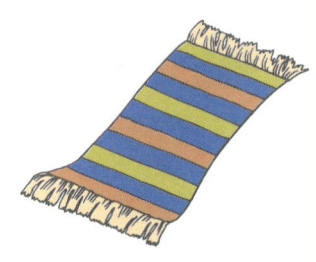

Mat is fibrous.

properties related to use

are the characteristics of a substance that affect its use, such as its chemical *properties*. For example, non-flammable substances are those that have a high fire resistance such as Kevlar, which is used for firefighters' clothes and wool for fire blankets. Another example is *corrosion*: metals that are exposed to moisture or other chemicals need to be non-corrosive or treated. See **rust proofing**.

property changes

result from changing the composition of a substance. This can alter the uses of the substance. For example, adding more sand or gravel to cement makes a weaker concrete, and adding baking powder to flour produces lighter dough than plain flour. See **rust proofing**.

protein

protein

is a *nutrient* needed for formation, growth and repair of body *tissues* (e.g. muscle and *enzyme* formation). It is found in meat, dairy products, cereal grain, nuts and *seeds*.

pulleys

are simple *machines* made up of wheels connected with ropes or chains. They are used to change the direction of a *force* or to lift a heavy load with a small effort.

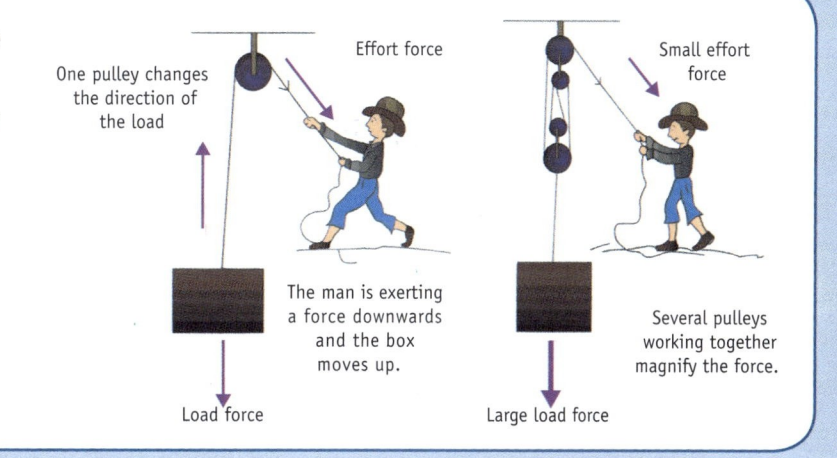

One pulley changes the direction of the load

Effort force

The man is exerting a force downwards and the box moves up.

Load force

Small effort force

Several pulleys working together magnify the force.

Large load force

pumice

is an *igneous rock* formed from frothy *lava* which has cooled very quickly. It is full of cavities which were caused by expanding gases trapped inside the lava as it solidified.

gas cavities

pupa

or chrysalis is a stage in the *life cycle* of some insects. It is usually the stage between the *larva* and the adult and is often found in a protective casing or cocoon. During this stage the larva develops into an adult. See **metamorphosis**.

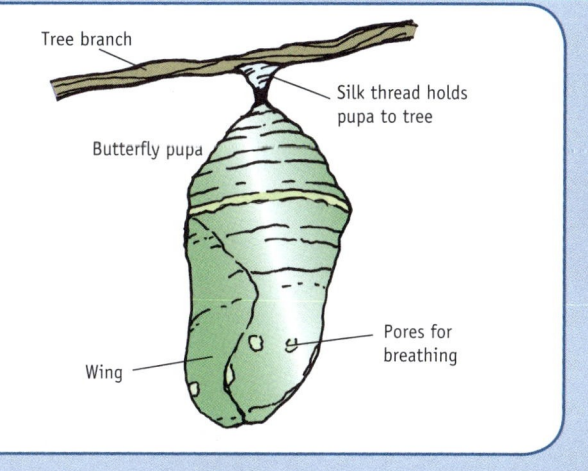

Tree branch

Silk thread holds pupa to tree

Butterfly pupa

Wing

Pores for breathing

Excel Illustrated Science Dictionary Years 5–8

109

pure substances

Compare with **mixture**. See **element**; **compound**.

pyramid of numbers

See **food pyramid**.

radiant energy

radiant energy

can travel through empty space. It includes gamma waves, *X-rays*, *ultraviolet* rays, microwaves, radio waves, infra-red rays and visible light. The *Sun* is our main source of radiant energy.

radiation of heat

See **heat radiation**.

radio telescope

collects the radio waves emitted by some objects in space (e.g. quasars and pulsars) with a large dish. The radio waves are converted to pictures. Radio telescopes can detect objects that are not visible (do not produce or reflect visible *light*). Compare **optical telescope**.

rain

occurs when fine water particles in the *clouds* combine and become heavy so that they fall. Water frozen slowly forms snow and frozen quickly forms hail. See **rain gauge**.

rain gauge

measures the amount of rainfall. A funnel collects the *rain*, which passes into a cylinder where it is measured in millimetres (mm).

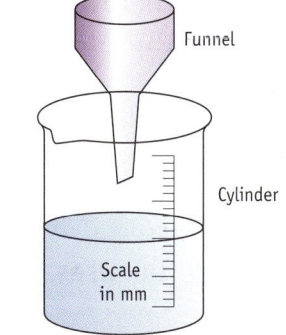

Excel Illustrated Science Dictionary Years 5–8

rainbow

occurs because sunlight is made up of different *colours*. As sunlight passes through a prism or raindrops, the colours are separated and reflected, and are seen as a rainbow.

ramp or inclined plane

is a simple *machine*. It is easier to move a heavy object up a ramp than to lift it. A gentle slope requires less effort than a steep one. A staircase is a type of ramp.

Less force is needed to roll the carpet up the ramp than to lift it.

recycle

means to reuse something or remake it so that it can be used again. For example, paper and glass can be broken down into their basic parts to form raw materials. The raw materials can be used to make new products. See **bacteria**; **waste disposal**.

red giant

is a huge red *star*. It forms when the nuclear fuel in a star begins to run out. The star expands, becomes cooler and glows red. Compare **white dwarf**. See **star life span**.

refining

is the process of removing impurities from a substance. For example, *ores* are refined to extract *metal*, sugar cane is refined to obtain sugar and *petroleum* is refined to obtain petrol. See **processed materials**; **fossil fuel uses**.

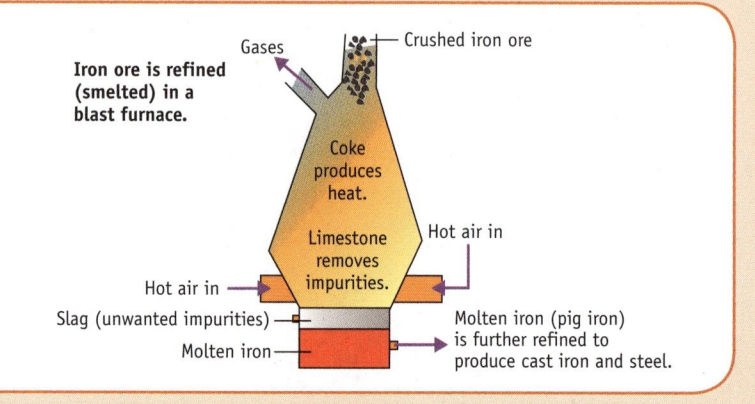

Iron ore is refined (smelted) in a blast furnace.
- Crushed iron ore
- Gases
- Coke produces heat.
- Limestone removes impurities.
- Hot air in
- Slag (unwanted impurities)
- Molten iron
- Molten iron (pig iron) is further refined to produce cast iron and steel.

reflection

reflection

is bouncing off. *Light*, *heat* and *sound* are reflected from certain hard surfaces. See **mirror reflections**.

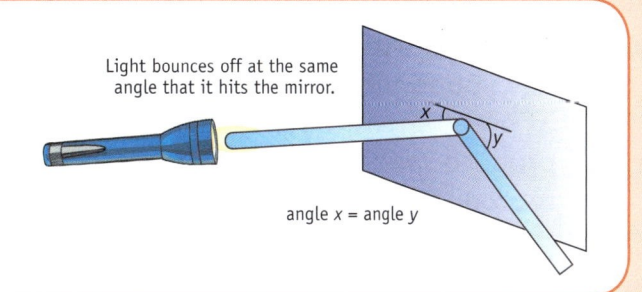

Light bounces off at the same angle that it hits the mirror.

angle *x* = angle *y*

refraction

is the bending of *light* rays as they pass from one substance to another (e.g. from *air* to glass). Some sunglasses use refraction which polarises the light and reduces it. Microscopes use light refraction to observe small objects. See **lens**.

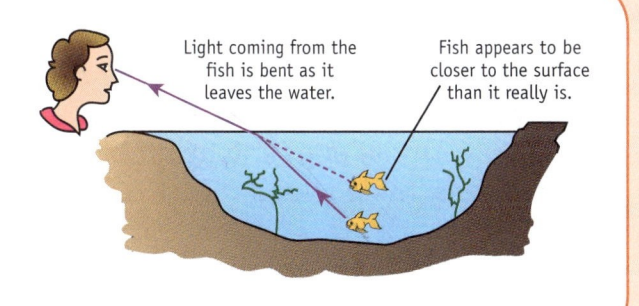

Light coming from the fish is bent as it leaves the water.

Fish appears to be closer to the surface than it really is.

renewable energy sources

include *hydroelectricity*, *wave energy*, *tidal energy*, *solar energy*, *wind energy*, *geothermal energy* and *biofuels*. They can be used to help conserve *fossil fuels*. Compare **non-renewable energy sources**. See **renewable resources**.

renewable resources

are *materials* such as food, *fibres*, wood and water. They are formed fairly quickly and so can be readily replaced (e.g. by growing vegetables, breeding sheep for wool). Compare **non-renewable resources**. See **renewable energy sources**.

Riding a bike uses energy supplied by food which is renewable.

A car uses energy supplied by petrol which is non-renewable.

reproduction

reproduction

is the process that forms new *organisms*. The young produced are the same kind of organism as the parent (e.g. rabbits produce rabbits). See **asexual reproduction; sexual reproduction**.

reproduction in flowering plants

occurs in the *flowers*. The male reproductive *cells* in pollen grains are transferred to the female part of the flower by *pollination*. The male cells unite with the *eggs* and an embryo develops inside a *seed*.

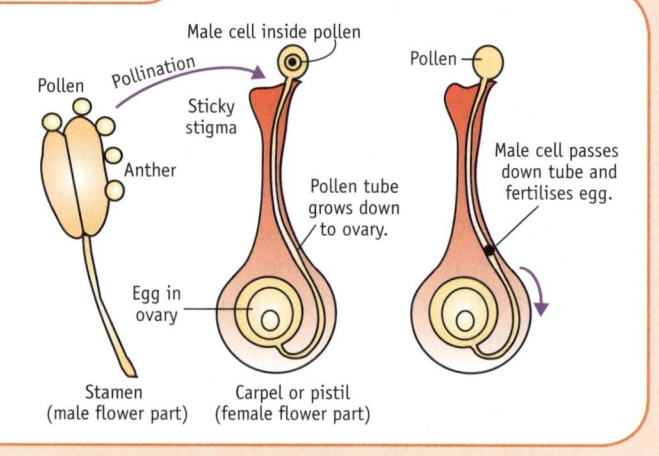

reproductive adaptations

occur in many *animals* and *plants* to ensure that they can reproduce and their young can survive.

- Fish and frogs: *Eggs* and *sperm* are released into the water but many are eaten by other animals. These animals produce large numbers of eggs/sperm to ensure their survival.

- Birds and lizards: *Eggs* are fertilised inside the animal and a shell is formed to protect the egg. This increases the survival rate.

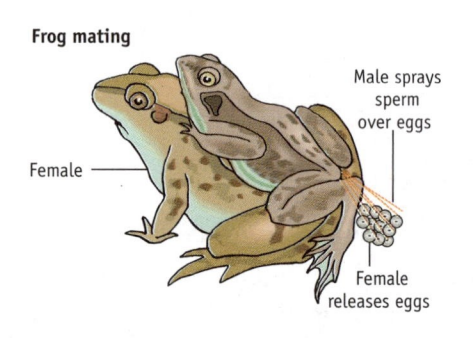

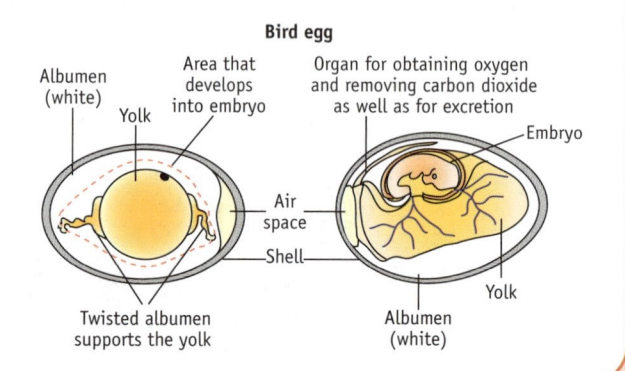

reproductive adaptations (cont.)

- *Mammals*: Fertilisation is internal and this increases the chances of successful mating. The embryo develops in the womb or a pouch, where it is protected.
- *Flowering plants*: Most pollen and *seeds* perish. Plants produce huge amounts of pollen and large numbers of *flowers*, *fruits* and seeds to increase the chances of *reproduction* and survival of the *species*.

See **courtship; parental care; reproduction in flowering plants; reproductive system**.

reproductive system

in higher *animals* is made up of *organs* that produce sex *cells* (*eggs* and *sperm*) and, in the female, a place for development of the fertilised egg and the young before birth.

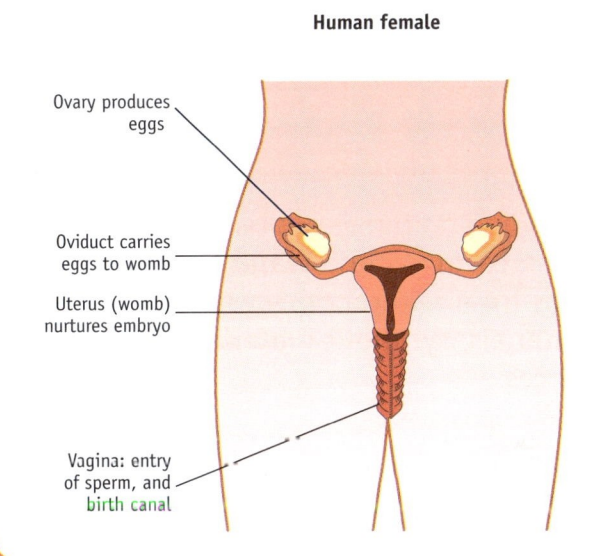

Human female

- Ovary produces eggs
- Oviduct carries eggs to womb
- Uterus (womb) nurtures embryo
- Vagina: entry of sperm, and birth canal

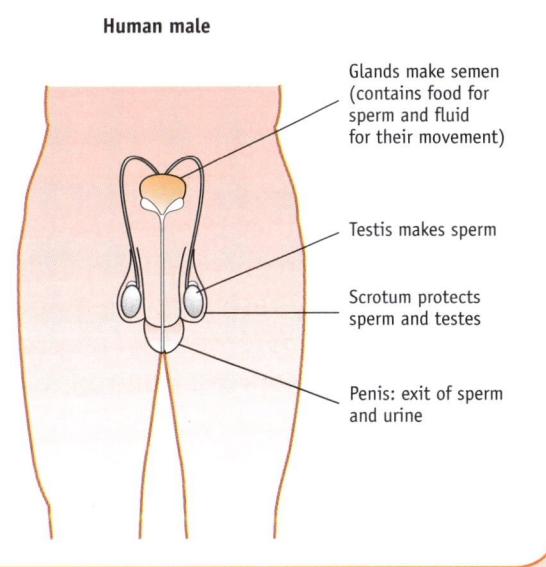

Human male

- Glands make semen (contains food for sperm and fluid for their movement)
- Testis makes sperm
- Scrotum protects sperm and testes
- Penis: exit of sperm and urine

reproductive system in plants

See **flower; reproduction in flowering plants**.

reproductive technology

such as *cloning* and *genetic engineering* is used to select the characteristics of new *organisms*.

Excel Illustrated Science Dictionary Years 5–8

R resource management

resource management

consists of plans set up to:
- slow down the use of *non-renewable resources* and to make supplies last longer
- reduce harmful waste production
- repair damage done to the land and the *environment*.

See **sustainable**; **conservation of non-renewable resources**; **waste disposal**; **water management**.

resource management by Aboriginal and Torres Strait Islander peoples

shows a great respect for the environment. They do not damage the environment in a useless way and they care for it so that it will keep on living for future use. For example, they have used back-burning for thousands of years to protect the environment from bushfires and to promote new growth. The new growth attracts animals which provide food. They are not allowed to hunt in sacred places; these give animals refuges and shelter. See **sustainable**.

resources

are *materials* that humans use (e.g. *food*, building materials, water, *fuels*). Natural resources come from *living things*, the earth, *air* and water (e.g. wood, *metals*). Many resources are made by humans from natural or raw materials (e.g. *plastics*, *detergents*). See **processed materials**; **synthetic materials**; **biofuel**; **renewable resources**; **non-renewable resources**.

Resources from the air

Carbon dioxide is used in fire extinguishers and as 'dry ice'.

'Dry ice' keeps ice cream and drinks cold.

Nitrogen is used in dyes and fertilisers and to remove skin growths.

Oxygen is used in respiration, rocket fuel and refining.

Resources from water and the oceans

Food

Pearls and shells

Water for irrigation, drinking and industry

Salt

Seaweed for food and fertiliser

resources (cont.)

Resources from the earth
Rocks, sand, soil, gravel, ores
Gold, gems
Oil and coal gas

Resources from living things
Timber for building and firewood
Fibre
Food
Coal
Medicines
Leather
Fossil fuels
Flowers
Oils

Aboriginal and Torres Strait Islander peoples prepared remedies using native plants (e.g. tea trees, eucalypt bark, lemongrass).

respiration

is a series of *chemical reactions* in *cells* of *organisms*. During respiration, cells use glucose (*food*) and *oxygen* to produce *energy* needed for the organism's activities (*life processes*). At the same time, *carbon dioxide* and water are formed.

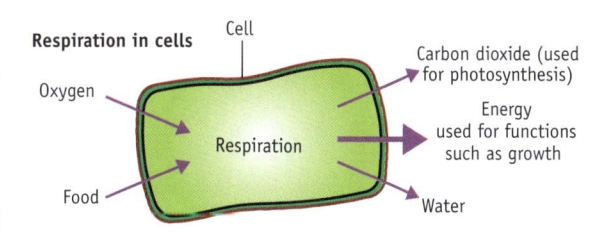

Respiration in cells
Cell
Oxygen
Food
Respiration
Carbon dioxide (used for photosynthesis)
Energy used for functions such as growth
Water

respiratory system in humans

consists of windpipe and lungs. The lungs pass *oxygen* to the blood and remove waste *carbon dioxide* from it.
See **breathing; respiration; excretory system.**

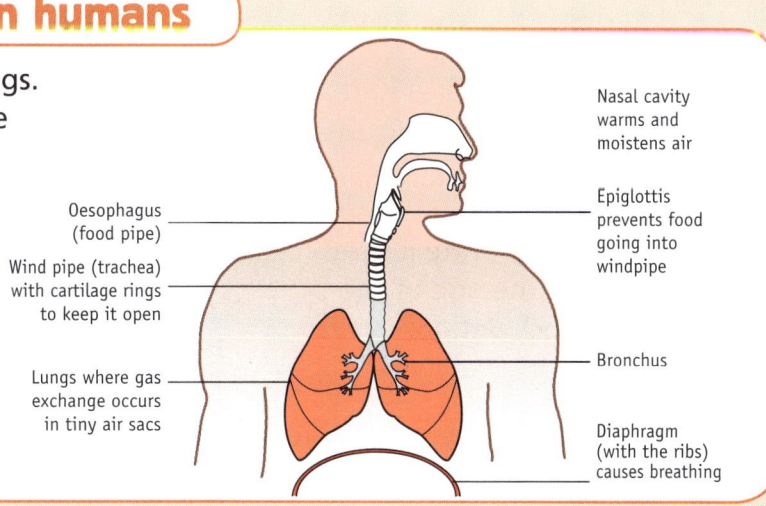

Oesophagus (food pipe)
Wind pipe (trachea) with cartilage rings to keep it open
Lungs where gas exchange occurs in tiny air sacs
Nasal cavity warms and moistens air
Epiglottis prevents food going into windpipe
Bronchus
Diaphragm (with the ribs) causes breathing

Excel Illustrated Science Dictionary Years 5–8

R respiratory system in fish

respiratory system in fish

is made up of gills. Each gill is composed of two rows of filaments containing blood vessels. When water passes over the gill filaments, oxygen passes into the blood from the water and waste carbon dioxide passes into the water from the blood.

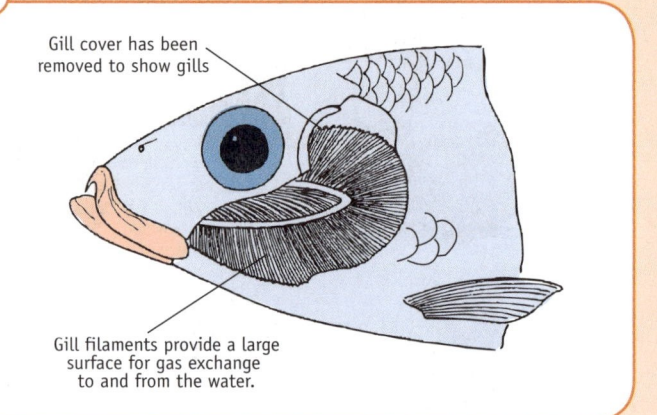

Gill cover has been removed to show gills

Gill filaments provide a large surface for gas exchange to and from the water.

rock

is a *mixture* of *minerals*. Rocks are classified by the way they are formed and their composition. There are three groups of rocks: *sedimentary*, *igneous* and *metamorphic*. See **rock use**; **rock cycle**.

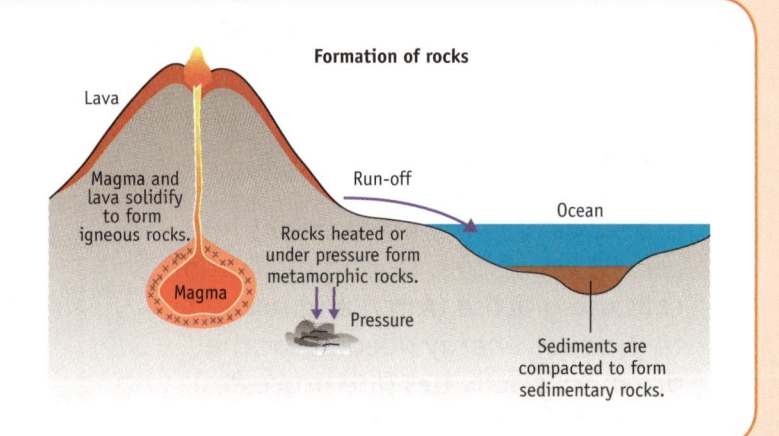

Formation of rocks

Lava

Magma and lava solidify to form igneous rocks.

Magma

Run-off

Rocks heated or under pressure form metamorphic rocks.

Pressure

Ocean

Sediments are compacted to form sedimentary rocks.

rock age

is determined by the *fossils* or radioactive *elements* in the *rock*. Radioactive elements (e.g. *uranium* or carbon-14) present in rocks and their fossils break down or decay. The breakdown rate is used to calculate the age of the rock. See **rock dating**.

Sections through rock layers from two different areas showing fossils present

This organism lived 15 000 years ago. So the rock is 15 000 years old.

These layers have the same fossil present so the rocks are the same age.

rock cycle

rock cycle

shows that the *rocks* in the *Earth's crust* are continually changing. These cycles may take millions of *years* to complete.

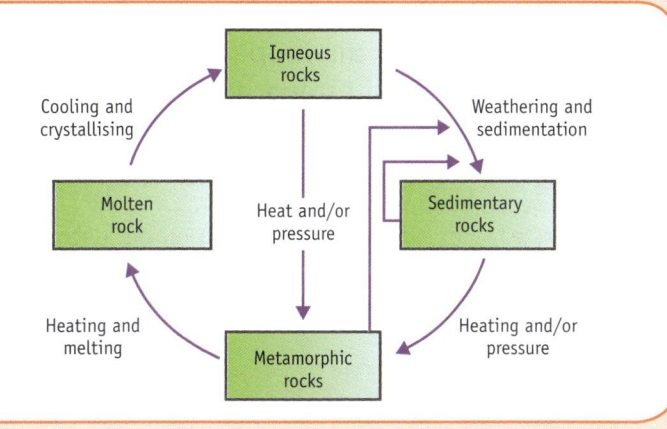

rock dating

involves determining the absolute or actual ages of rock formations by:
- radioactive *elements* that decay very slowly
- *fossils* present (e.g. trilobites existed 590 to 250 million years ago).

Relative dating places the rocks in order of their formation (in relation to other rocks). The following are some examples of relative dating.

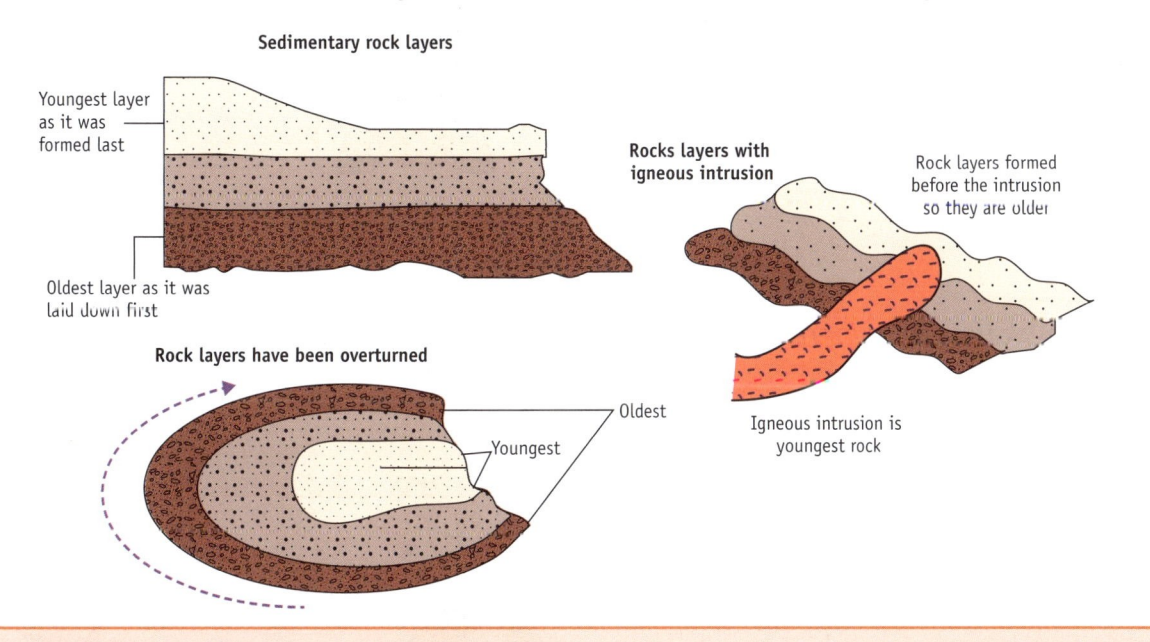

rock minerals

make up the rocks. Common rock *minerals* are quartz, feldspar, calcite, haematite and mica. Compare **ore minerals**.

Excel Illustrated Science Dictionary Years 5–8

rock use

is determined by the *properties* of the *rocks*. Rocks used for building need to be strong, able to withstand *weathering* and easy to shape (e.g. *sandstone*, granite).

Rock	Property	Use
shale	forms clay	pipes, bricks
granite	breaks into building blocks; decorative	buildings; bench tops
slate	hard and splits into sheets	roofs and floors

rocket

is a strong jet propulsion engine used to place *satellite*s into *orbit* and to take *spacecraft* beyond the *Earth's gravity* and into space. The first humans into space travelled in rockets made up of stages and modules (e.g. the Apollo spacecraft, which landed on the *Moon*).

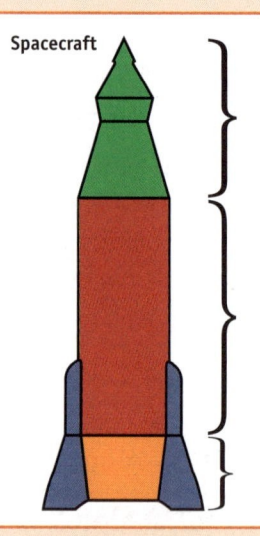

Spacecraft

Spacecraft or module for astronauts has its own built-in rockets.

The 2nd-stage rocket puts the craft into orbit, then drops off and burns in the atmosphere.

The 1st-stage rocket launches the craft, then drops off and falls back to Earth.

roots

absorb water and *minerals* and anchor the *plant* in the *soil*. They hold the soil together and reduce *soil erosion*. See **physical weathering**.

rotate

means spin on an axis. The *Earth* rotates once every 24 hours. The *Sun*, *Moon* and *stars* appear to move across the sky every 24 hours because of this rotation.
See **day and night**.

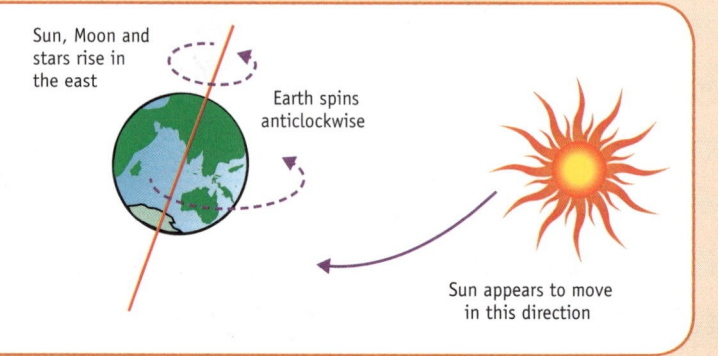

Sun, Moon and stars rise in the east

Earth spins anticlockwise

Sun appears to move in this direction

rust

See **corrosion**; **rust proofing**.

rust proofing

involves painting iron to stop water and *oxygen* coming in contact with it. This prevents the *chemical reaction* that forms rust. Coating iron with a more reactive *metal* such as zinc also prevents rusting. This is called galvanising.

salt lakes

form in the desert. Heavy *rains* make lakes that contain *dissolved* salt from the weathered rocks. When the water dries up, a crust of salt remains, forming a lake of salt (e.g. Lake Eyre).

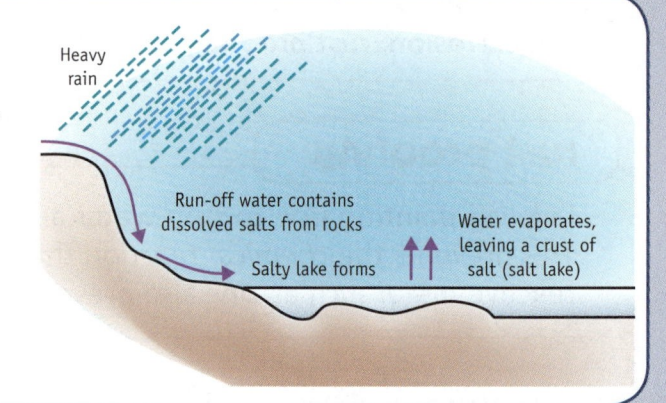

sandstone

is a *sedimentary rock* made of sand particles cemented together. It is formed in oceans, riverbeds and deserts.

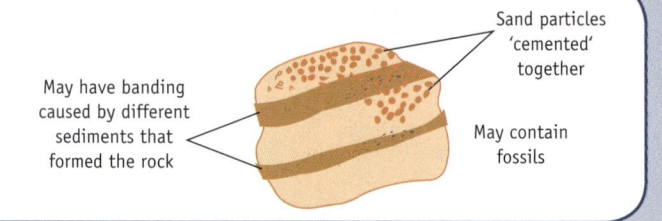

satellite

is a body that travels around another body in *space*. The *Moon* is a satellite that travels around the *Earth*. See **satellites (artificial)**.

satellites (artificial)

are *spacecraft* that have been made by humans and *orbit* the *Earth* (e.g. Landsat). They make observations, take photographs and collect useful information (e.g. for *weather forecasting*). They also transmit television and telephone messages to other parts of *Earth*. See **satellite**.

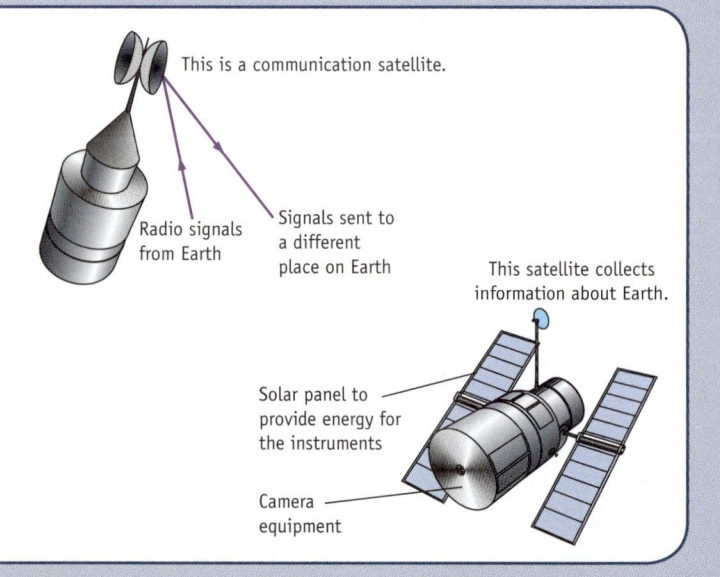

saturated solution

saturated solution

is a *solution* when no more *solid* will *dissolve* in the *liquid*. Increasing the *temperature* of the water will allow more solid to dissolve. Compare **dilute solution**; **concentrated solution**.

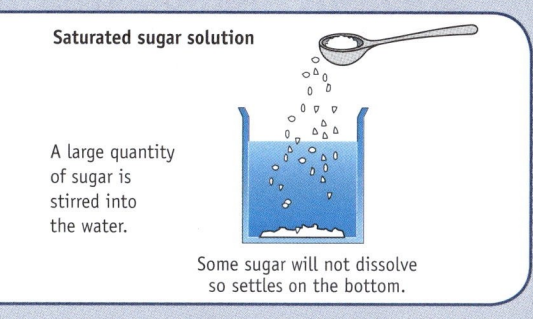

Saturated sugar solution

A large quantity of sugar is stirred into the water.

Some sugar will not dissolve so settles on the bottom.

Saturn

is a large *planet* made mainly of *gas*. It is surrounded by a system of rings of ice and rock. The outer surface of gas has belts, ovals and spots (storms). Saturn has many *moons*. Currently 63 have been identified.

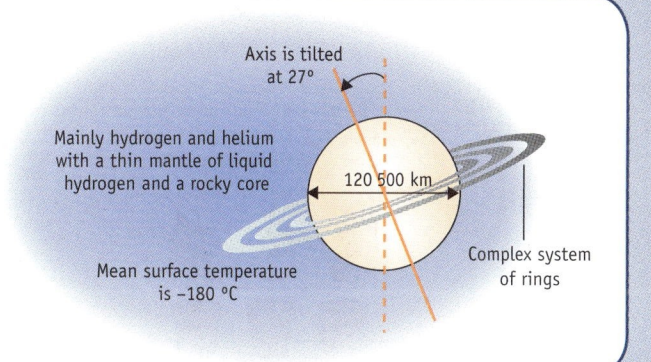

Axis is tilted at 27°

Mainly hydrogen and helium with a thin mantle of liquid hydrogen and a rocky core

120 500 km

Mean surface temperature is −180 °C

Complex system of rings

scavenger

is an *animal* that eats dead or decaying animals. Hyenas, crows and ants are scavengers. See **food chain**.

science

is one way we obtain knowledge and solve problems. The word 'science' comes from the Latin word meaning 'knowledge'. There are many areas of science and some of these are included in the table.

Science	Scientist	Area of study
astronomy	astronomer	solar system, celestial bodies and space
biology	biologist	living things
botany	botanist	plants
chemistry	chemist	chemicals that make up the world
geology or Earth science	geologist	rocks, montains, Earth movements and structure
palaeontology	palaeontologist	fossils
physics	physicist	the behaviour of matter (e.g. forces, electricity)
zoology	zoologist	animals

Excel Illustrated Science Dictionary Years 5–8

scientific method

scientific method (fair test)

is a set of steps scientists use to investigate problems and test ideas. See **control**; **variable**.

Step 1: Observe a problem

Plants are dying.

Step 2: Suggest a reason (i.e. make an hypothesis)

Perhaps they are not getting enough light.

Step 3: Design and set up an experiment to test this idea

Experimental group of plants

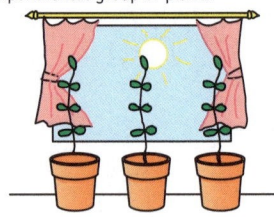

Control group of plants for comparison

Set up several healthy plants in light and several in shade. Soil, water, temperature are kept the same for both groups of plants.

Step 4: Repeat the experiment
Step 5: Make conclusions from results

Possible result 1

Alive

Dead

Conclusion: The plants died because they did not have enough light.

Possible result 2

Dead

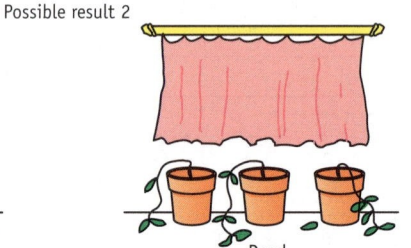

Dead

Conclusion: Dim light did not kill the plants. Perhaps they did not have enough water (new hypothesis).

seasons

are caused by the *Earth* revolving around the *Sun*. The Earth is tilted on its axis. This means that the area that is tilted towards the Sun gets the most direct *heat* and is in *summer*. The area tilted away from the Sun is in *winter*.

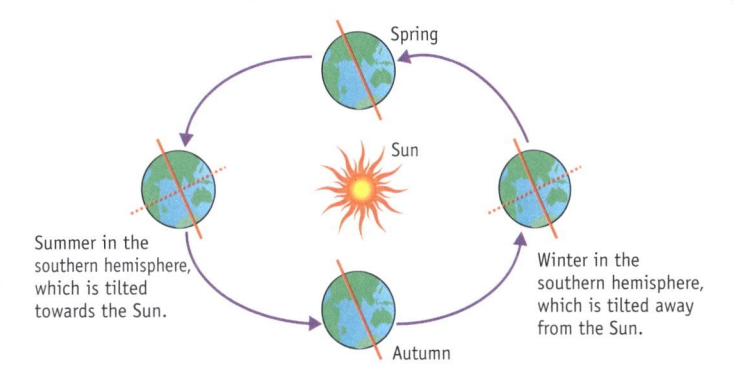

Seasons are different in different parts of the world. These different seasonal conditions relate to latitude. The Sun's rays hit the ground vertically and are very concentrated at the equator. They hit at a low angle near the poles so the ground receives less radiant energy. See **summer** and **winter**.

sediment

is a layer of *solid* particles that have settled at the bottom of a *liquid*. Sediments forming in lakes and oceans may eventually form *sedimentary rocks*.

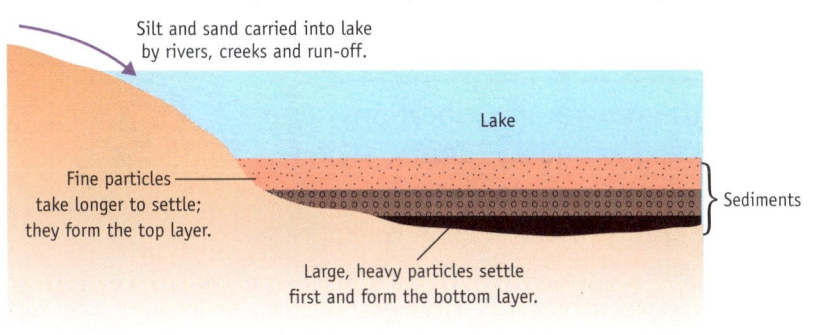

sedimentary rocks

are made from particles of other *rocks*. These particles settle in layers (*sediments*). They are compressed and become cemented together. They may show layers and contain *fossils*. See **sandstone**; **shale**; **conglomerate**; **weathering**.

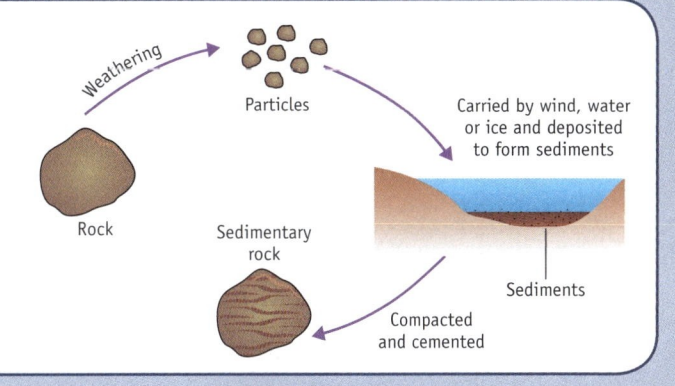

Excel Illustrated Science Dictionary Years 5–8

sedimentation and decanting

are methods used to separate mixtures of *liquid* and undissolved (*insoluble*) substances (e.g. water and *soil*). See **water treatment**.

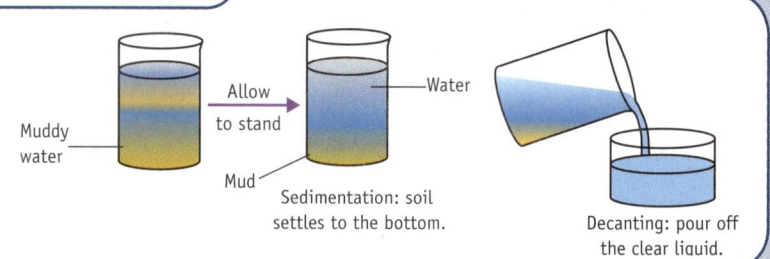

seed

forms after *fertilisation* in flowering and cone plants. It is enclosed in a *fruit*. The seed contains a small *plant* (embryo) that grows when the seed germinates. See **germination**.

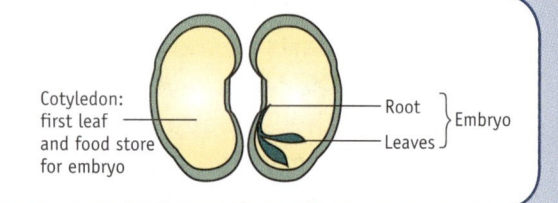

seed capsules

See **fruit**.

seismograph (seismometer)

is an instrument that measures vibrations caused by *earthquakes* and *volcanoes*. When the ground shakes the pen stays still because of the heavy weight. A drum, which is slowly turning, moves with the vibrations and the pen records the vibrations on it. Chinese astronomer Zhang Heng invented the first seismograph in 132 AD.

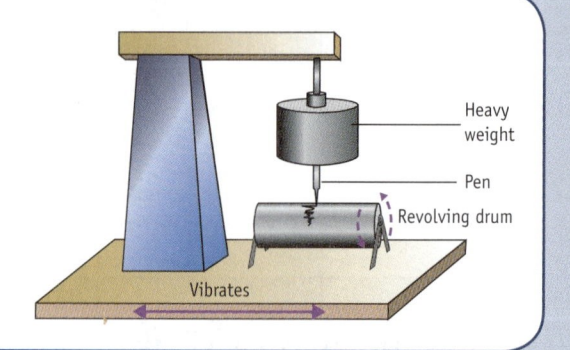

separation methods

are used to obtain useful substances from *mixtures* (e.g. *metals* from *ores*, sugar *crystals* from sugar plant, cream from milk). The substances can be separated because of their different *properties*.

Methods used to separate substances include *centrifuging*, *evaporation*, *crystallisation*, *sedimentation and decanting*, *distillation*, *filtration*, *condensation*, *magnetic separation* and *chromatography*.

separation methods (cont.)

separation methods (cont.)

Sand and rocks have different particle sizes.

They can be separated with a sieve.

Methylated spirits (metho) and water have different boiling points.

Metho vapourises first

Metho and water

Metho condenses

Water

They can be separated by heating.

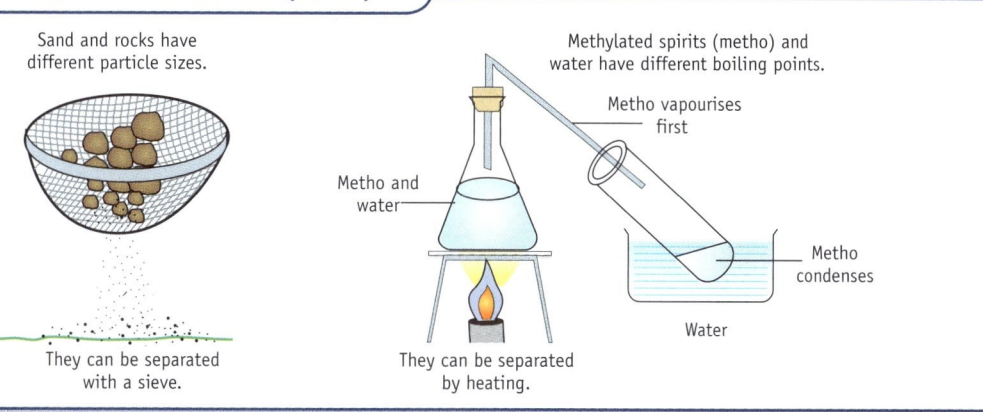

sexual reproduction

occurs when new *organisms* develop after *egg* and *sperm* combine (*fertilisation*). The new individual will have characteristics of both parents. Compare **asexual reproduction**.

shadow

is formed when *light* hits an object it cannot pass through (an *opaque* object). See **shadow stick; sundial**.

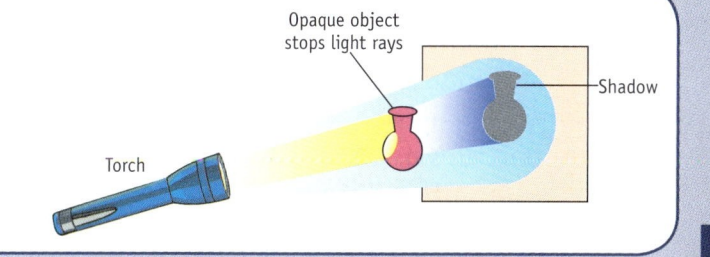

Opaque object stops light rays

Shadow

Torch

shadow stick

is an upright stick used to produce *shadows* in sunlight. The shadow's length and position changes during the *day*. It can be used to indicate the time. The shadow is long at dawn and dusk and short at midday. See **sundial**.

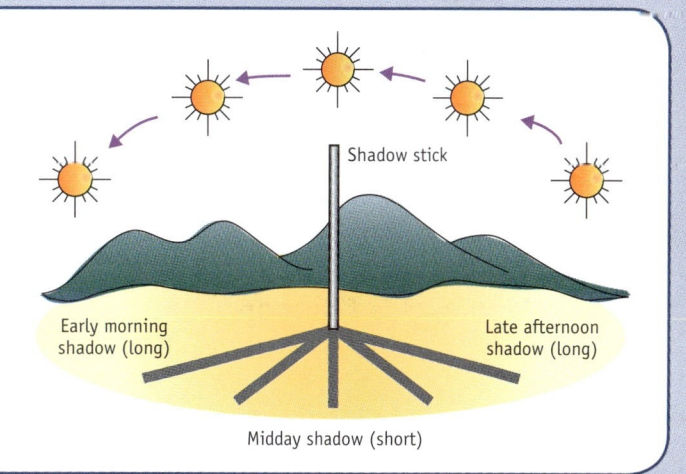

Shadow stick

Early morning shadow (long)

Late afternoon shadow (long)

Midday shadow (short)

Excel Illustrated Science Dictionary Years 5–8

127

shadows from different light sources

shadows from different light sources

have different types of outlines. A point source of *light* such as a small torch globe creates *shadows* with a sharp outline.

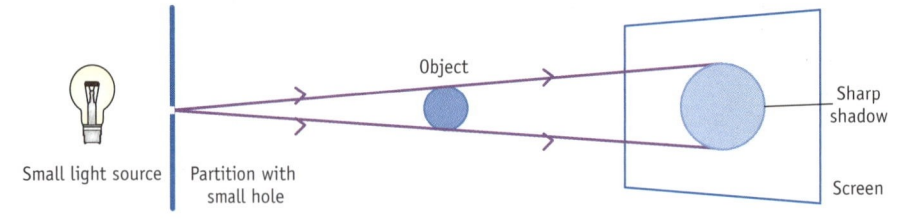

Small light source | Partition with small hole | Object | Sharp shadow | Screen

An extended or large light source such as a *fluorescent globe* produces a shadow with two distinct regions.

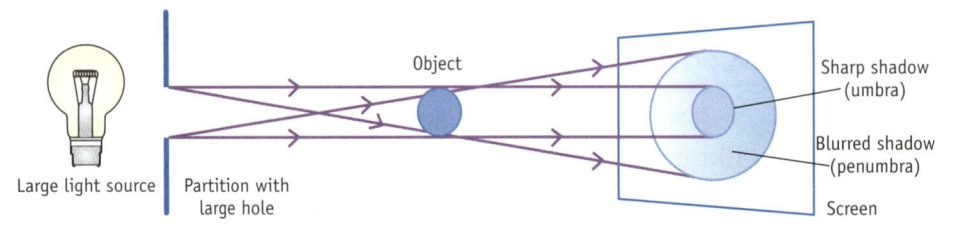

Large light source | Partition with large hole | Object | Sharp shadow (umbra) | Blurred shadow (penumbra) | Screen

shale

is a *sedimentary rock* made of clay and mud particles. It is formed in still water where these fine particles are able to settle. *Fossils* are often found in shale.

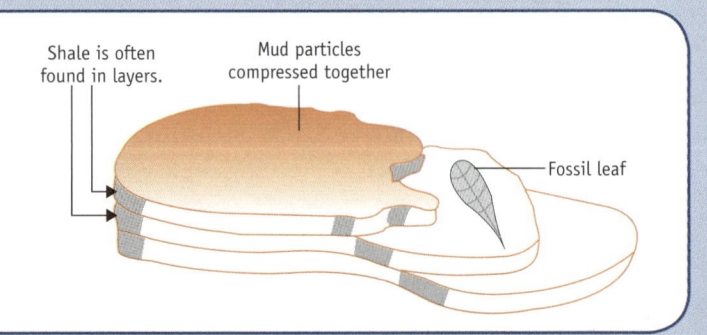

Shale is often found in layers. Mud particles compressed together. Fossil leaf

sieving

is one method used to separate substances in a *mixture*. It separates large particles from small ones. It will also separate *solids* from *liquids*. See **filtration**.

Sand is separated from rocks by using a mesh or sieve.

Peas are separated from the water by using a strainer.

sink

is to fall gradually. An object that is denser than water (heavier than the same amount of water) will sink. Compare **float**.

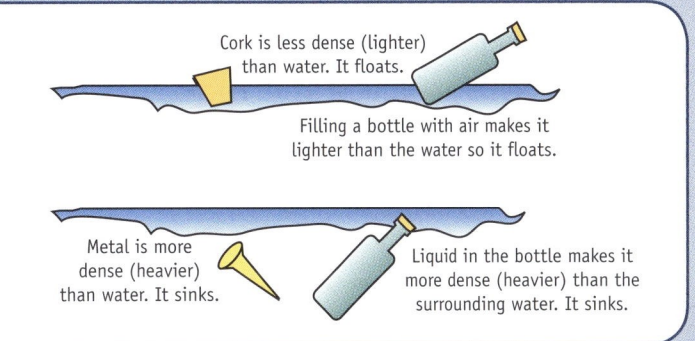

Cork is less dense (lighter) than water. It floats.

Filling a bottle with air makes it lighter than the water so it floats.

Metal is more dense (heavier) than water. It sinks.

Liquid in the bottle makes it more dense (heavier) than the surrounding water. It sinks.

skeletal system

is the skeleton. It supports the body and protects *organs*. For example, the rib cage protects the heart and lungs. Muscles are attached to the skeleton and together they make the body move. See **levers in the human body**.

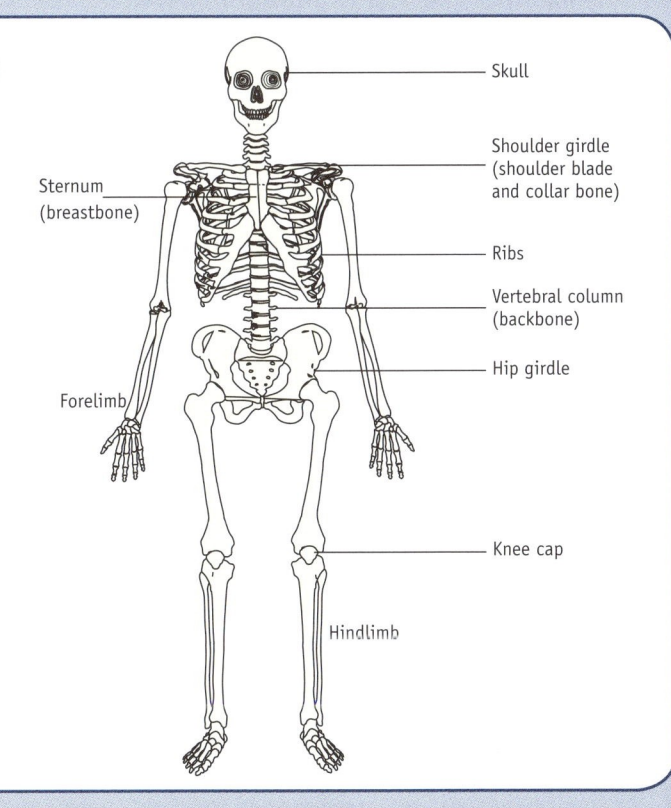

- Skull
- Shoulder girdle (shoulder blade and collar bone)
- Sternum (breastbone)
- Ribs
- Vertebral column (backbone)
- Hip girdle
- Forelimb
- Knee cap
- Hindlimb

skeleton

See **skeletal system**.

slate

is a *metamorphic rock* formed by *pressure* on *shale*. Layers are sometimes visible in the rock, which splits easily into sheets.

Excel Illustrated Science Dictionary Years 5–8

soaps and detergents

are used for cleaning. Soap is made from an alkali and oils or *fats*. Modern detergents are made from *petroleum* products. Many soaps and detergents have polluted the *environment*. *Biodegradable* soaps and detergents are now being manufactured. *Microorganisms* change them to harmless products.

soil

consists of weathered rock particles (sand, silt and clay) and decaying *plant* and *animal matter* (humus). The diagram shows a cutting through soil layers, showing the different stages in soil formation. Soil is important for *ecosystems* as it provides *nutrients* and support for plants and shelter for burrowing animals. See **soil composition**.

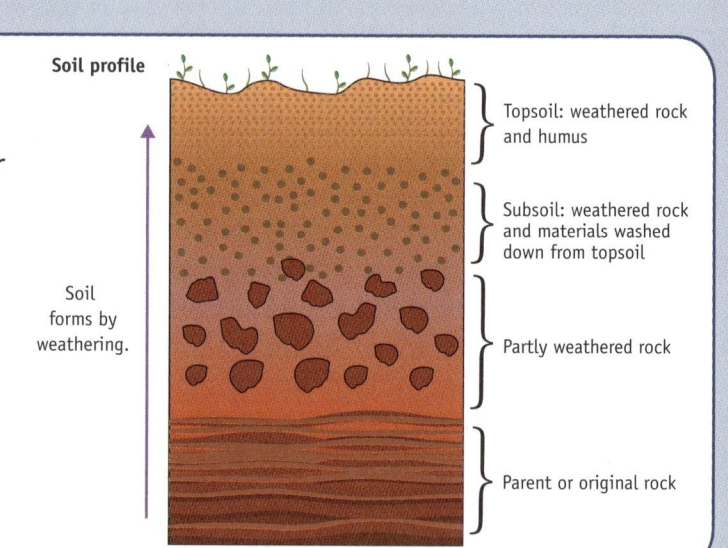

Soil profile

Soil forms by weathering.

Topsoil: weathered rock and humus

Subsoil: weathered rock and materials washed down from topsoil

Partly weathered rock

Parent or original rock

soil composition

is the amount of clay, silt and sand present in soil, which is classified by its composition. For example, loams are rich soils with about equal amounts of sand, silt and clay with humus. Clay, silt and sand give the soil its texture and make it *porous* (allowing air spaces). See **soil water retention**.

soil conservation

is protecting or preserving the *soil* against *erosion* and depletion of *nutrients*. Erosion is reduced by growing *plants*, by reducing grazing and by farming on terraces and in contours around a hill rather than ploughing down it. Nutrients can be replaced by *composting* and mulching. See **soil erosion**.

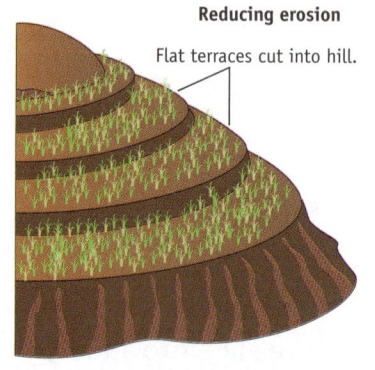

Reducing erosion

Flat terraces cut into hill.

Ploughing around a hill reduces erosion.

soil erosion

soil erosion

occurs when rich topsoil is washed away, leaving behind land with poor *soil* and trenches. It is caused by removing *plants* from the land and by overgrazing. See **soil conservation**.

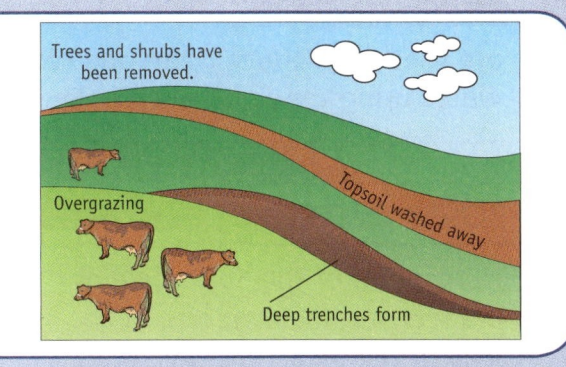

soil water retention

is better in some soils than others. Sandy soils are very porous and do not hold water. Clay soils hold onto water and tend to become waterlogged. See **soil composition**.

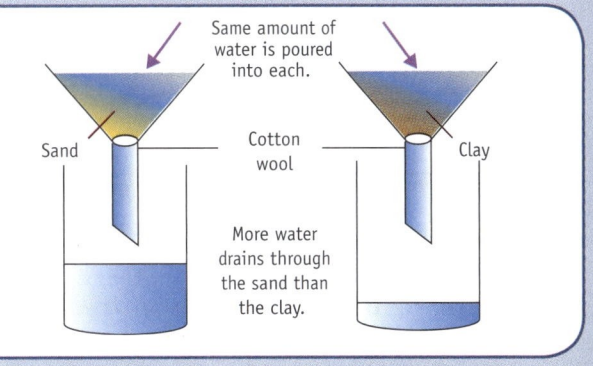

solar energy

is *radiant energy* from the *Sun* (e.g. *heat, light and ultraviolet rays*). It is the main source of energy on *Earth* and is responsible for natural activities such as *wind*, *rain* and *photosynthesis*. Solar energy can also be used to heat the household water supply and can be changed to *electricity* by solar cells. Solar-powered cars and boats are now being designed. See **renewable energy sources; energy transfer; energy transformation in living things**.

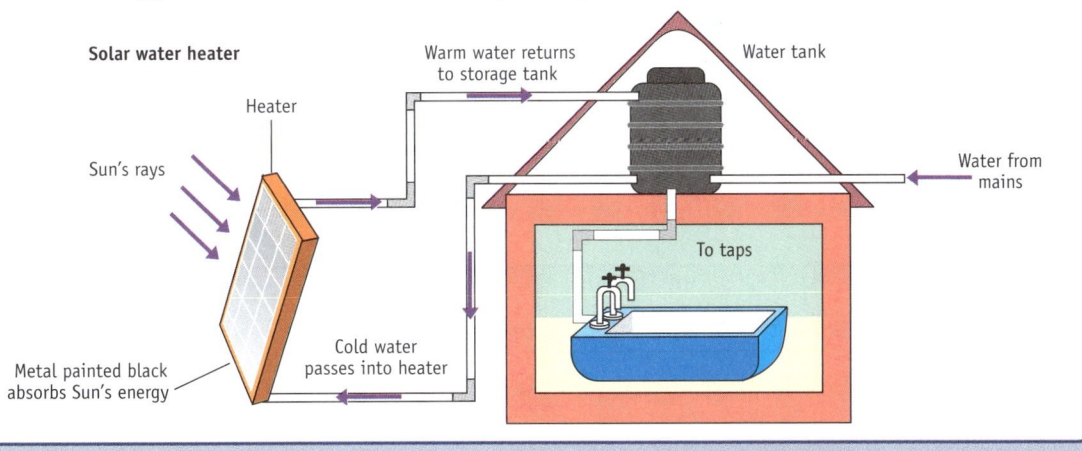

Excel Illustrated Science Dictionary Years 5–8

131

solar panels

are used to produce clean and renewable *energy* (*electricity*) and to heat water using the *Sun's* energy. See **solar energy**.

solar system

is made up of the *Sun*, the eight *planets* and their *moons*, at least three dwarf planets, the *asteroids* and *comets* that all move around the Sun. See **astronomy**; **galaxy**.

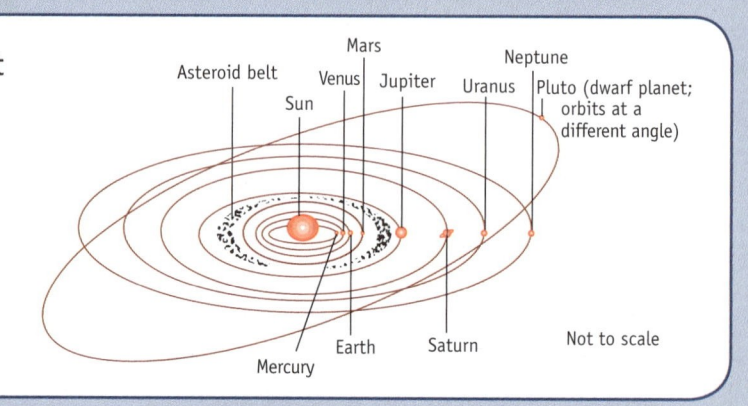

solid

is one of the three *states of matter*. The particles in a solid cannot move freely so solids have a definite shape and size, or *volume*. See **particle theory of matter**.

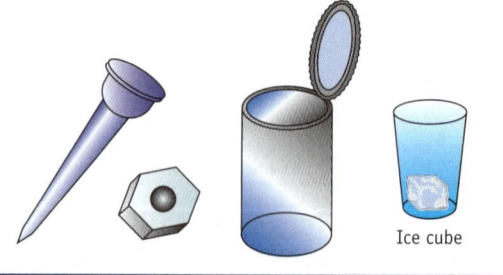

soluble

describes a substance that *dissolves* in another. A substance that does not dissolve is *insoluble*. For example, sugar is soluble in water, but oil *floats* on water and so oil is insoluble in water. See **solution**.

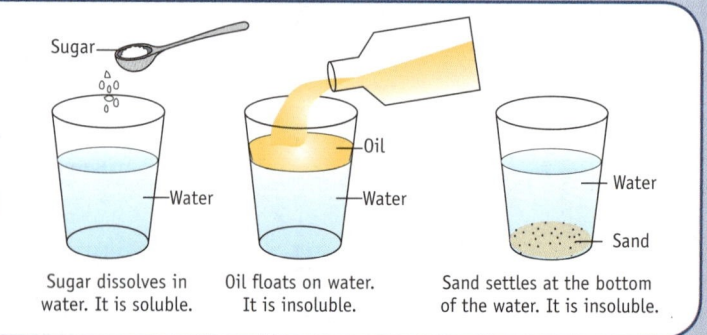

Sugar dissolves in water. It is soluble.

Oil floats on water. It is insoluble.

Sand settles at the bottom of the water. It is insoluble.

solute

See **solution**.

132

Excel Illustrated Science Dictionary Years 5–8

solution

solution

is formed when a substance *dissolves* in a *liquid*. The liquid is called a *solvent*. The dissolving *solid* is called a solute. See **dilute solution; concentrated solution; saturated solution**.

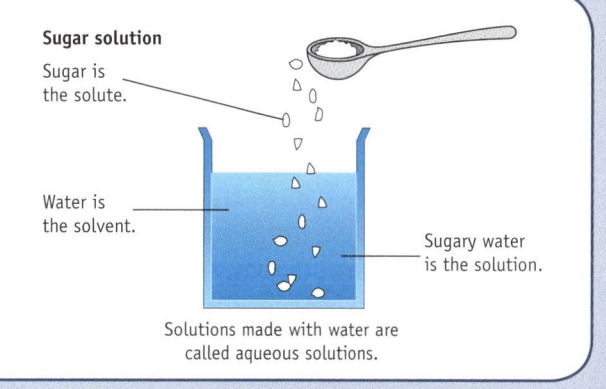

Sugar solution
Sugar is the solute.
Water is the solvent.
Sugary water is the solution.
Solutions made with water are called aqueous solutions.

solvent

is a *liquid* that *dissolves* substances. Water dissolves many substances and forms aqueous *solutions*. Turpentine is a solvent used to dissolve oil paint; acetone in nail polish remover is a solvent that dissolves nail polish.

Turpentine

Nail polish remover (acetone)

sound

is caused by vibrations. These vibrations make *air* particles move in waves, which travel to your ear. Sound will not travel through a *vacuum*. See **pitch of a sound; loudness; energy transfer; energy transformation; echo**.

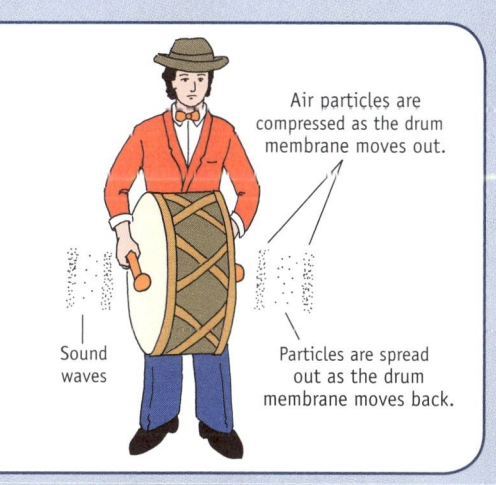

Air particles are compressed as the drum membrane moves out.
Sound waves
Particles are spread out as the drum membrane moves back.

sources of energy

See **energy sources**.

Excel Illustrated Science Dictionary Years 5–8

133

S space probes

space probes

are unmanned *spacecraft*. They travel into space and collect information about the *solar system* and space without interference caused by the *atmosphere*. The probes carry instruments to measure conditions and send this information back to *Earth*. For example, Voyager 2 travelled to *Saturn* and *Jupiter*.

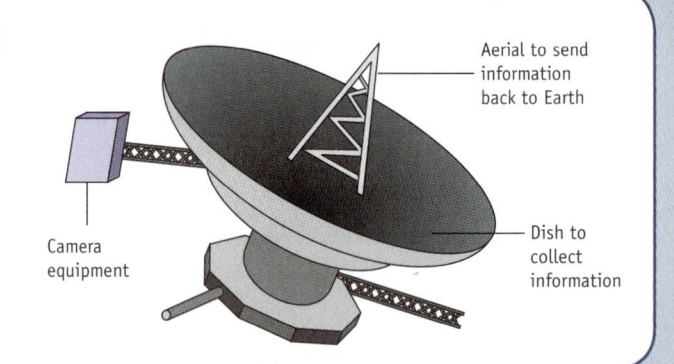

Aerial to send information back to Earth

Camera equipment

Dish to collect information

space shuttle

consisted of a launch *rocket* and a manned *spacecraft*, which returned to *Earth* like a plane and was able to be reused. The space shuttle was used to take *satellites* and *space stations* into space, carry crews and equipment to and from space stations and take crews out to repair satellites. The last shuttle mission was in 2011.

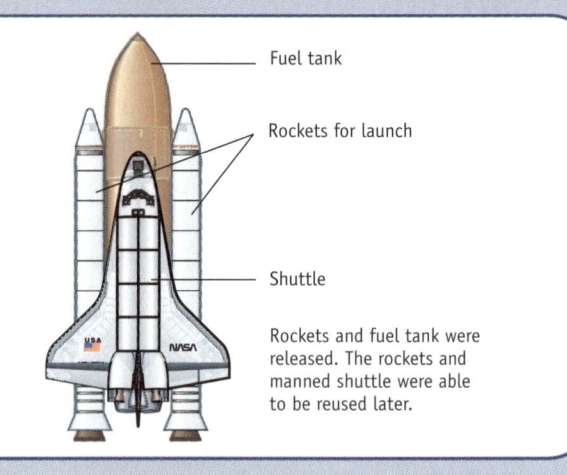

Fuel tank

Rockets for launch

Shuttle

Rockets and fuel tank were released. The rockets and manned shuttle were able to be reused later.

space stations and laboratories

are manned by scientists who make observations and can carry out research and *experiments* in space (e.g. Skylab, Mir and the International Space Station, ISS).

space technology

is the *technology* developed for exploring space (e.g. *telescopes* and *spacecraft*). The items are used for collecting information and carrying out research.

spacecraft

include *rockets*, *satellites*, *space probes*, *space shuttles* and *space stations and laboratories*. They are used to explore and collect information about the *Earth*, the *solar system* and space (i.e. beyond the Earth's atmosphere).

species

species

is a group of *living things* that can breed and produce young in nature. For example, lions and tigers do not naturally interbreed; they belong to different species. See **variations within a species; classification groups; species name; evolution**.

Do not naturally interbreed

species name

of an organism is made up of its genus and specific or descriptive name. It is in Latin. For example, the scientific or species name for a domestic cat is

Felis catus

The genus has a capital letter.

The specific or descriptive name has a small letter.

The name is in italics or underlined.

speed

is the distance travelled in a certain time. It is measured in metres per second (m/s) or kilometres per hour (km/h).

$$\text{average speed} = \frac{\text{distance travelled}}{\text{time taken}}$$

The girl and her dog take 10 seconds to travel 10 metres. They have a speed of 1 metre per second.

sperm

is the male reproductive *cell*. In higher *animals* sperm is formed in the **testes**. See **fertilisation**.

star

is a glowing ball of *gas*. It forms from a cloud of dust and gas, which contracts and is held together by *gravity*. Nuclear reactions occur in stars, releasing *heat* and *light*. Our *Sun* is a star. See **red giant; white dwarf; star life span**.

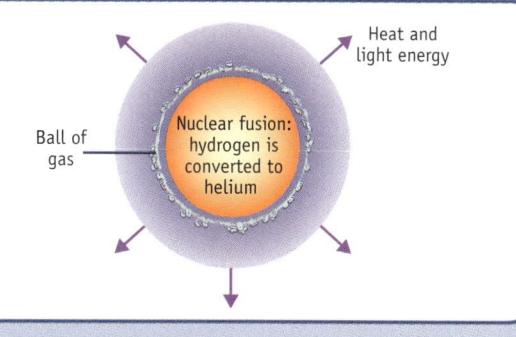

Heat and light energy

Ball of gas

Nuclear fusion: hydrogen is converted to helium

Excel Illustrated Science Dictionary Years 5–8

star life span

Stars last for thousands of millions of years and change with age. At the end of its life, the star may become a *white dwarf* which becomes cold and fades. Some stars erupt with a violent explosion (supernova) to form a *nebula*. Sometimes very large stars contract to form a *black hole*.

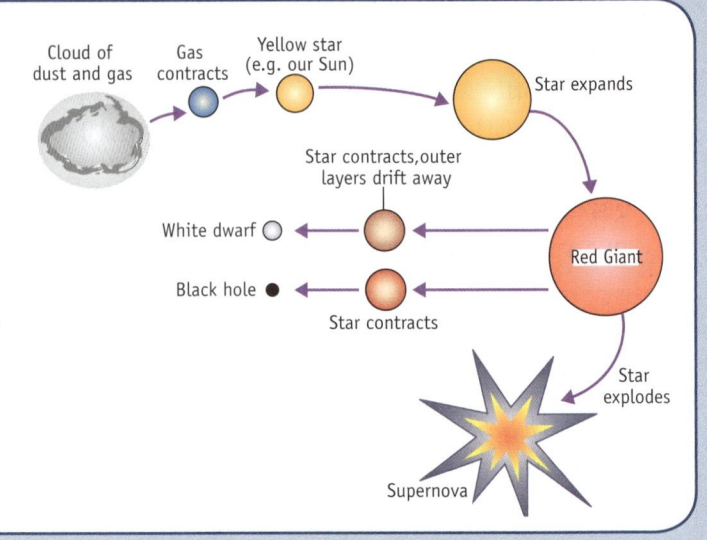

state of matter

There are the three states in which matter exists: *solid*, *liquid* and *gas*. For instance, water exists as a liquid, as solid ice or as a gas, when it is steam. Some substances (e.g. foam, rubber and polystyrene) exist as a combination of a solid, liquid and/or gas.
See **state of matter, change; particle theory of matter**.

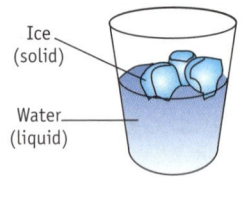

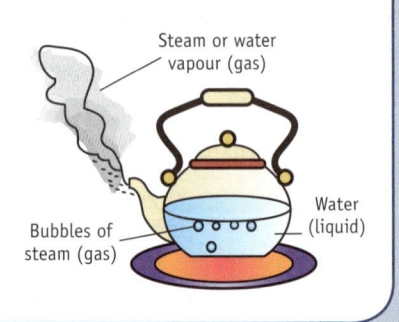

state of matter, change

occurs when a *solid* becomes a *liquid*, a liquid becomes a *gas*, a gas forms a liquid or a liquid becomes a solid. A few substances will change from a solid to a gas without becoming a liquid (e.g. dry ice, iodine). This is called sublimation. See **state of matter; bonds**.

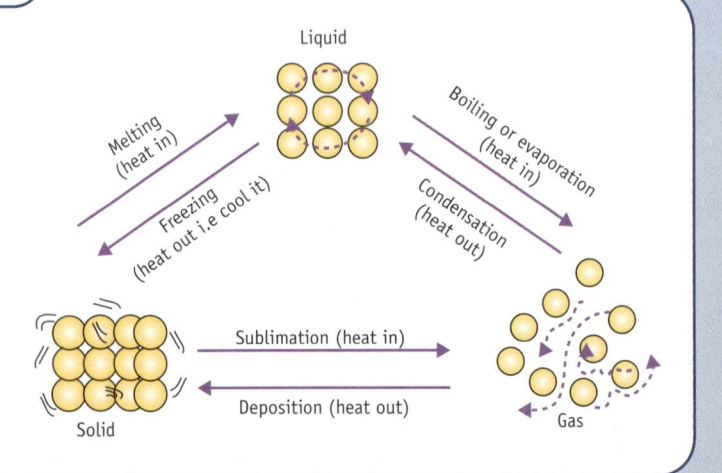

static electricity

is the *charge* collecting on objects. The charge causes attractive and repulsive *forces*. Lightning is an example of static electricity. See **electrostatic force**; **charging an object**.

stems

support the *plant* so that its *leaves* receive sunlight. They carry water and *minerals* in *xylem* tissue from the *roots* to *cells* where they are needed. *Phloem* tissue carries *food* that has been made in the leaves to cells.

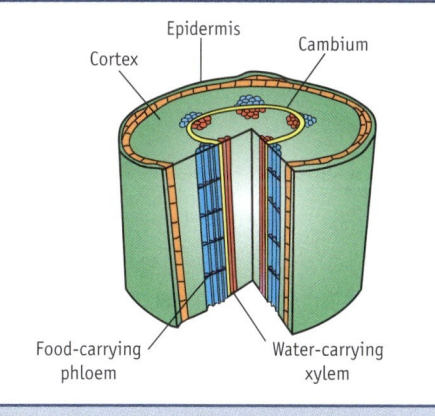

Epidermis, Cortex, Cambium, Food-carrying phloem, Water-carrying xylem

stomates

are pores in the surfaces of *leaves* (and sometimes *stems*). They allow water to evaporate and *carbon dioxide* and *oxygen* to pass into and out of *plants*. See **transpiration**; **respiration**; **photosynthesis**.

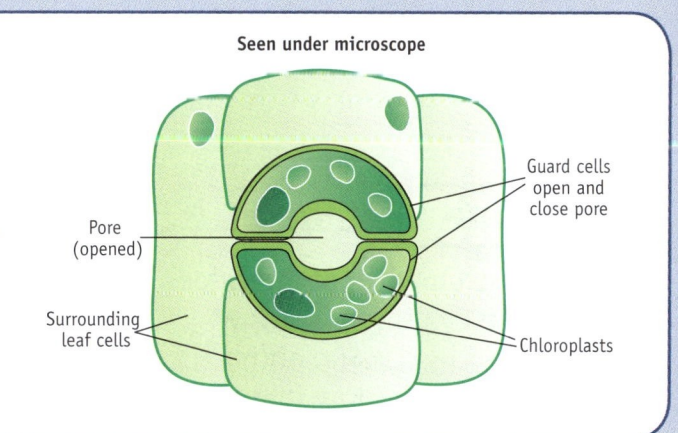

Seen under microscope

Pore (opened), Surrounding leaf cells, Guard cells open and close pore, Chloroplasts

sublimation

See **state of matter, change**.

Excel Illustrated Science Dictionary Years 5–8

summer and winter

summer and winter are determined by the angle at which the *Sun's* rays hit the *Earth*. In summer, the southern hemisphere is tilted towards the Sun and is closer to it. The Sun's rays are concentrated in a smaller area and the ground heats readily. In winter, the southern hemisphere is tilted away from the Sun. The rays hitting the Earth are spread over a large area and so heating is less. See **seasons**.

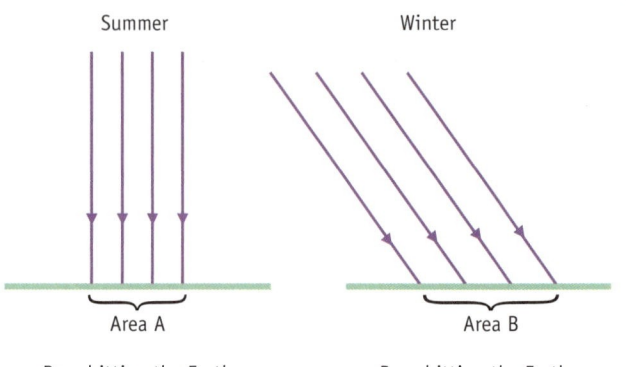

Summer — Area A — Rays hitting the Earth directly heat a smaller area and make it hot.

Winter — Area B — Rays hitting the Earth are spread and so the ground heats less.

Area A is smaller than Area B.

Sun

Sun is a yellow *star* at the centre of our *solar system* that will eventually swell to form a *red giant*. It is made of hydrogen and helium *gas*. Nuclear reactions in the centre of the Sun convert hydrogen to helium and produce *heat* and *light* energy.

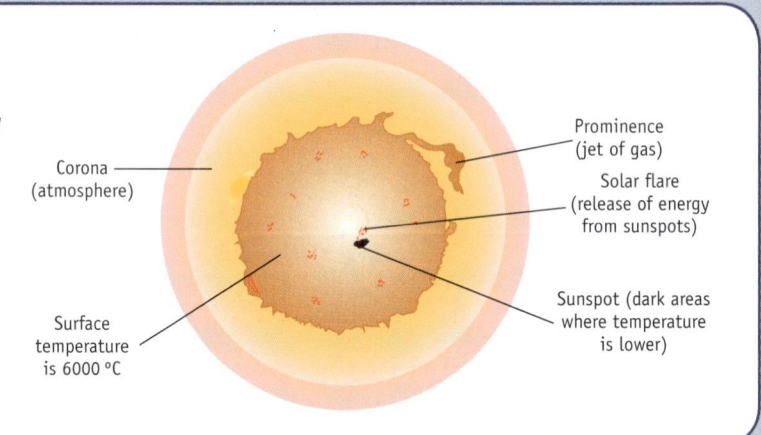

- Corona (atmosphere)
- Surface temperature is 6000 °C
- Prominence (jet of gas)
- Solar flare (release of energy from sunspots)
- Sunspot (dark areas where temperature is lower)

sundial

sundial is an instrument that indicates the time by using a *shadow* produced by the *Sun* and a pointer. The shadow falls on different parts of the dial at different times of the *day*. See **shadow stick**.

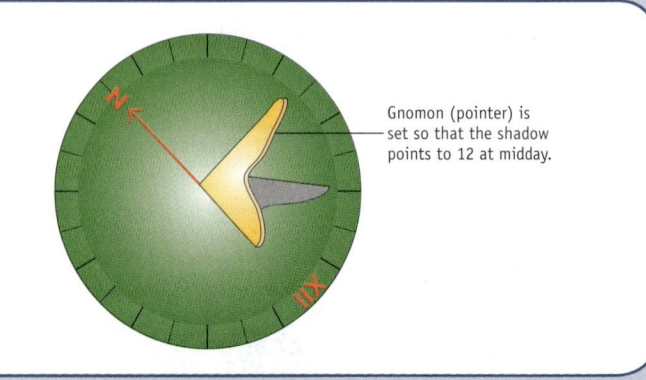

Gnomon (pointer) is set so that the shadow points to 12 at midday.

Excel Illustrated Science Dictionary Years 5–8

survival features

survival features

have evolved and they help *living things* survive. For example, birds have evolved beaks that enable them to eat different *food*s. See **adaptation**.

Pelicans have a beak that can scoop up flesh.

Cockatoos have beaks that can crack seeds and nuts.

Eagles and hawks have beaks that can tear flesh.

suspension

is a *mixture* made up of a *liquid* containing *solid*, *insoluble* particles that will eventually settle on the bottom. Compare **solution**.

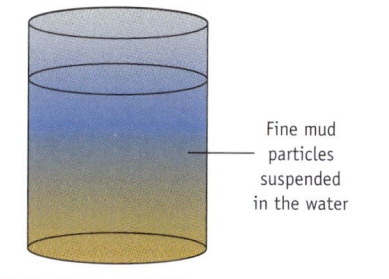

Fine mud particles suspended in the water

sustainable

is making supplies last longer by methods such as *recycling*, reusing and using alternatives. Aboriginal and Torres Strait Islander peoples cared for the land so that it could recover between periods of use. Their nomadic lifestyle gave time for *food* supplies (e.g. fish, *plants*) in an area to regrow. See **resource management**.

switch

operates a *circuit*. Turning an electrical switch off makes a gap in the circuit so that *current* will not flow. This is called an open circuit. Turning a switch on closes the gap and allows *electricity* to flow. This is a closed circuit.

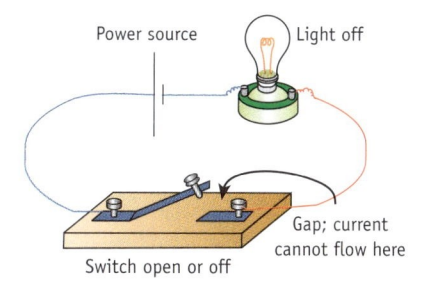

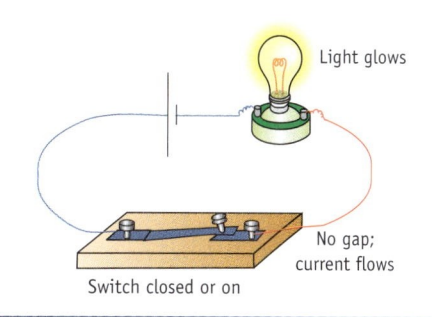

Power source — Light off
Gap; current cannot flow here
Switch open or off

Light glows
No gap; current flows
Switch closed or on

Excel **Illustrated Science Dictionary Years 5–8**

139

symbiosis

symbiosis

is a close association between *organisms* of different *species*. See **ecosystem interactions**.

Staghorn fern perched on tree trunk helps it to get light.

Sucker fish attach to shark and eat its food scraps.

symbols

See **electrical symbols**; **element symbols**.

synthetic materials

are artificial *materials* made by humans from natural or raw materials (e.g. *plastics* and *detergents* are made from *petroleum* products). They are often used instead of *natural materials* because of their different characteristics, or *properties*. See **impact**.

Fibreglass boat (glass embedded in plastic) is lighter than metal and more durable than wood.

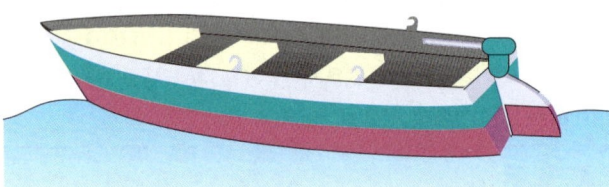

technology

refers to the tools and techniques used to carry out a plan. Sticks to dig up yams, string bags made from bark fibre and fishing hooks made from shells are examples of technology. Modern technology allows scientists to collect information and monitor and manage events on *Earth*. It includes complex *machines*, such as cars, computers and *satellites*. Electronic optical sensors are used for procedures such as medical imaging and monitoring contamination of water.

Technology used by the traditional Australian Aboriginals
- Stone axes
- Wooden boomerangs
- Baskets made from hair, grass or bark

Modern technology

telescope

See **radio telescope**; **optical telescope**; **Hubble Space Telescope**.

temperature

indicates the hotness of a substance. It is measured with a *thermometer* in degrees Celsius (°C). In some countries it is measured in degrees Fahrenheit (°F). Scientists often use the Kelvin scale of temperature. The temperature of a substance in Kelvin is found by adding 273 to the Celsius temperature. Absolute zero is 0 K and is equal to −273 °C. This is the temperature at which the molecules and atoms have minimal energy and movement.

tension and compression

affect all structures. All building structures are under *forces* of tension (pulling forces) and compression (pushing forces).

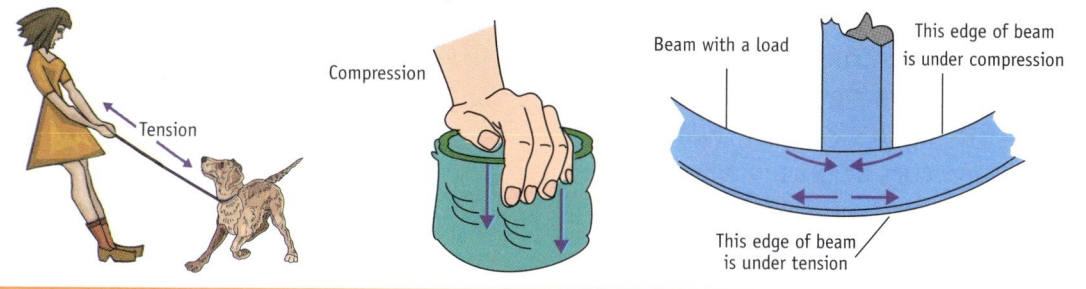

- Tension
- Compression
- Beam with a load
- This edge of beam is under compression
- This edge of beam is under tension

Excel Illustrated Science Dictionary Years 5–8

141

terrestrial

means living or growing on land. Terrestrial *environments* include deserts, mountains, grasslands, farms and cities.

thermometer

is used to measure the *temperature* of a substance. Most thermometers are glass tubes containing mercury or coloured alcohol. See **temperature**.

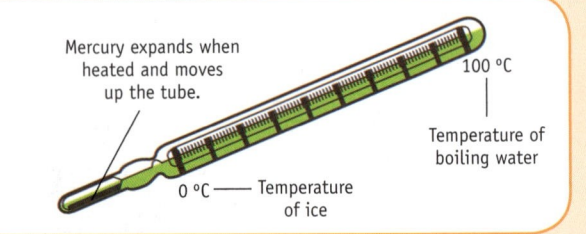

Mercury expands when heated and moves up the tube.
100 °C
Temperature of boiling water
0 °C — Temperature of ice

thermos flask

keeps its contents from losing or gaining heat by *heat conservation*. It is designed to reduce heat loss by *conduction*, *convection* and *radiation*.

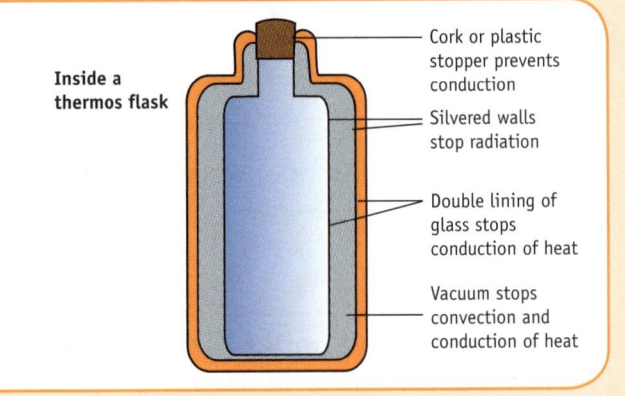

Inside a thermos flask

- Cork or plastic stopper prevents conduction
- Silvered walls stop radiation
- Double lining of glass stops conduction of heat
- Vacuum stops convection and conduction of heat

tidal energy

can be used to produce *electricity*. The moving water from large *tides* rotates *turbines*, which drive *generators* and produce electricity. See **renewable energy sources**.

tides

occur as the height of the *ocean* rises and falls twice a *day*, causing high and low tides. A high tide occurs when the *Moon's* gravitational pull moves the *Earth's* water towards it. Low tide occurs at places where the water is moving away. The *Sun* also has a small effect on tides.

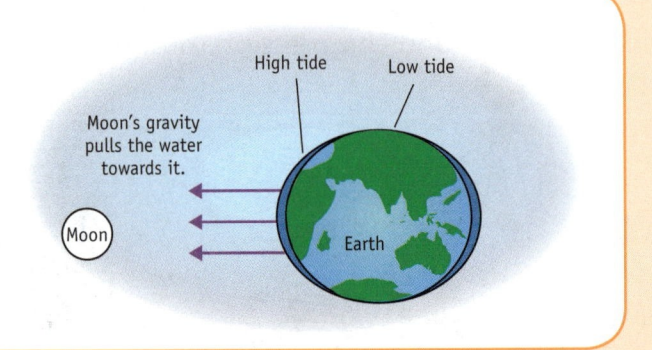

High tide   Low tide
Moon's gravity pulls the water towards it.
Moon   Earth

time scales

vary. Changes and events on *Earth* occur on a different time scale from those in space. Human time is very short when compared with geological and astronomical time. See **Earth history**.

Human time: events related to humans involve minutes, hours, weeks and years.

Humans have been on Earth for about 80 000 years.

Geological time: mountains, canyons and landforms take millions of years to form.

Mountains in the Kosciusko area formed about 10 million years ago.

Astronomical time: events in space take many millions of years.

It is believed the universe began about 13.7 billion years ago and our Sun is 4600 million years old.

tissues

are formed when similar *cells* are grouped together (e.g. to form skin). The cells in a tissue have the same function (job). Different tissues are grouped together to form *organs*.

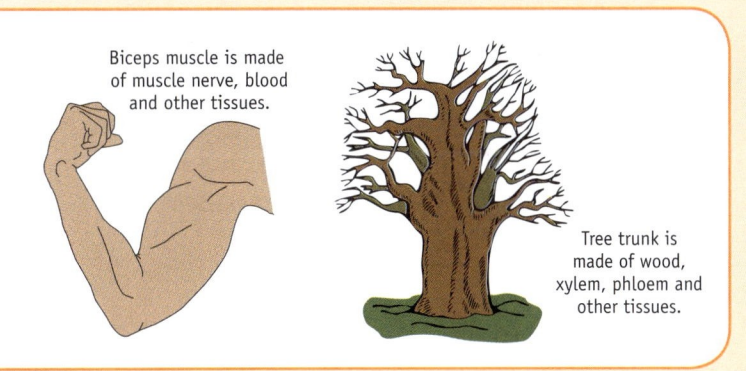

Biceps muscle is made of muscle nerve, blood and other tissues.

Tree trunk is made of wood, xylem, phloem and other tissues.

transfer of energy

See **energy transfer**.

transformation of energy

See **energy transformation**.

translucent

objects are those that scatter *light* as it passes through them (e.g. frosted glass). Compare **transparent**; **opaque**.

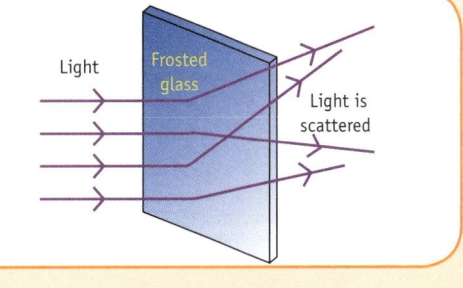

Light → Frosted glass → Light is scattered

transparent

objects are those that *light* will pass straight through (e.g. glass and water). Compare **translucent**; **opaque**.

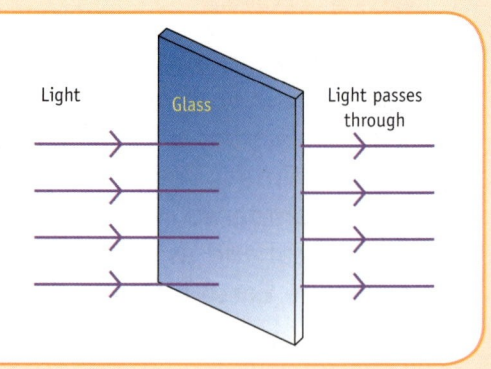

transpiration

is the loss of water from *plants* by *evaporation*. Most transpiration occurs through pores (*stomates*) in the *leaves*. When water evaporates from the pores, more water is drawn into the plant from the *soil*. *Wind* and *heat* from the *Sun* increase transpiration. See **transport systems in plants**.

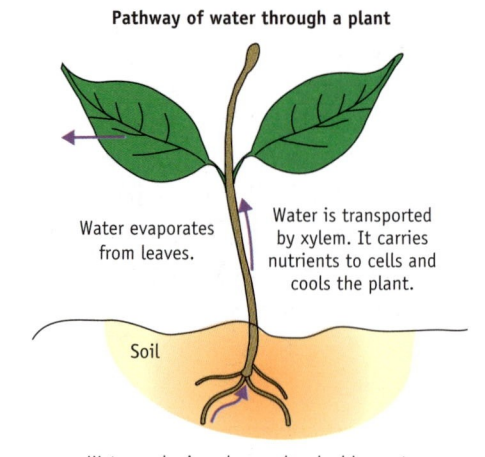

Pathway of water through a plant

transport systems in plants

carry *food* and water through the plant. Water and *minerals* are transported or carried from the *soil* through the *plant*, in *xylem* tissue. Food made in *leaves* is transported by *phloem* tissue to other cells.

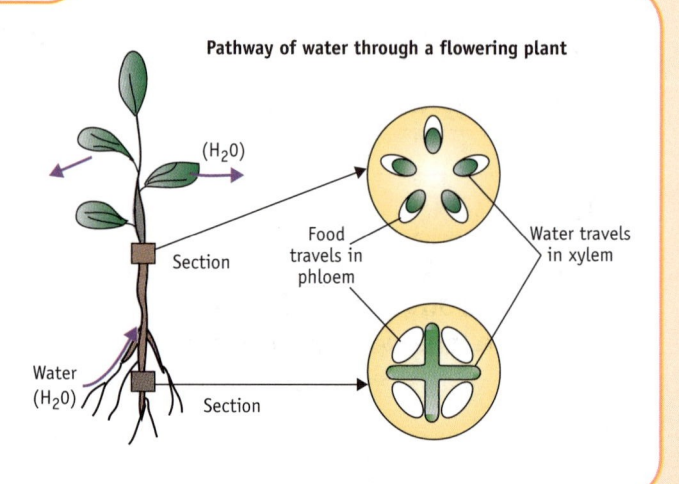

Pathway of water through a flowering plant

tsunami

tsunami

is a huge wave caused by an earth movement or *earthquake* in the sea floor. Tsunamis can travel at 700 km/h and can be over 10 m high near the shore. *Seismograph*s are used to detect the position of the earthquake causing the wave. See **earthquake zones**.

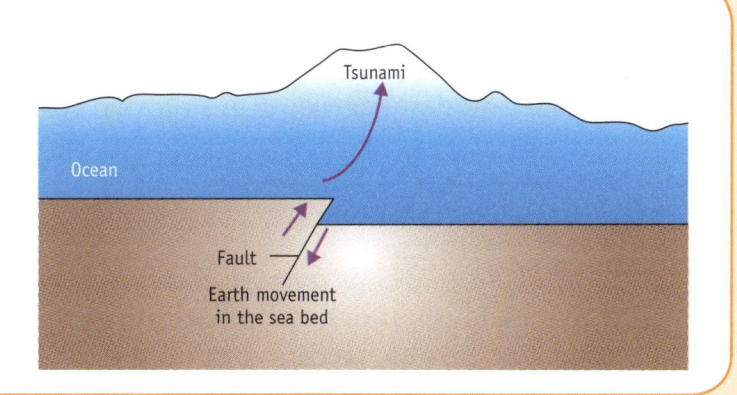

turbidity

is the cloudiness of water caused by living and non-living particles suspended in it.

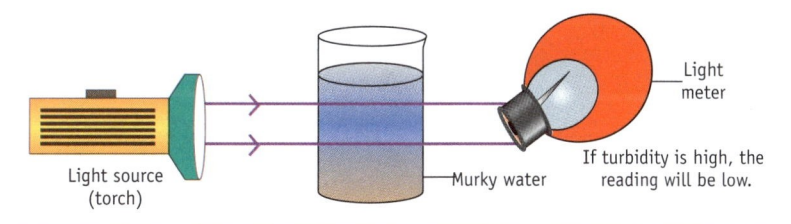

turbine

is a set of curved blades mounted on a shaft that is attached to machinery such as a *generator* or pump. *Wind*, steam or water is used to move the blades and rotate the shaft, which in turn powers the *machine*. See **windmill**; **water wheels**.

Excel Illustrated Science Dictionary Years 5–8

U

ultraviolet rays

ultraviolet rays

are one type of radiant energy from the *Sun*. Ultraviolet rays are also produced by fluorescent lights and arc welders. They carry more *energy* than *light* and can penetrate and damage skin (causing skin cancer) and eyes. See **ozone**.

unicellular organisms

are tiny *living things* or *microorganisms* that are made up of one *cell*. This one cell needs to be able to carry out all the *life processes* that are necessary for survival (e.g. *respiration* and obtaining *food*). Compare **multicellular organisms**.

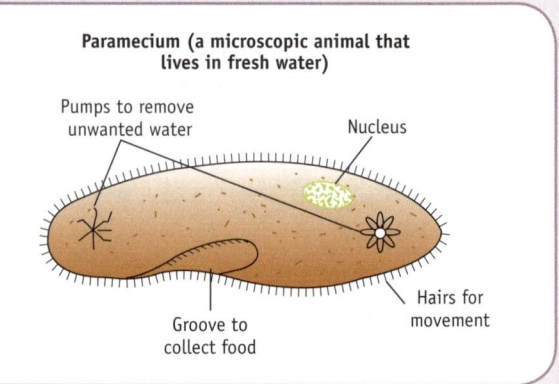

Paramecium (a microscopic animal that lives in fresh water)
- Pumps to remove unwanted water
- Nucleus
- Groove to collect food
- Hairs for movement

universe

is everything that exists. It refers to all space, *matter* and *energy*. Scientists believe an explosion (the Big Bang) produced the universe about 13.7 billion years ago and it has been expanding ever since.

upthrust

is the upward *force* on an object which is in a fluid (*liquid* or *air*). It causes ships and balloons to *float* and parachutes to work and gives an object *buoyancy*. See **float**.

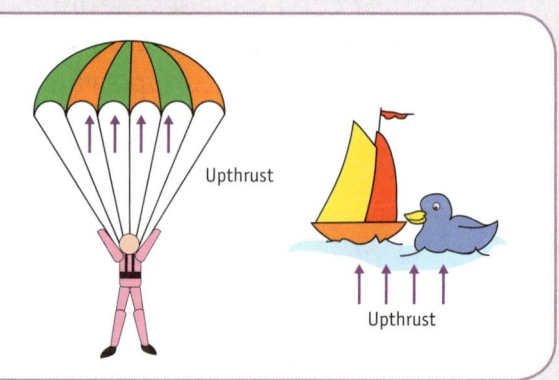

Upthrust

Upthrust

uranium (U)

is a radioactive *metal*. It is used in nuclear weapons and as a fuel in most types of nuclear reactors. *Mining* and *refining* of uranium and its use in reactors produce radioactive waste, which is difficult to dispose of.

146

Excel Illustrated Science Dictionary Years 5–8

Uranus

Uranus is one of the *planet*s furthest from the *Sun* in our *solar system*. It consists of a *mixture* of *gas* and ice around a *solid core* and has a bluish tinge. The axis is almost horizontal. It has a system of rings and currently has 27 known *moon*s.

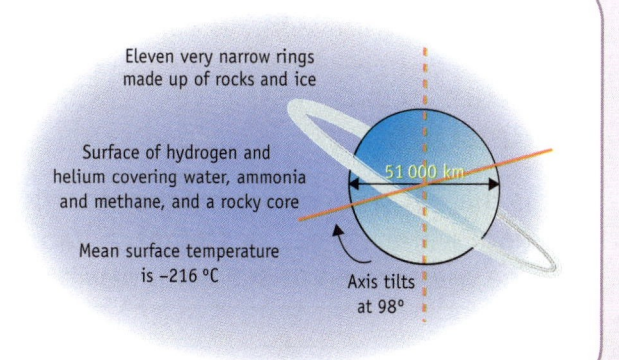

Eleven very narrow rings made up of rocks and ice

Surface of hydrogen and helium covering water, ammonia and methane, and a rocky core

51 000 km

Mean surface temperature is −216 °C

Axis tilts at 98°

V

vacuum

is a space with very few particles of *matter*. A true vacuum is completely empty.

vapour

is the *gas* state of a substance that is usually solid or liquid at room temperature (e.g. water vapour or steam). A vapour can be changed to a liquid by increasing the pressure on it. See **compression of matter**.

variable (in an experiment or fair test)

is a factor that can change. In an experiment to see how wing shape affects the flight of a toy plane, the planes would be identical except for the wing shape The wing shape is the variable. See **scientific method**.

These model planes are made from the same wood and are the same size and weight. They are tested in the same conditions (wind, moisture).

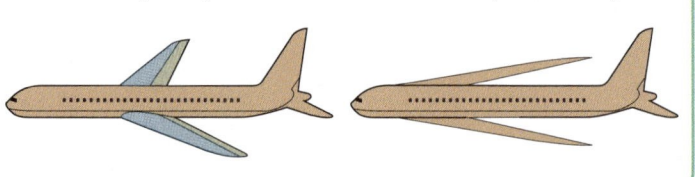

variations

are the different features *organisms* possess. See **invertebrates; vertebrates; variations within a species**.

Most birds fly.

Others are flightless.

variations within a species

are the differences between individuals belonging to the same *species*. They may be produced by genes (e.g. eye and skin colour) and/or by the *environment* (e.g. body size and build caused by different diets and exercise).

148

Excel **Illustrated Science Dictionary Years 5–8**

Venus

Venus

(the 'morning star' and 'evening star') is a rocky *planet* with gentle hills and several active *volcanoes*. The planet is covered with dense clouds made of sulphur dust and drops of concentrated sulphuric acid. It has no moons or water.

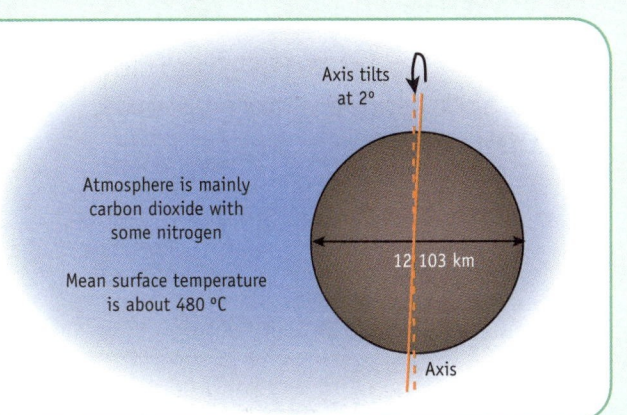

Axis tilts at 2°
Atmosphere is mainly carbon dioxide with some nitrogen
Mean surface temperature is about 480 °C
12 103 km
Axis

vertebrates

are *animals* that have a backbone and internal skeleton. They are subdivided into five groups.

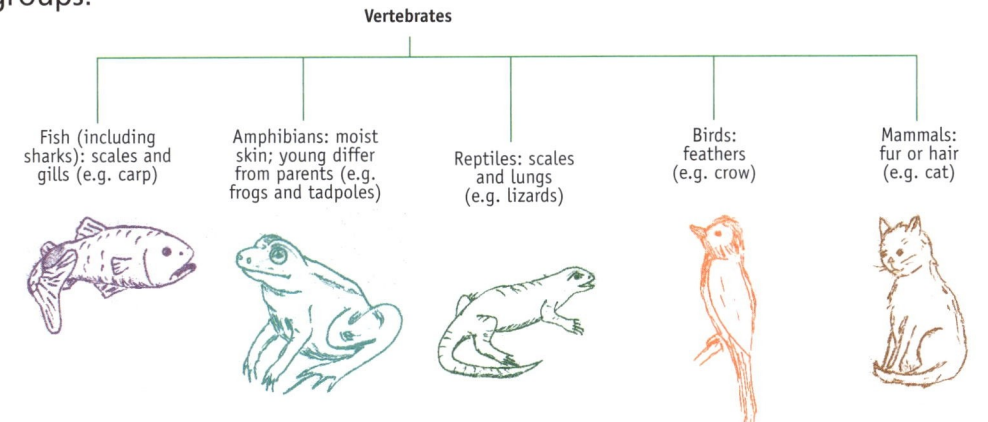

Vertebrates

- Fish (including sharks): scales and gills (e.g. carp)
- Amphibians: moist skin; young differ from parents (e.g. frogs and tadpoles)
- Reptiles: scales and lungs (e.g. lizards)
- Birds: feathers (e.g. crow)
- Mammals: fur or hair (e.g. cat)

virus

is an extremely small particle and can be seen only with an electron microscope. Viruses are *parasites*. They cause disease and reproduce only when inside living *cells*.

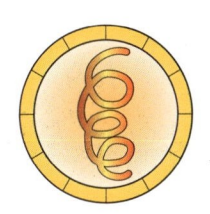

Influenza virus  | Herpes virus  | Hepatitis virus 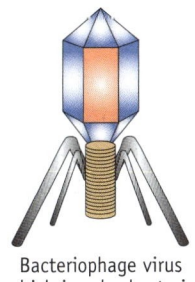 | Bacteriophage virus which invades bacteria

Excel Illustrated Science Dictionary Years 5–8

V

viscous

means thick and sticky, and slow to pour. Honey is more viscous than water.

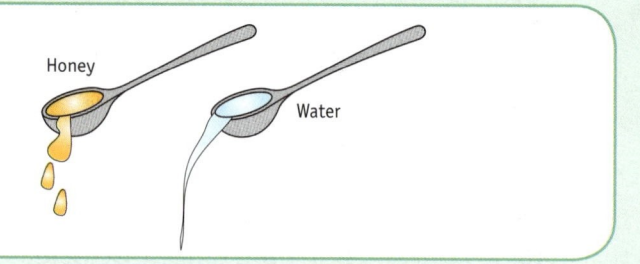

vision

relies on *light* travelling from an object to the eye passing through a *lens*. This forms an inverted image on the retina. The brain makes the image appear upright.

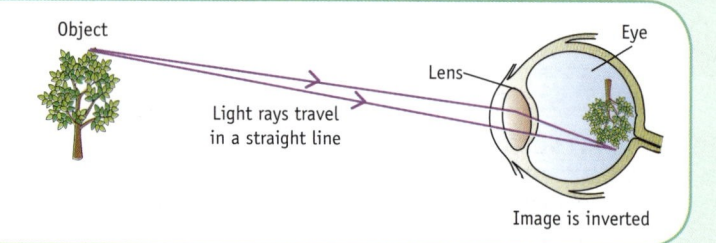

vitamins

are *nutrients* needed in small amounts for body growth, *chemical reactions* and body functioning. *Plants* make their own. *Animals* obtain most from their *food*.

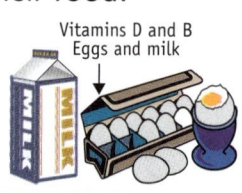

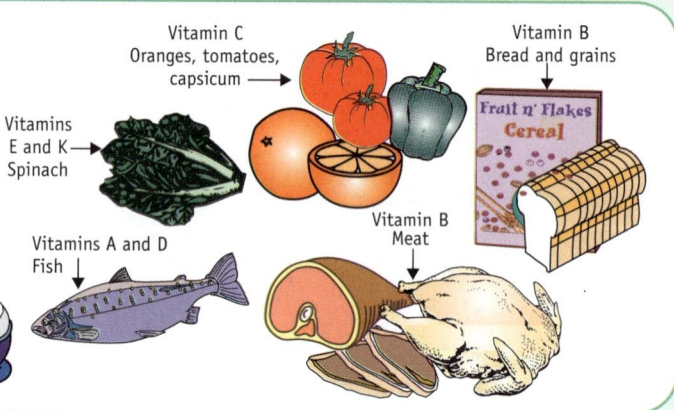

volcano

is an opening in the *Earth's crust* through which *lava*, ash and *gases* flow from the inside the Earth. If the vent is blocked by lava solidifying, pressures build up inside the volcano, causing an explosive eruption and severe devastation. See **seismograph**; **earthquake zones**.

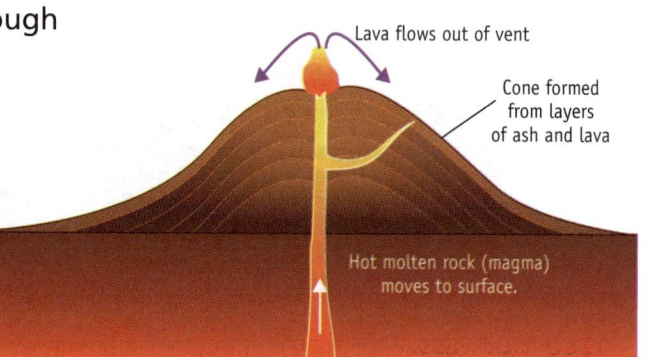

voltage

voltage

is electrical push and is measured in *volts*. It is the difference in *charge* between two parts of a *circuit* and is provided by an *electric cell*, battery or *generator*. It causes charge or *current* to move through the wires in a circuit. See **voltage in batteries**.

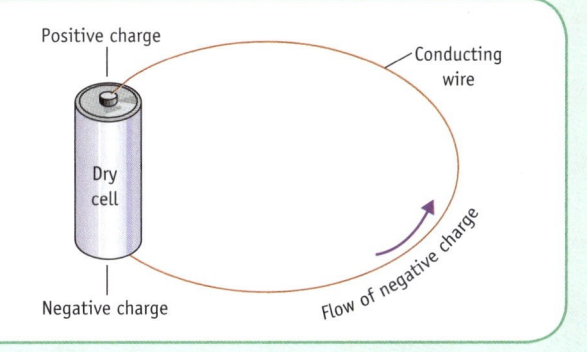

voltage in batteries

determines the strength of the battery. A battery with a high *voltage* has a high negative *charge* on its negative terminal. It is capable of 'pushing' more *current* through the *circuit* than a battery with a low voltage. See **batteries in series**; **batteries in parallel**.

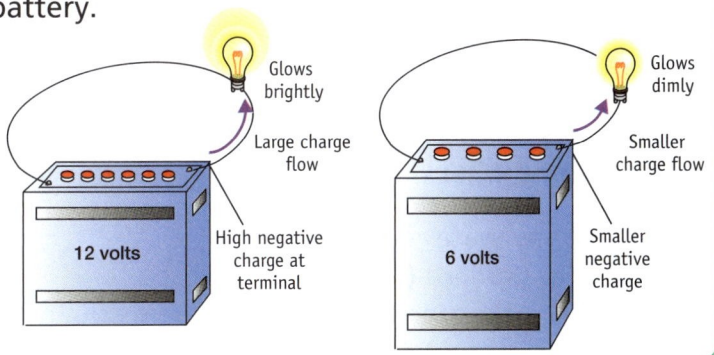

volts (V)

are a measure of electrical pressure or voltage. They are measured with a voltmeter. See **voltage**.

volume

is the space an object or substance occupies. It is measured in litres (L), millilitres (mL) or cubic centimetres (cm³ or cc). A gas has no definite volume but spreads out to fill its container.

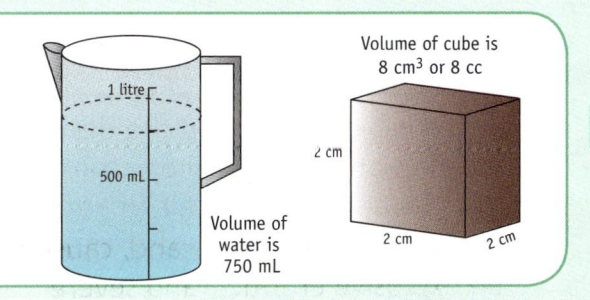

volume of a sound

See **loudness**.

Excel Illustrated Science Dictionary Years 5-8

W waste disposal

waste disposal

in many cases consists of recycling or reusing waste *materials*. *Soluble* materials that will not pollute the waterways are often washed down the sink. *Insoluble matter* and poisonous substances (e.g. paints, pesticides, oil, *solvents*) need to be disposed of by special collection. They are treated to make them safe, and useful substances are recovered.

Paper, plastic, metals and glass are recycled and reused.

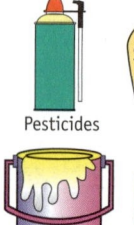

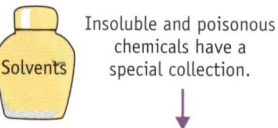

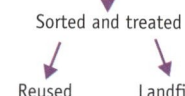

Plant matter is used for compost and mulch.

Insoluble and poisonous chemicals have a special collection.

Sorted and treated → Reused / Landfill

water cycle

is the way water cycles between the *hydrosphere* (sea, rivers, oceans), *lithosphere* (land) and *atmosphere* (air). The cycle involves *evaporation* from bodies of water on Earth and *condensation* to form clouds, then rain, hail and snow. Both evaporation and condensation are affected by *temperature*.

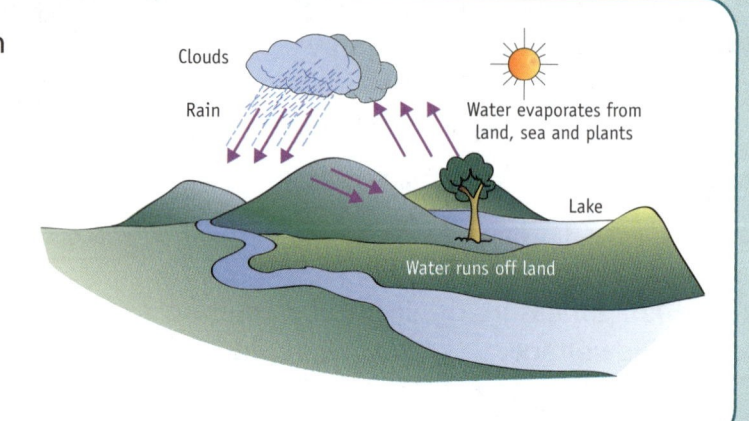

Clouds, Rain, Water evaporates from land, sea and plants, Lake, Water runs off land

water management

is carried out to obtain the best use of water and to reduce the effects of its use by man on the natural *environment*. It includes such objectives as pollution control and waste *water treatment*. Fresh water is used by humans for drinking, agriculture, *manufacture*, industry and leisure (pools).

water retention

See **soil water retention**.

152

Excel Illustrated Science Dictionary Years 5–8

water treatment

is the process of purifying town water. *Sedimentation* is the first step: the water stands in large reservoirs to allow mud and silt to settle to the bottom. The water is then taken from the upper layers and filtered and chemically treated.

water wheels

are turned by the *force* of the water on blades that are set across the rim of the wheel. The rotating wheel can be used to drive machinery. Water wheels were commonly used to drive machinery in the first factories. Compare **windmill**. See **turbine**.

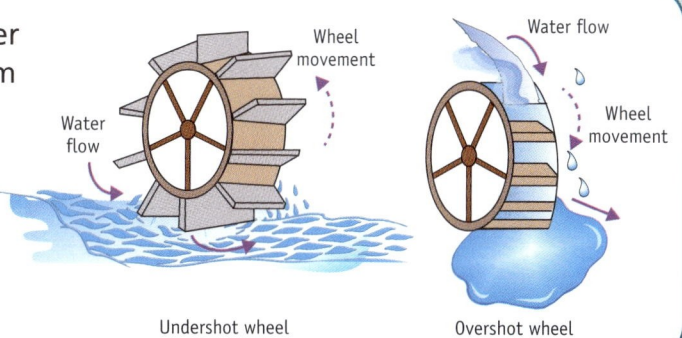

Undershot wheel

Overshot wheel

watt (W)

is a measure of *power*. The watts on the label of an appliance show how much power it draws from the *electricity* supply. An 800-watt toaster uses 800 units of *energy* every second. See **electrical energy used by an appliance**.

wave energy

is the *kinetic energy* in ocean waves and may be used to produce *electricity*. One design uses a line of floats. As they bob up and down with the water, the motion drives a *generator*, which produces electricity. See **renewable energy sources**.

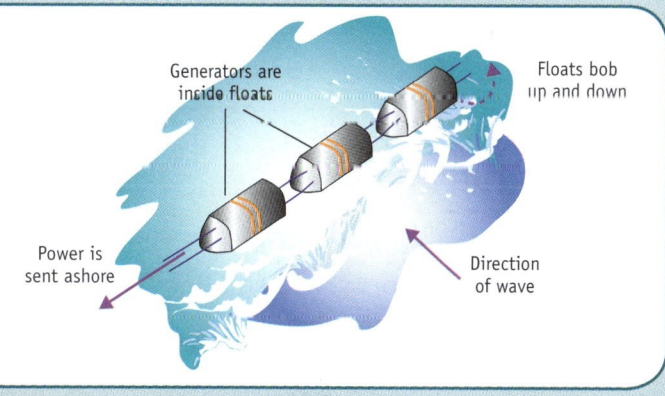

weather

is the conditions in the *atmosphere*. It includes *temperature* of the *air*, *air pressure*, *cloud* cover, *winds*, *humidity* and *rainfall*. See **oceans and weather; high pressure system; low pressure system; El Niño**.

Excel Illustrated Science Dictionary Years 5–8

W weather balloons and satellites

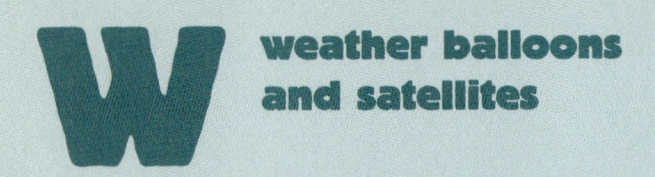

weather balloons and satellites

carry instruments that take photographs of climatic conditions and record *temperature*s, *air pressures* and *humidity* at different heights in the *atmosphere*. The information is sent by radio transmitters to *Earth*, where it is analysed, allowing meteorologists to predict the *weather*.

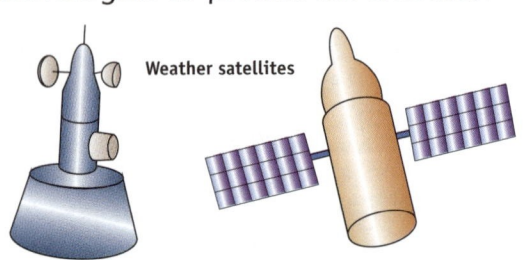

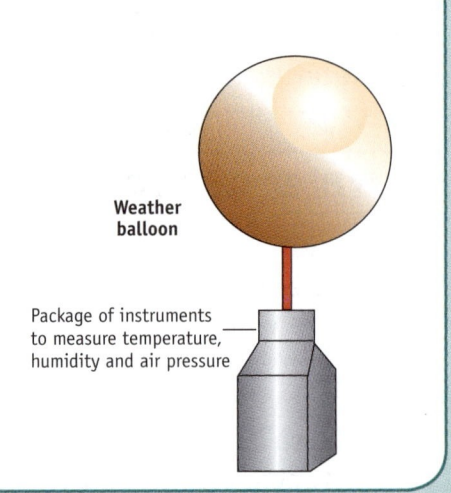

Weather satellites

Weather balloon

Package of instruments to measure temperature, humidity and air pressure

weather forecasting

is making predictions about future *weather* trends. Information about the *atmosphere* and the oceans is collected by radar, aircraft, ships, weather stations, *weather balloons and satellites*.

weathering

is the breaking down and crumbling of *rocks* into smaller particles. This forms *soil* or *sediments*, which may eventually form *sedimentary rocks*. See **physical (mechanical) weathering; chemical weathering**.

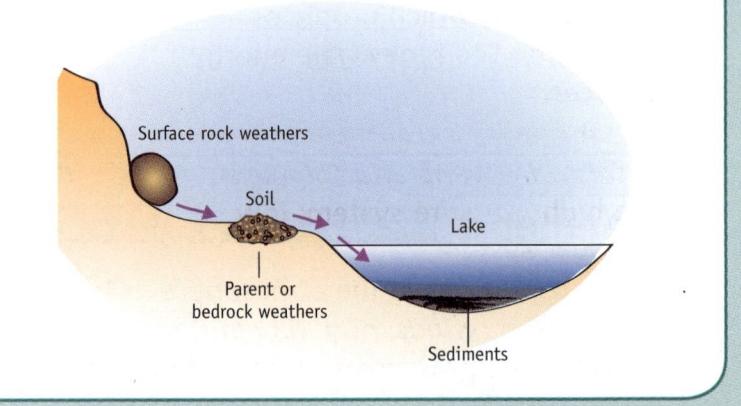

Surface rock weathers
Soil
Parent or bedrock weathers
Lake
Sediments

Excel Illustrated Science Dictionary Years 5–8

weight

weight

is the downward *force* of an object caused by *gravity*. The *Earth's* gravitational force is six times stronger than the *Moon's*, so an object will weigh six times more on Earth than on the Moon.

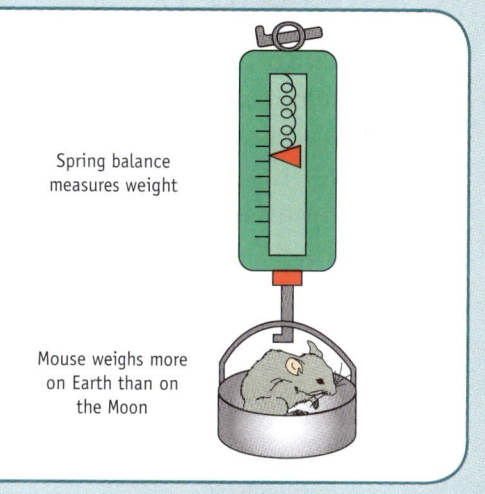

Spring balance measures weight

Mouse weighs more on Earth than on the Moon

white dwarf

is a *star* at the end of its life. It is formed from a *red giant*. As the red giant cools, the outer layers drift away and the inner layers compress, leaving a tiny *core* that shines with a white *light*. The white dwarf shrinks away and the star dies. See **star life span**.

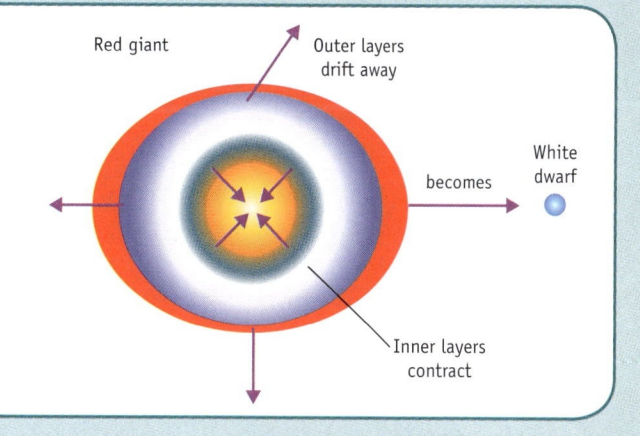

Red giant — Outer layers drift away — becomes — White dwarf — Inner layers contract

wind

is moving *air* caused by local heating. Air moves from areas with high *air pressure* to areas with low pressure. The *speed* of the wind is measured with an *anemometer* and the direction is measured with a *wind vane* and compass. See **high pressure system; low pressure system**.

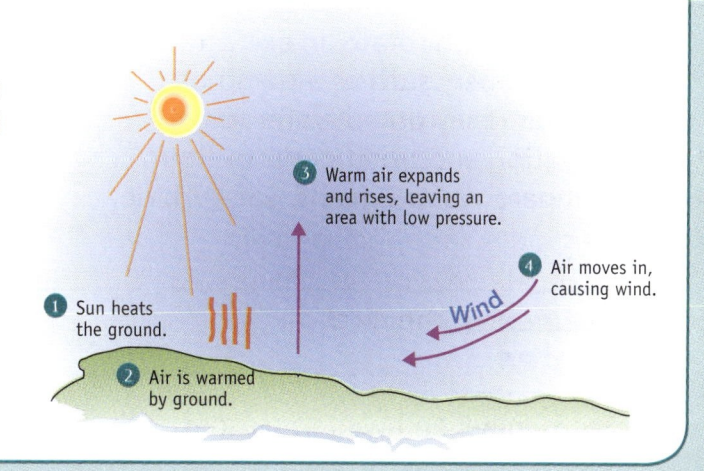

1. Sun heats the ground.
2. Air is warmed by ground.
3. Warm air expands and rises, leaving an area with low pressure.
4. Air moves in, causing wind.

Wind

Excel Illustrated Science Dictionary Years 5–8

155

W wind energy

wind energy

is used to pump water by turning the propellers of *windmills*. This *energy* can also be channelled to a *generator*, where it is changed to *electrical energy*. See **renewable energy sources**; **turbine**; **windmill**.

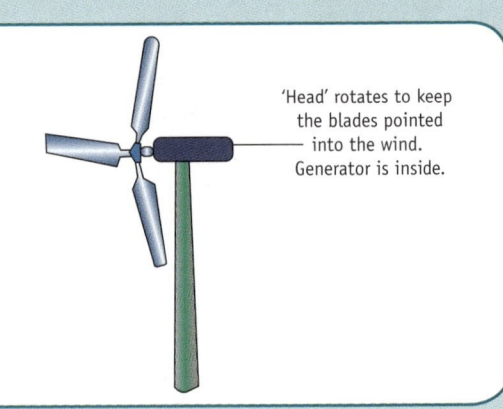

'Head' rotates to keep the blades pointed into the wind. Generator is inside.

wind vane

measures the direction of the *wind*. It indicates where the wind is coming from (e.g. a westerly wind is coming from the west). The arrow points into the wind.

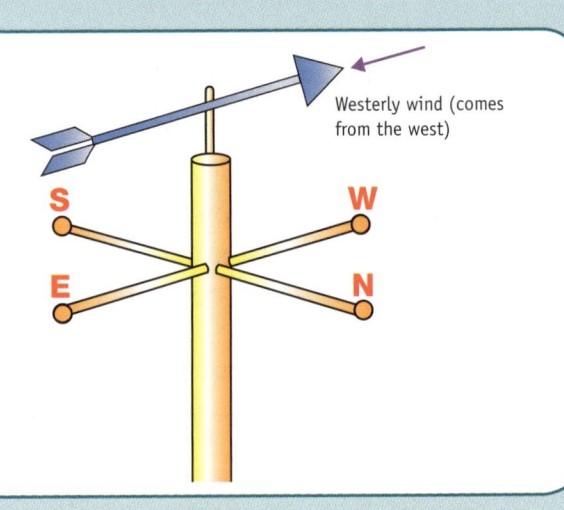

Westerly wind (comes from the west)

windmill

uses the *wind's energy* to drive *machines*. The wind turns angled blades, which rotate an axis attached to machinery such as a pump or grinder. They pump water for irrigation and grind grain to flour. Compare **water wheels**. See **turbine**.

winter

See **summer and winter**; **seasons**.

word equations

are used to show the chemicals that react (the reactants) and those that are produced (the products) in a *chemical reaction*. For example:

$$\text{oxygen} + \text{hydrogen} \longrightarrow \text{water}$$

Oxygen and hydrogen are the reactants; water is the product.

work

is done on an object when it is changed or moved by a *force*. *Energy* is transferred (moved) or transformed (changed). See **energy transfer; energy transformation**.

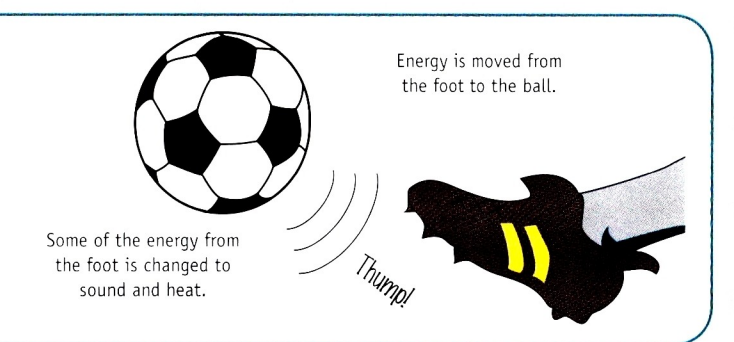

Energy is moved from the foot to the ball.

Some of the energy from the foot is changed to sound and heat.

Thump!

Excel Illustrated Science Dictionary Years 5–8

X-rays

are one type of radiant energy produced by the *Sun*. Humans produce them with an X-ray tube. They readily penetrate many materials and are useful in *science*, medicine and industry. For instance, they are used to see inside the body. Bones and teeth stop the X-rays and they appear as a shadow on the photographic plate.

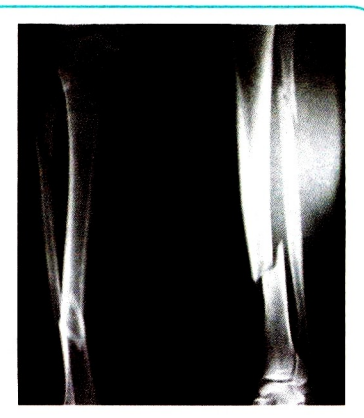

X-ray of broken bones

xylem

tissues carry water in *plants*. The *cells* in this tissue are dead and hollow and function like microscopic pipes. See **transport systems in plants**.

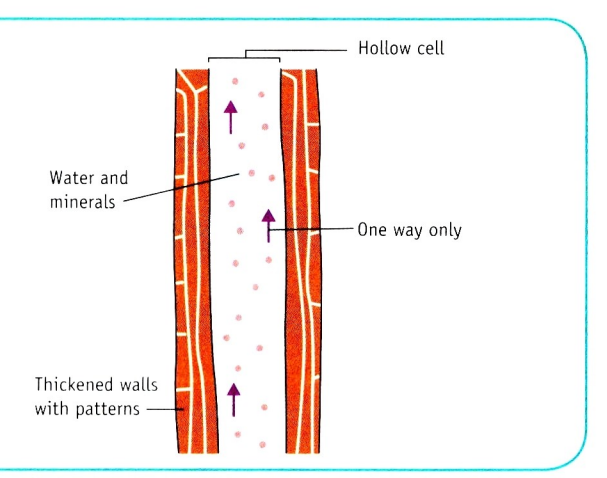

- Hollow cell
- Water and minerals
- One way only
- Thickened walls with patterns

year

year is the time taken for a *planet* to travel around the *Sun*. *Earth* takes 365 *days* to *orbit* the Sun. *Mercury* takes 88 days and has the shortest year of the *planets*. *Pluto* takes 248 Earth years and has the longest year.

Planet	Time taken to revolve around the Sun
Mercury	88 Earth days
Venus	225 Earth days
Earth	365 Earth days
Mars	687 Earth days
Jupiter	12 Earth years
Saturn	30 Earth years
Uranus	84 Earth years
Neptune	165 Earth years
Pluto (dwarf)	248 Earth years

See **solar system**.

Notes